Tipping Out of Trouble

What kind of trouble lies ahead? How can we successfully transition toward a sustainable future? Drawing on a remarkably broad range of insights from complex systems and the functioning of the brain to the history of civilizations and the workings of modern societies, the distinguished scientist Marten Scheffer addresses these key questions of our times. He looks to the past to show how societies have tipped out of trouble before, the mechanisms that drive social transformations, and the invisible hands holding us back. He traces how longstanding practices such as the slave trade and foot binding were suddenly abandoned and how entire civilizations have collapsed to make way for something new. Could we be heading for a similarly dramatic change? Marten Scheffer argues that a dark future is plausible but not yet inevitable and he provides us instead with a hopeful roadmap to steer ourselves away from collapse – and toward renewal.

Marten Scheffer is a Distinguished Professor at Wageningen University and an expert on stability of complex systems ranging from the climate and the brain to societies and ecosystems. His work is highly cited and he is associated to the Dutch as well as the US academies of sciences.

"In approachable writing, as over coffee with a friend, this book uses recent science and deep knowledge to show the ways out of current global crises."

Stephen R. Carpenter, winner of the Blue Planet Prize

"This page-turner makes a convincing case of how the widely perceived values of nature could now well become key drivers of long-needed change. I couldn't stop reading."

Gretchen Daily, author of *The New Economy of Nature* and winner of the Volvo Environment Prize

"Some find the possibility of a bright planetary future naive. This book proves them wrong. Marten Scheffer takes us on an exciting journey with hope, not wishful thinking, with numerous insights into the significance of agency and collective action throughout human history and civilizations, and by seeing the future as open rather than pre-determined. *Tipping Out of Trouble* is simply a brilliant book! A must-read for anyone and everyone interested and engaged with the future of humankind in our beautiful biosphere."

Carl Folke, founder of the Stockholm Resilience Center

"Scheffer is no stranger to the worst that climate change may bring – his renown work has brought urgency and alarm to the world's scientific understanding. And yet here he offers cause for hope, in a novel text that recognizes the complex and interwoven social and political forces shaping our reaction to global change and points to the tipping points that lead to a positive outcome to this crisis."

Abrahm Lustgarten, author of *On the Move: The Overheating Earth and the Uprooting of America*

"Scheffer brings a lifetime of study of complex systems to our knottiest problems, such as climate destabilization, biodiversity loss, and erosion of democracy. The result is a timely, fascinating, and accessible study of how societies have plunged into crises and occasionally climbed out again."

John McNeill, author of *Something New Under the Sun: An Environmental History of the Twentieth-Century World*

"In this eye-opening book, Marten Scheffer shows that the 'good Anthropocene' is within our reach, but that it will require bold collective action and massive wealth redistribution. A must-read."
Thomas Piketty, author of *Capital in the Twenty-First Century*

"We often speak of tipping points with fear, as signals of collapse or crisis. But as this book reminds us, their true power lies in their potential to transform systems for the better. Marten Scheffer helps us understand how this change happens and how we can harness positive tipping points to shift our trajectory toward a more just and sustainable future."
Paul Polman, former CEO of Unilever and co-author of *Net Positive: How Courageous Companies Thrive by Giving More Than They Take*

Marten Scheffer

Tipping Out of Trouble

How Societies Transformed and How We Can Do So Again

Shaftesbury Road, Cambridge CB2 8EA, United Kingdom

One Liberty Plaza, 20th Floor, New York, NY 10006, USA

477 Williamstown Road, Port Melbourne, VIC 3207, Australia

314–321, 3rd Floor, Plot 3, Splendor Forum, Jasola District Centre,
New Delhi – 110025, India

103 Penang Road, #05–06/07, Visioncrest Commercial, Singapore 238467

Cambridge University Press is part of Cambridge University Press & Assessment,
a department of the University of Cambridge.

We share the University's mission to contribute to society through the pursuit of
education, learning and research at the highest international levels of excellence.

www.cambridge.org
Information on this title: www.cambridge.org/9781009699754

DOI: 10.1017/9781009699785

When citing this work, please include a reference to the DOI 10.1017/9781009699785

First published 2026

A catalogue record for this publication is available from the British Library

A Cataloging-in-Publication data record for this book is available from the Library of
Congress

ISBN 978-1-009-69975-4 Hardback

CONTENTS

PROLOGUE: CHANGE IS IN THE AIR

A few years ago I recovered a time capsule: the diaries of my great-grandfather. I shared daily life with him when I was little and he was quite old. A family doctor, he lived through two world wars and the Spanish flu, among much other turbulence, yet his writings remain focused on nature. As he wrote in an entry during World War I: "While the cannon roar rumbles our windows, a robin is singing in the garden amidst a flock of long-tailed tits, marvelous purple-brown backs, and white heads with elegant black linings." More than a century later I now enjoy the same birds, flowers, wines, meals, and sunshine that he did. Yet the world looks very different. When he started his diary, fishing boats on the river were powered by sails, and he traveled to see his patients in a cart pulled by a dog, made to his design by the local blacksmith (Figure 0.1). Soundscapes were untouched by the roar of machinery. There were four times fewer people on Earth, and their ecological footprints were small. Humans have radically changed the planet in just a few generations. The world feels as if we could be headed for trouble. Still, our emotional anchors in life seem deceptively solid. Fruit trees bloom, wine is wonderful, and a robin sings brilliantly.

What kind of trouble awaits? Are we approaching a profound transformation for humanity? If so, could we recognize that? Change is constant. Yet the fabric of trends and adjustments is occasionally ruptured by transformations that upend the rules of the game. These periods stand out so markedly that we call them revolutions or collapses, depending on the point of view. Could we

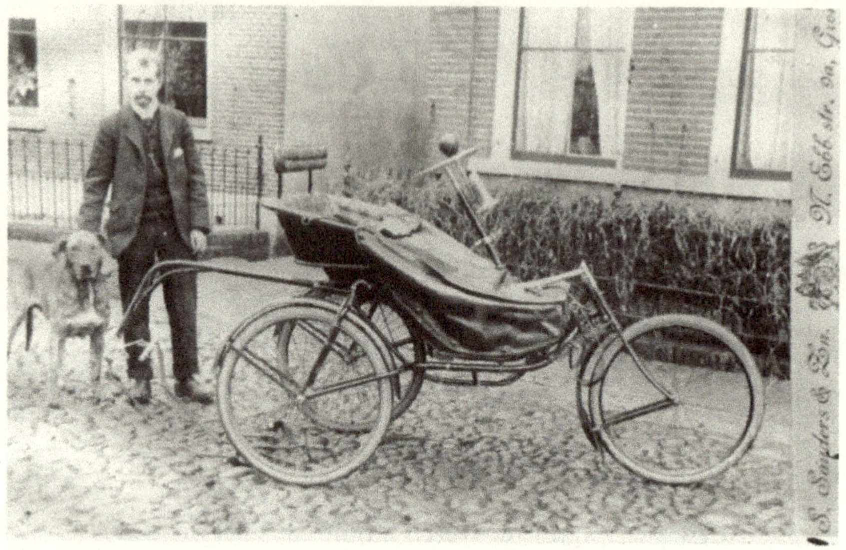

Figure 0.1 My great-grandfather with his dog-propelled cart.

be heading for a massive change of our global civilization over the next century? Humanity has come a long way. Looking at lifespan, disease burden, poverty, and many other indicators of well-being, we live in the best of times,[1] but there are also troubling trends. Wilderness and the biodiversity it nurtures is shrinking every day, and the Earth is warming at such a rate that, fifty years from now, a third of humanity may be displaced as their homelands become uninhabitable.[2] At the same time, there is an unprecedented accumulation of wealth in the hands of a tiny fraction of humanity. Against this backdrop, we have entered a global wave of turbulence. The Covid-19 pandemic, fundamentalist movements, the election of extreme leaders, the rise of far-right populism, wars, and waves of street protests have shaken the globe. But there have also been new lifestyle movements such as veganism and voluntary simplicity, together with novel economic experiments such as platforms for bartering and sharing. All these changes, good and bad, suggest tensions in the status quo and a widespread search for new ways of thinking and living.[3] Why? Where are we heading? Nobody knows, of course. We are traversing entirely new ground. We face a changed climate that humanity has never experienced. We possess technologies that would have been unimaginable just years ago.

Despite this unprecedented moment, can we say anything definitive or even productive about humanity's near future? I think so. In this book I argue that a fundamental transformation of our societies is inevitable, and that we are better placed than ever to make that transformation graceful. First, there is a lot to learn from our past. "History never repeats itself, but it often rhymes." That quotation is often falsely attributed to Mark Twain, but it has popped up many times in different forms over the years.[4] Wherever it comes from, its persistence suggests that it captures some truth. Certainly, time after time, societies have become fragile as they age. Their elites and the institutions they shaped – beliefs, taxes, rituals, worldviews – eventually lose credibility as the system no longer delivers. What will it take for humanity to break its love affair with the aging way we run the world? With the things we think we want? What will it take for that attraction to be lost? It can be surprisingly hard to break a loving relationship, even if you see that it is destructive, leading nowhere. Nonetheless, love affairs end. Every once in a while, longstanding practices such as the slave trade, foot binding, or smoking in public spaces are suddenly abandoned. Even entire civilizations have collapsed to make way for something new.

Transformation requires a good deal of discontent with the way things are. There is evidence that discontent has skyrocketed over the past decades, driven by growing awareness of wealth inequality, unfairness, fear of runaway climate change, mass migration, and other worries, catalyzed partly by populist rhetoric and the dynamics of social media. But where will our discontent drive us? Will it make society tumble in the wrong direction, as it did, for instance, in Nazi Germany? Or could the resulting instability caused by discontent help push us in a beneficial direction? Consider the Progressive Era, over a century ago, when the USA helped itself out of the social trap caused by the Industrial Revolution.[5] The country solved a seemingly unescapable tangle of environmental and social crises by creating anticorruption laws, environmental regulations, access to schooling, and more. All within a decade. Could a similar transformation help us escape from the unsustainable trap we are currently in? Could we transition toward a happier setting where our ecological footprint and social tensions are much smaller, allowing future generations to flourish? What could such a utopia realistically look like? And importantly: could the transformation happen swiftly? I will try to convince you that the answer is yes, but only if we reach a tipping point where change suddenly starts speeding up.

Tipping points have been at the core of my work as a scientist. It all started with lakes. In my first job we were tasked with finding out how to make murky Dutch lakes clear again. We discovered that they were trapped in a turbid state, and that we could tip them back to clarity through shock therapy. If we removed the fish, the lake became clear. Then, after reintroducing the fish, the clear state persisted in many lakes. This suggested that those ecosystems could have alternative stable states. The same lake could get stuck in a turbid state or a clear state. Historically, pollution from wastewater and farming had pushed the lakes to a tipping point where the clear state became unstable, causing the lake to shift into the turbid state. Reducing pollution was the first step to make the clear state possible again, but our shock therapy was necessary to provide a push out of the turbidity trap.[6] This became fundamental in much follow-up work on coral reefs, tropical forests, and other ecosystems, showing that they had tipping points where they could flip to an alternative state.[7] I could have happily stayed in ecology if not for a nagging question that gradually started taking over my thoughts: could humanity reach a tipping point? In search of answers, I worked with economists, archaeologists, mathematicians, historians, psychologists, physicians, journalists, sculptors, novelists, and others ranging from students to Nobel laureates. This extended adventure resulted in numerous scientific articles; but meanwhile, something more valuable unfolded. Each experience opened my eyes to new questions and strikingly different ways of investigating and seeing the world. I became an expert in none of those fields, but I got a look behind the scenes everywhere. On this winding path I picked up a remarkably diverse collection of insights, ranging from the mathematical theory of dynamical systems to the functioning of the brain, the history of civilizations, and the workings of modern societies. In this book I combine those elements to address what I see as the big question of our times: how might our global industrialized civilization reach a tipping point for runaway change toward a future where humans and other species can thrive in the centuries to come?

The structure of the argument is straightforward. First, I will show the many ways in which societies have tipped out of trouble before and summarize the mechanisms that drive such social transformations. Then, I will take you through a set of scary as well as hopeful world trends over the past decades. After that, putting the pieces together, I will argue that a dark future is plausible but not at all inevitable. In the end, I will offer an evidence-based set of strategies for maximizing the chances that we may tip into a good Anthropocene. A world we can be proud of.

1

THE TROUBLE

First, a word about the trouble. I won't dwell too long on this, as it gets too much press already. Not a day goes by without headlines suggesting that the world is heading for disaster if we don't act swiftly and profoundly. Is that really true? And if so, what should be done about it?

A Planetary Crisis

It may seem that the world is entangled in endless problems, but things are really not so complicated when it comes to sustainability. Perhaps that was the thought of Johan Rockström when, in 2008, he invited a bunch of us to get together in a quiet place in the Swedish countryside to try and define the "safe operating space for humanity." I was doubtful. How were we going to do that? But I attended, and surprisingly, after a few days of deliberation, we wrote a paper concluding that there were essentially only nine environmental problems that could cause serious trouble on a planetary scale if a critical threshold was passed. We called them our nine "planetary boundaries."[1] We tried to get to ten but couldn't come up with a final one. Little did we suspect that this would become the most influential paper in any of our careers. I still wonder why that was. You never know. Sometimes, a paper that you consider a fabulous eye-opener remains ignored, while another unexpectedly becomes a 'hit' as measured by public attention and scientific citations. My guess is that there were two elements that caused our planetary boundaries paper to cause such a splash. First, we painted things from a positive angle, framing the possibility of a safe operating space for humanity. Instead of warning what could go wrong, we showed how things could go right. Second, we offered a "corridor of clarity,"[2] attempting to keep things simple and constructive. Overwhelmingly complex problems can be paralyzing, especially when some aspects are uncertain. Clarifying the core of the matter and leaving out the uncertainties and unimportant sidetracks helps. In hindsight, summarizing nine planetary boundaries was remarkably effective; but in fact, the core of the matter may be even simpler.

Our planetary boundaries had to do with the disruption of global cycles of phosphorus and nitrogen, the health of the ozone layer, the pervasiveness of polluting chemicals, the quality of fresh water, ocean acidification, and the concentration of aerosols in the atmosphere. Simplifying even further, however, one could say that there are two key issues: climate and nature. More precisely, the future of humanity is threatened by global warming and by the deterioration of ecosystems. Many updates later, details have changed, but the overall picture remains the same.[3] Humanity's job is to ensure that climate change stays within safe limits and that we don't undermine the integrity of the biosphere. Perhaps surprisingly, despite all the complexity in the details, we already know the solutions to both problems: stop mining fossil fuels and eat a largely plant-based diet. The big question, of course, is how to achieve those goals. That will be the focus of this book. But first, let's ask how big and fast the change needs to be to prevent serious trouble for humanity. Are things really that urgent?

In terms of the loss of nature, this is not so easily answered. Certainly, the scale of the change incurred by humanity is daunting.[4] To get an impression, humanity is only one among roughly 5,400 mammal species. Yet we represent one-third of the mammalian biomass globally, and our livestock and pets occupy most of the remaining two-thirds. Only 4 percent of the global mammalian biomass is made up by the remaining thousands of wild species. We have transformed about half of the Earth's ice-free land surface and are using about half the available fresh water. Meanwhile, we have polluted soil, air, and water in countless ways. As a result, the Earth has entered its sixth mass extinction event, losing species at a rate faster than during any of the five previous such events in the history of our planet, when much of life vanished.[5] But is our ravaging of nature really a problem? Certainly not for life on the planet in the long run. Upon each of the previous mass extinction events, evolution allowed the diversity of life to recover, often surpassing previous diversity (even if it took millions of years).[6] The question is rather whether the extent to which we are eradicating nature might imply a lurking crisis for humanity. More specifically, will it be a problem for our children, or for the grandchildren of our grandchildren? Certainly, the world would be more boring if so many species were lost and few natural ecosystems survived. But would humans still be able to live safely and feed themselves even if most of nature is lost? Surely we'll still have our hamburgers and be able to watch movies? Yes, the loss of forests may lead to erosion. Lost plant species could have contained potential medicines, or genes that might have helped produce more resilient crops. Loss of natural habitats may trigger pandemics of unforeseen lethality. But does this all really pose an existential problem? Can we do with fewer species and fewer forests and wetlands? Intuitively it may seem so. However, our intuition gets things terribly wrong.[7] It may feel as if economy is what sustains society, and that nature is a luxury add-on. But it is the other way around. Society cannot exist without a functioning biosphere, and economy is irrelevant without society (Figure 1.1). We depend entirely on a functioning biosphere, even if it is hard to determine the critical limit to the destruction of nature that we should avoid.[8]

While the implications of the loss of nature remain difficult to pinpoint, climate change is a different story. The impacts of megadroughts, unprecedented floods, and heatwaves are starting to speak

Figure 1.1 It may seem that everything, including nature, is part of the economy. In fact, economy exists without society and no society can exist without a functioning biosphere.

for themselves. There are many ways of sketching the potentially devastating impacts of climate change. Focusing on the economic cost reveals that doing something now is much cheaper than waiting.[9] But there is also a human cost.[10] The problem really dawned on me in 2017 when I was at a conference on tropical biology on the Yucatan peninsula. The tremendous heat and humidity got my cold-adapted Dutch mind wondering: Surely these conditions can't be good for humans? At what temperatures do humans actually function best? I started looking for literature, and found surprisingly little about this fundamental question. Some papers showed declining cognitive capacity or rising aggression at elevated temperatures, but those were just a few scattered studies. Home in Holland, my friend Xu Chi from Nanjing University happened to come and visit our lab for several months. We pondered the issue, and, both being rooted in ecology, started wondering whether humans have a definable climate niche. We know the global distribution of species ranging from penguins to palms is restricted to specific conditions, but what about humans? We didn't expect much of a niche limitation, given that people live from the poles to the tropics. After all, clothes, heating, and air conditioning can make life comfortable almost anywhere. Nonetheless, we did what ecologists looking for niche evidence do: plot human population density as a function of environmental conditions such as mean annual temperature and rainfall. To our surprise, the data indeed suggested a distinct climate niche for our species.[11] People live almost everywhere, yet the vast bulk of our species is concentrated in a relatively narrow range of conditions around a mean annual temperature of around 13 °C. Was that just a coincidence? To dig a bit deeper, with the help of colleagues steeped in archaeology and climate history, we reconstructed the climate conditions under which most humans lived up to 6,000 years ago. Strangely, it turned out that, despite all technological advances and increases in ease of migration, the human climate niche seemed unaltered over the millennia. Humans still flock together in the same climate sweet spot as thousands of years ago. Could there be some fundamental mechanism making humans seek out those conditions? Support for this somewhat radical idea came from an unexpected direction. Economists had independently started looking into the effects of climate variations on economic production in 166 countries. Rather than simply plotting GDP against climate, they looked for economic outputs for each individual country as it varied between warmer and colder years. It turned out that any

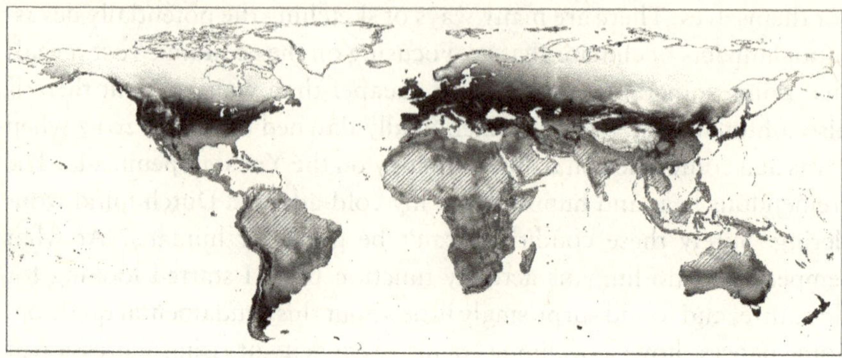

Figure 1.2 Climate suitability in 2070 for a business-as-usual scenario. The striped area – home to about one-third of the world population – is where global warming would cause near-uninhabitable conditions. (By Xu Chi, based on analysis in Lenton *et al.*, "Quantifying the human cost of global warming."[12])

deviation pushing a country further away from a mean annual temperature of around 13 °C reduced its output.[13] This was true globally across agricultural and nonagricultural activity in rich and poor countries. Stunningly, this indicated the same optimal temperature we had inferred.

Of course, the robustness of those findings raised a further question: What could this imply for our future? As the planet keeps warming, how many people will be left outside their climate niche fifty years from now? Our estimate was around 3 billion.[14] Of course, this estimation involved many assumptions and complicated computations. We therefore took a different angle to double-check the order of magnitude. We asked what the hottest places on Earth were – so hot that few people live there. Mean annual temperatures of above 29.0 °C seemed a good threshold. Such temperature extremes are found in only 0.8 percent of the global land surface, mostly concentrated in the Sahara. Fast-forward half a century from now, those conditions seem likely to prevail on one-fifth of the world's land, exposing about 3.5 billion humans to potentially uninhabitable conditions (Figure 1.2). A third of humanity is a lot of people. Will they be able to adapt? It's hard to say, but the fact that those happen to be also the poorest regions will not make it easier. Of course, one way of adapting to the new reality is migration. As some places become too hot to live, others will actually get more livable. Think of Siberia and northern Canada. As argued in Chapter 6 (Buying Time), migration must be part of the adaptation, just as it is for other species and just as it has been for humans for hundreds of thousands of years. If done well, the benefits can be great, both for migrants and for the receiving communities.[15] Nonetheless, the social challenge of relocating one-third of humanity within half a century is huge.

A Societal Crisis

Clearly, a planetary crisis driven by humans is starting to endanger humanity. This book is about turning the ship. As we will see, there are different reasons why that is challenging, but one stands out: excessive concentration of wealth in the hands of a few.

Wealth is not so much a problem of consumption. Bill Gates's favorite food is cheeseburgers, but he can only eat so many of them. Nor is it a problem of unfairness. True, the wealthiest 1 percent own almost half of the world's wealth, while the bottom half possess only around 0.75 percent.[16] Poverty is a huge problem, but the very existence of wealthy people is not usually considered unfair. The real problem of excessive wealth concentration is that it results in 'state capture.' Excessively wealthy people change the rules and manipulate perceptions in ways that make it easier to gain even more wealth, often at the cost of the planet and society. Connecting back to climate change, for more than half a century, wealthy parties in the fossil-fuel industry have been working to discredit the science that warns against climate change.[17] Those strategies worked. Society still pays an annual $6 trillion worth of explicit and implicit subsidies for fossil-fuel use,[18] funding its own demise. Such problems turn out to be difficult to solve, mainly because powerful parties with vested interests work against any solution. We will get back to how this works in detail, but the key point is simple: while lucrative industries are ruining the planet, the resulting concentration of wealth and power also make it hard to do something about that.

As wealth becomes more concentrated, it unavoidably starts affecting democracy. That has been known for millennia. The economist Joseph Stigler received the Nobel Prize for his work in the 1970s analyzing the problem of wealth concentration.[19] Half a century earlier the Italian polymath Vilfredo Pareto also suggested that wealth inequality was an inevitable threat to democracy – a young Benito Mussolini attended some of his classes.[20] But the problem was noted long before that. In his *Politics*, Aristotle approves of the practice in ancient Greece of ostracizing individuals who "seemed to predominate too much through their wealth," noting that "the encroachments of the rich are more destructive to the state than those of the people." In the *Laws*, Plato states that the richest should not possess more than four times what the poorest have. Any surplus should be handed over to the state.[21] Throughout history, the worry was not so much the unfairness of inequality as how excessive wealth concentration threatens the functioning of societies.

Wealth concentration arose when humans changed from being hunter-gatherers to a sedentary lifestyle.[22] You simply cannot carry much around in a nomadic hunter-gatherer life, so there was no way to accumulate substantial property. Interviews with the few remaining hunter-gatherers reveal that they do not see the point of possessing things. That changed with the rise of civilizations.[23] Wealth inequality has been with us ever since. What is new is the scale. When the playing field is a village, wealth concentration is less pronounced than in a kingdom or a nation. Nowadays mechanisms of wealth concentration work on a global scale, with spectacular results.[24] Not only do the richest 1 percent own most of the wealth, they also produce the same carbon emissions as the poorest 66 percent.[25] Moreover, a small group of billionaires globally owns most of the news media,[26] and billionaires are heavily overrepresented in political positions, especially in autocracies.[27, 28] This is best known for countries such as Russia, Venezuela, Angola, Myanmar, and Sudan. But in 2023 China had 116 billionaires in government, representing 36 percent of political positions.[29] And for the USA the link became obvious in 2025 with the massive attack on democratic institutions by the wealthiest person in the world, Elon Musk, together with the freshly elected president and fellow billionaire Donald Trump.

Is wealth concentration inevitable? The short answer is yes. Surprisingly, the laws of mathematics tell us that, even if everyone is equal in intelligence and temperament, large wealth inequality may arise solely by chance.[30] That may seem strange, but picture a simple game: everyone in a group starts with $100. Then, in each round, a roll of the dice decides the percentage of cash each player gains or loses. (The total amount of money in the group is kept constant by applying a correction tax after each round; a fixed fraction of each player's stack is redistributed.) What happens in the long run? By pure chance, one player usually ends up with almost all the cash – not because they are good at the game, but because of the way numbers work. The key is that the gains or losses are computed as a fraction of the capital. If you have very little, you can neither lose nor gain much. This makes poverty 'sticky.'[31] Most of us make an income by working for a salary, which does not depend upon capital. Work can make you rich, but never extremely rich. The game is entirely different when income is derived from capital, which it is for the very wealthy. For instance, for Elon Musk to earn his hundreds of billions on a yearly income of $150,000, he would have had to start working when the Egyptians were still building their pyramids. That is not the way extreme wealth is built up.

A curious fact we noted when we were working with economists and ecologists on the strange emergence of inequality is that patterns in nature look very similar to those in society.[32] Inequality between species resembles inequality between persons in society. Just as a small percentage of humans have most of the money, a small fraction of species form most of the biomass in nature. This is true whether you look at communities of mushrooms, rodents, birds, beetles, trees, or even intestinal bacteria. For instance, in the Amazon rainforest 1 percent of the approximately 4,000 tree species form around 50 percent of the biomass, and biologists cannot identify traits that explain this success.[33] Curiously, the dominance pattern of ranked species is almost indistinguishable from that of billionaires (Figure 1.3). Those are the simple pleasures of being a scientist. Finding a remarkable pattern and then trying to figure out why. Our first intuition was that the multiplication mechanism was at work again. Rodents can have good years when food or climate permit the doubling of their populations, or bad years when their population is halved. Indeed, the multiplication game may explain why rarity is a 'sticky state,' causing the vast majority of species to be very rare.[34] However, the parallel only goes so far. In nature, abundance comes at a cost. The more dominant you become, the more your natural enemies thrive. That is essentially why monocultures require so much pesticide to keep them intact. This is a well-studied mechanism that helps keep nature diverse.

In society, things work differently. The mechanism to prevent excessive wealth inequality is straightforward: wealth redistribution. This can be done, for instance, through taxation of wealth (taxation on income is much less effective, for reasons that should be obvious by now). However, the wealthier an individual, the easier it becomes to duck such

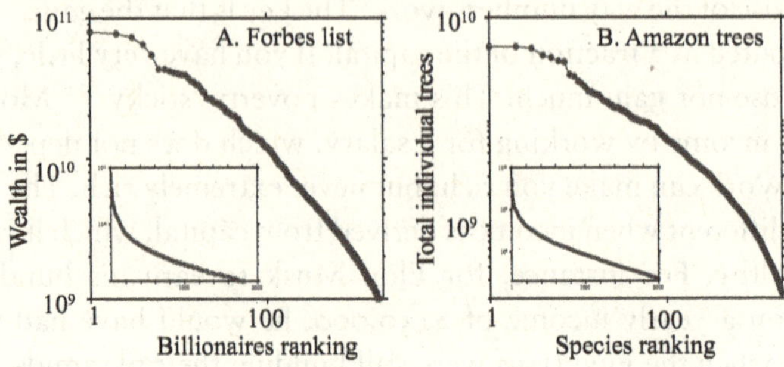

Figure 1.3 Runaway wealth concentration produces patterns resembling those found among species in nature. Just as 1 percent of the people own half the global wealth, 1 percent of the Amazon tree species accounts for 50 percent of the forest biomass. Adapted from Scheffer *et al.*, "Inequality in nature and society."[35]

redistribution by using the power afforded by wealth to shape the rules, or to find ways to circumvent them. Again, this does not require a wealthy individual to be smart. They simply have to hire people who are. Consequently, tax rates paid by the wealthiest people have decreased over the past half-century.[36] Wealth inequality also tends to increase during times of crisis, as the richest can better navigate trouble and influence how rules are reshaped during tumultuous periods.[37] The Covid-19 pandemic is just the latest example in a pattern that is discernible since medieval times. Billionaires' wealth has risen $5 trillion since the pandemic, the biggest surge since records began.[38]

The fact that wealth has become extremely concentrated in the hands of a few has changed the way the world works, and has therefore changed our options for future change. As we will see, the unprecedented wealth concentration of today has been facilitated by the rise of neoliberal policies since the 1970s. Such policies relax taxation and regulation, allowing corporations to thrive, often at the cost of planetary degradation and societal ills. For instance, large profits are made from addictive products such as tobacco, painkillers, and social media. The power that results from the associated wealth concentration leads to distortions of policies and perceptions that make it difficult to break away from the status quo. Meanwhile, rising inequality, weakening institutions, and perceived unfairness help fuel a trend toward far-right populism, xenophobia, and isolationism that is starting to challenge democracies and global cooperation. Also, runaway wealth concentration is increasingly powering autocracies and their opaque relationships with webs of billionaires and corporations, actively challenging the institutions meant to regulate the wealth concentration that threatens the climate, nature, and ordinary people worldwide.[39] Those trends and their causal linkages are the topic of Chapter 5. For now, it suffices to note that the trouble mentioned in the book's title consists of two closely intertwined strains: a planetary strain and a societal strain. Finding ways to tip out of trouble requires seeing the big picture. That is the aim of this book.

Who Are We?

As a last element, before we take off, let me reflect for a minute on the question of agency: what power do we have? What can we really do? And, equally important: whom do I mean when I say 'we'? When *The Economist* presented a special issue on the Anthropocene, its cover had a message: "Humans have changed the way the world works. Now they have to change the way they think about it, too."[40] That may seem very true, but if you try to unpack the word "they" it turns out to be a Pandora's box. Who precisely are the humans *The Economist* is talking about? Who are 'they' and who are 'we'? 'We' is a tricky word. As I use it, sometimes it means the reader and me. Sometimes, me and my colleagues. That should be clear from the context. The danger is when 'we' is used more broadly for humanity. When I write, "*We* are in climate trouble, so *we* should reduce our carbon footprint," it is reasonable to ask who I mean. Most of the climate change burden falls on the Global South's low-income countries, which are least able to cope and most exposed to dangerous new weather patterns. Their climate problem is caused almost entirely by the countries of the Global North. A small, wealthy section of humanity caused most of the climate change, while the most damaging effects hit the majority of people who hardly took part in causing it. So, what should 'we' do? A logical thought is there are too many people on the planet, but that misses the main point: consumption.[41] The carbon footprint of a citizen of a country such as Malawi, Niger, or Rwanda is more than a hundred times lower than that of the average person in the USA or Australia.[42] Family sizes are larger in Africa, but having a single child in the USA still produces an order of magnitude more carbon than a ten-child family in Malawi. A similar pattern holds for the loss of nature. The ecological footprint estimates how many Earths would be needed to sustain humanity in the long run. We would need eight Earths if all humans consumed at the US level. If the living standard of Eritrea was the norm, half an Earth would do.[43] It is thus easy to see that in the short run, reducing consumption and carbon emissions in the Global North is many times more effective than changing things in the Global South. You probably already know this, and I am very much aware of it too. I also know that I am a child of the Global North and cannot avoid thinking from that perspective. Throughout the book I will nonetheless keep using the term 'we,' broadly meaning citizens of the Global North unless otherwise specified.

So, to sum up: to pass the world on to our grandchildren in the best possible shape, we would need to curb global warming and the loss of nature as quickly as possible. To curb global warming, we need to stop mining fossil fuels. To stop the loss of nature, shifting to a largely plant-based diet is probably the single most effective step we can take, and it has benefits for climate neutrality, too. Of course, it is relevant how many people live on the planet, as humanity's ecological footprint is the sum of individual ones. Many things are moving in the right direction already. Family size, waste recycling, electric car sales, solar panels, wind turbines, house insulation, the rise of meat substitutes, vegan milk, etc. all contribute to the change we need. Yet, looking at the end result, the rise in atmospheric carbon and loss of nature show little sign of slowing down. Interpreting that isn't rocket science. We are not doing enough.

A fundamental shift of scale is needed in all those efforts. There are good ideas on what a sustainable economy should look like: a "doughnut economy,"[44] a "post-growth" or "degrowth" economy,[45] with a focus on well-being rather than economic output,[46] built on a different food-production system.[47] This work is hugely important, as it shows that a sustainable economy is possible. Yet so far there has been little thinking about how a shift to such a new economy may realistically happen.[48] In other words, we know roughly where we want to be, but not how to get there. Filling that gap is the goal of this book. Can we learn from the transformations of past civilizations? Does the information revolution make it easier to succeed? Do markets and transnational corporations make it harder? Should we abandon or tweak the system? I will get back to all of those questions. But first, there is a more fundamental question: Is there any evidence that it could be possible to achieve change that is both massive and fast enough to pass on the world to our grandchildren in good shape? As you will see, I am hopeful, if only because humanity has tipped out of trouble many times before. But before we get into too much detail, I should explain what I mean by tipping. The next chapter provides a simple, intuitive explanation of the tipping point theory on which much of my career has been based. It is also central to my argument, as tipping is the only thing that can deliver what humanity needs so urgently: big change fast.[49]

2 THE TIPPING

History is full of inspiring examples of social tipping. Let me start close to home. The wealth of my small country of Holland, like that of much of the Western world, was in part built by enslaving others. The business model of the transatlantic slave trade essentially consisted of buying enslaved people in West Africa and shipping them to the Americas. Millions died in the process, which was only the tip of an iceberg of suffering. Activists long stressed that slavery was blatantly dissonant with Christian morals. Yet the lucrative practice continued for about four centuries. Then suddenly, within a few decades, it completely vanished. How did that happen despite formidable economic interests? Meanwhile, in China, it was common to break and then bind the feet of young girls tightly in order to change their shape and size. Despite occasional bursts of objection, this ancient practice of foot binding lasted for about a millennium until it finally vanished within one generation. Why did it last so long, and how did it disappear so swiftly? While the Chinese were binding feet and Europeans were in their Middle Ages, social experimentation flourished in what is now the Southwestern United States. From roughly 500 till around 1300, the Pueblo people, also known as Anasazi, developed small but elaborate societies with beautiful pottery and architecture. Strikingly, archaeological evidence reveals five distinct waves of development, each ending with the sudden abandonment of the villages and practices before starting anew in other places. What drove those societies to abruptly stop what they were doing and start experimenting with new settlement locations, architecture, and pottery styles? I will get back to those and many other examples in detail, but first I want to introduce the universal phenomenon behind those and many other surprising shifts: tipping points.

The expression 'tipping point' is easy to understand. Though he didn't originate it, we must thank the journalist Malcolm Gladwell for popularizing this intuitive term. In his bestseller *The Tipping Point* he describes it as "that magic moment when an idea, trend, or social behavior crosses a threshold, tips, and spreads like wildfire."[1] Fittingly, the exponential spread of the term after the publication of his book illustrates the very phenomenon that fascinated him (Figure 2.1). The term had been introduced in the scientific literature of the 1950s to describe a mechanism of racial segregation.[2] Beyond a certain threshold fraction of nonwhite inhabitants, white residents would start to leave a neighborhood, driving a self-amplifying feedback. Fascination with the mathematics of tipping points also existed well before the term became popular. In the 1960s the French mathematician René Thom developed the 'catastrophe theory' describing the fundamentals of why sometimes a tiny event may set into motion an irreversible sea-change. Popularized by his charismatic British colleague Christopher Zeeman, Thom's ideas triggered a wave of interest.[3] The magic also reached the painter Salvador Dalí, who was so struck by the idea that

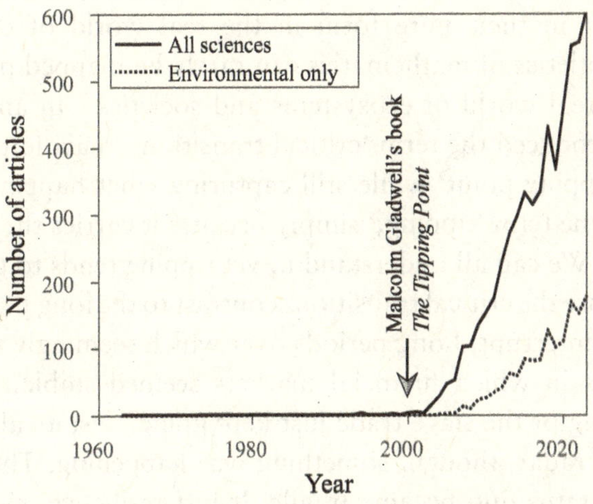

Figure 2.1 The frequency of the term 'tipping point' in scientific literature.

decades later he depicted a mathematical graph of it in his final painting, *The Swallow's Tail*. He posed in front of the painting for his last portrait before he died. It is easy to see why Dalí and so many others were struck by the tipping point theory. It captures something that we can all relate to, and yet it keeps surprising us.

It may seem strange that the same mathematical laws of dynamic systems can describe those very different examples, as well as many others, including the onset of a migraine, the termination of glaciations, the capsizing of a canoe, and the abolition of slavery. Yet, on an abstract level, all those phenomena correspond to essentially the same situation: a critical point where change becomes self-reinforcing, where change starts invoking ever more change, propelling a rapidly accelerating transition to a contrasting state.[4] That is the definition of 'tipping point' we will use in this book.

Some scholars criticize the broad term 'tipping point' as lacking precision.[5] It's true that mathematical theory distinguishes between many types of such critical situations,[6] and indeed, it would be mathematically more precise to speak of phenomena such as saddle-node bifurcation, torus destruction, a zero Eigenvalue, a homoclinic bifurcation, a noise-induced transition, symmetry-breaking, or even a subcritical Poincaré–Andronov–Hopf bifurcation. Alas, there are two problems with that. First, there will be very few people who understand what you mean. Second, none of those fantastic mathematical phenomena exist in their pure form in the real world of complex systems. The subtleties of mathematics can rarely be mapped precisely onto the messy real world of ecosystems and societies.[7] In an earlier book, I have introduced the term 'critical transition' to avoid the contentious term 'tipping point' while still capturing what happens.[8] But now I return to the term 'tipping,' simply because it carries the correct intuitive feeling. We can all understand it, yet tipping tends to takes us by surprise because the critical transitions contrast to the long periods of inertia that they interrupt. Long periods over which seemingly nothing changed. Periods in which financial markets seemed stable, periods when foot binding or the slave trade just kept going, despite all objections. Under the radar, though, something was happening. The seemingly unaltered status quo became fragile. It lost resilience, making it invisibly vulnerable.

Loss of Resilience

What circumstances are needed to trigger a tipping point? Why did a street vendor setting himself on fire in an act of protest cause the Arab Spring, a wave of protests that uprooted seemingly stable regimes across North Africa and the Middle East? Why did the bankruptcy of Lehman Brothers bank trigger a global financial collapse? Why did Covid-19 infections spread worldwide and lead to the deaths of so many elderly people? Words that come to mind are 'fragility' and 'vulnerability'. Or, seen from the other side, a lack of resilience. The Arab strongman regimes had apparently lost resilience, becoming fragile enough for a single protest to precipitate a cascade of revolutions throughout the region. The network of financial institutions had quietly become vulnerable, allowing a crisis in a single bank to trigger a series of collapses. Elderly persons can be frail, with little surplus capacity of vital systems such as their lungs, cognition, and immune systems, allowing disruptions to cause systemic failure more easily.

To get a feel for what I mean by resilience in this context, here is a thought experiment. You rented a cabin to spend a week with friends on an island. To get to the island, you have a very small rowboat. Ten crates of beer and other goodies must be transported. How many will you take each trip? You put the first crate on the bottom of the boat. That will be an easy and safe trip, but you would need to row back and forth ten times. Could you put another crate on top? Or two, three, four, five? Each extra crate will save you rowing effort, at the cost of stability. The resilience of the boat's upright position decreases, making it more likely that a wave could cause the boat to capsize.

Another way to imagine how the loss of resilience works is through marble-in-a-cup diagrams (Figure 2.2). In this view, the status quo is at the bottom of the cup. Perturbations may push the marble around, but if the cup is deep the marble will always roll back to the bottom. The status quo is resilient. By contrast, when the cup is small and shallow even a minor perturbation may flip the marble out of it. How tipping points work in society is the fundamental question at the heart of the book. It is the topic of Chapter 4, where we ask how current theory could help understand and enact social change. But for now, the intuitive notion of how tipping works is enough.

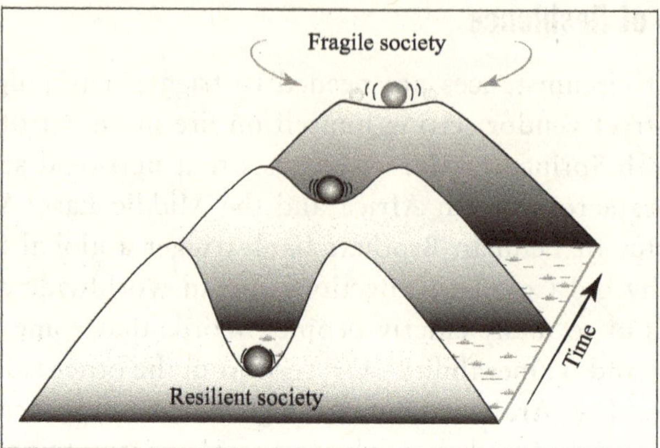

Figure 2.2 Loss of resilience depicted in stability landscapes. (See Scheffer *et al.*, "Loss of resilience preceded transformations of pre-Hispanic Pueblo societies."[9])

Early Warning Signals

One of the big questions is whether we can see tipping points coming. Could we have foreseen the end of slavery or of foot binding, the onset of the Arab Spring, the global financial crisis, or the sudden burnout of a productive young scientist? The status quo usually seems stable until the very last moment. Centuries of attacks on practices such as slavery or foot binding seemed ineffective, but they slowly eroded the resilience of settled ways of doing things. In the end, most transitions are triggered by chance events, making their precise timing fundamentally unpredictable. On the other hand, the likelihood of a given event triggering a critical transition are larger if resilience of the status quo is low. Scientists are starting to see how resilience of complex systems can be probed. The same math that helps us understand tipping points also points to symptoms that may reveal the loss of resilience that precedes tipping. These symptoms are universal, applying across varied systems ranging from the brain to the climate system or societies.

How is that possible? It is not as mysterious as it seems. The basic idea can be grasped simply from stability landscapes. As resilience decreases, the stability basin around the status quo shrinks, and the slopes around the equilibrium flatten. This means that the ball rolls back more slowly if you push it a bit away from the bottom of the valley. In other words, the return rate to the equilibrium after small perturbations becomes slower. Doing such experiments can be impossible in practice, because creating such a perturbation may be problematic. It is unethical to perturb the financial market to see what happens, or a person to see if they might get a burnout. However, natural fluctuations can also reflect the change in resilience. This is because reduced vigor of recovery (low return rate to equilibrium) implies that the system lingers longer in states to which it has become pushed by random events and fluctuations. This is reflected in larger fluctuations (higher 'variance'), but also in slower change (higher 'temporal autocorrelation'). As the tendency to return to the equilibrium becomes weaker, the 'memory' of previous states in the signal increases (Figure 2.3). The state of the system now starts looking more like that in the recent past. As an intuitive example, think of the perturbation of someone's mood by a nasty telephone call. If the good mood returns in a few hours, that indicates greater resilience than if it takes days to get over it.[10]

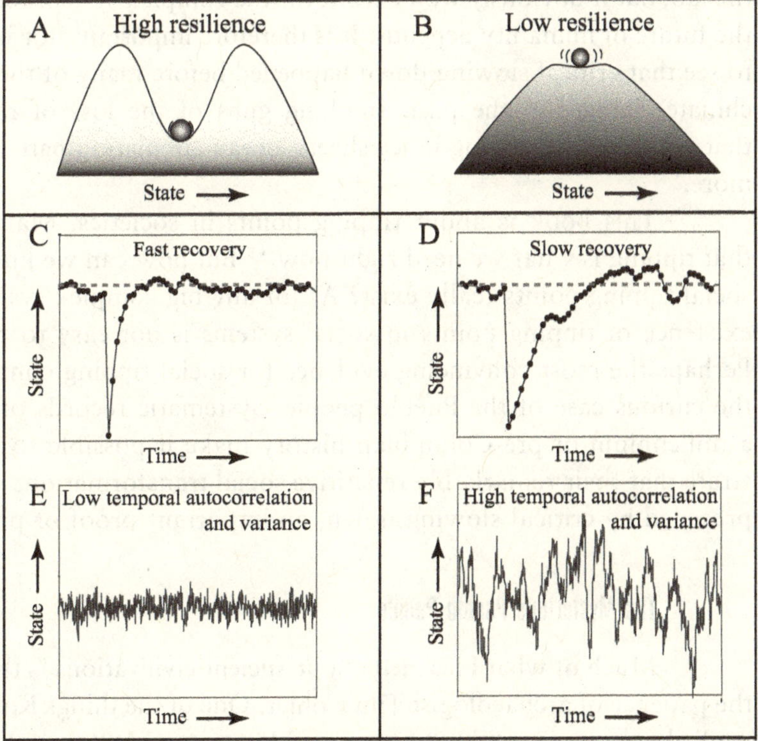

Figure 2.3 Dynamic indicators of resilience.

In the technical literature, the underlying phenomenon is known as 'critical slowing down.' 'Critical' because the slower recovery begins when the system approaches a critical threshold, a tipping point. Dynamic indicators of resilience (DIORs) based on this phenomenon have been used to identify loss of resilience in systems as diverse as the climate, human postural balance, mood, and ecosystems.[11] This may all sound a bit technical, but I bring it up for a reason. At first, within the small community of researchers working on this topic, we thought of those indicators basically as useful early warning signals for tipping.[12] But later we realized that evidence of critical slowing down before a major transition may also be a smoking gun, suggesting that the transition was related to a tipping point. That is not a minor feat. The existence of tipping points in complex systems such as the climate, society, or ecosystems is not easy to prove.[13] Ideally, a scientist does many replicated experiments under controlled conditions to reach a conclusion. That is great if you can hold your system in a test tube in the lab, but it obviously won't work for the complex systems on which the future of humanity depends. It is therefore important, for instance, to see that critical slowing down happened before many of the abrupt climate changes in the past, smoking guns of the loss of resilience that preceded the tipping in ice sheets, ocean circulation patterns, and more.[14]

This book is about tipping points in societies. Many agree that tipping is what we need right now.[15] But how can we know that social tipping points really exist? As for any big complex system, the existence of tipping points in social systems is not easy to prove.[16] Perhaps the most convincing evidence for social tipping comes from the curious case of the Pueblo people. Systematic records of almost a millennium of pre-Columbian history make it possible to demonstrate that their remarkably repetitive social transformations were all preceded by critical slowing down, an important proof of principle.

The Mysterious Pueblo People

Much of what I learned about ancient civilizations is thanks to the patience of archaeologist Tim Kohler. One of the things Kohler has studied is known as "the greatest vanishing act in American history," the end of the famous Pueblo people's culture in the American Southwest. These people – known as the Anasazi in older literature –

Figure 2.4 Remains of Pueblo people architecture (www.flickr.com/photos/natio
nalparkservice/26938954403).

constructed elaborate cliff dwellings in the Mesa Verde region for about
a millennium until they suddenly vanished (Figure 2.4). Abandoning
everything, they moved to the Rio Grande and other places.[17] The
mystery of why they abandoned their settlements is well known, but
equally fascinating is what happened over the preceding millennium. It
turns out that smaller versions of the Great Vanishing Act had happened
about five times before. The archaeological evidence suggests that on
each of those occasions the people abandoned not just their villages but
also their old ways of doing things – pottery styles, rituals, and architecture. Why? We do not know for certain, and there are multiple possible
interpretations. Yet there are clues, such as rising numbers of broken
skulls and other signs of violence, suggesting that the societies became
unstable. Eventually, the people abruptly abandoned their buildings and
started new settlements in other places, experimenting with new ways of
art, agriculture, and construction. The most successful settlements grew,
attracting more people and kicking off a new cycle of rise and fall.

The reason the Pueblo people are important in the context
of this book is that, with Tim Kohler and others, we found proof
that those societal transformations were related to real tipping points.[18]
The dynamic indicators revealed that a gradual decline in resilience

started decades before the critical moments when people decided to abandon the old way of doing things. Tim Kohler and his colleagues painstakingly quantified a unique uninterrupted time series of annual building activity over more than eight hundred years, using tree rings to reconstruct the year in which each of the trees used for wood in the buildings was felled. The variation in the width of growth rings reflects annual differences in growing conditions for the trees due to year-to-year differences in climatological conditions. The unique sequence of good and bad years makes it possible to align the history of all individual trees in the region and reconstruct the number of trees harvested each year, thus creating a record of construction activity that we used to probe the dynamic indicators of resilience. Leading up to each collapse, the year-to-year fluctuations in building activity became wider and slower, precisely the dynamical indicators of slowing down predicted by the mathematical theory. Thus, the collapses didn't come out of the blue. They happened as those societies became fragile. With their resilience lost, they became easily pushed over the tipping point for collapse. The probability of getting those results by chance was less than 1 in 250.[19] In other words, we found a convincing smoking gun for social tipping.

We could also reveal the role of rising vulnerability by looking more closely at how the crashes aligned with climatic fluctuations. Tree growth rings made it possible to trace good and bad years for agriculture. The Pueblo people did not use irrigation, so harvests depended on having rainfall at the right time of the year. Our rainfall reconstruction revealed that while years of failed harvest likely triggered some of the collapses, this happened during times of fragility. In times when they were resilient, the societies could easily handle worse droughts than the ones that finally did them in. In conclusion, the time series that the archaeologists assembled to reconstruct the repeated transformations of the Pueblo societies over a millennium provided a unique opportunity to test the tipping point hypothesis. The fact that each of the transformations was preceded by signs of critical slowing down, together with the observation that eventually even small perturbations triggered collapse, implies quantitative support for the idea that gradual loss of resilience of the status quo can prime societies for big transformations. A reason for fear perhaps, but also a reason for hope.

3 HOW CIVILIZATIONS TRANSFORMED

The case of the Pueblo people is unique because it covers a millennium of repeated transformations, but the lack of written sources means that we don't know in great detail what happened. Moreover, abandoning settlements during or after a crisis is just one of the many ways societies can tip. Time to look deeper. With examples ranging from state turnover to technological revolutions and norm shifts, this chapter is a helicopter view over humanity's history of social tipping. As we will see, past tipping events were a mixed bag. Sometimes, people suffered in the wake of change. But often, transformations kicked off better times in which problems that had plagued societies were overcome. There is a lot to learn from that when determining how to tip humanity out of trouble now. Mechanisms differ widely, and in most cases there is debate about what happened precisely. Nonetheless, history rhymes, and as you will see the past is a treasure trove for our quest to find the rules of the rhyme. Those rules are important because, as the English philosopher and historian R. G. Collingwood famously wrote:[1] "The only clue to what man can do is what man has done."

The Birth of Civilization

The earliest and perhaps most fundamental transitions in human history were those from small and mobile hunter-gatherer groups to large, sedentary 'civilizations.' The word 'civilized' has a positive connotation, but let's get it straight that civilization is not something inherently good or bad. It is simply what happens when humans get organized in large groups and start living in urban settings. This invariably comes with specialization, hierarchy, and the development of an elite that concentrates wealth and power. It also comes with a move away from animistic beliefs toward more human-like gods, with a system of rituals and beliefs that reinforces the power of the elite. Curiously, all this seems to be an inevitable package deal.[2]

It only dawned on me how miraculous that is when I was sitting on a big block in a Mayan ruin, staring at the pillars and representations of gods. Why was it so similar to the ruins I had seen in Greece? Of course, I had seen pictures of Mayan remains in books, but it is one thing to read about them and quite another thing to be there. As far as we know, the hunter-gatherers who colonized the Americas started to build structures with pillars, invent gods, and create a monetary system independently from anything happening in Eurasia. There is a large literature on the question of how complex societies developed, but the mere fact that roughly the same thing emerged independently in about six areas worldwide is food for thought. My complexity-attuned scientist's mind tells me that this type of organization is an 'attractor' to which systems inevitably move, like a marble rolling to the bottom of a cup. Or consider the emergence of eyes in animals. The eye has evolved many times independently in different lineages of organisms.[3] The remarkable camera-like eye of humans and other vertebrates evolved independently in animals such squids and octopuses. The eye's design was apparently something that had to happen, an accident in waiting. Civilization turns out to be a massive attractor too. It simply had to happen. This is not to say that the hunter-gatherer life cannot be an attractor too. Under some conditions it is clearly a stable societal setting. For instance, Australian aboriginals maintained their hunter-gatherer lifestyle up till the colonization by the British, despite the fact that they had been in frequent contact with Polynesians for centuries.[4] Their organizational structure was thus a stable attractor rather than something maintained by naivety about alternatives. Nevertheless, under most conditions the package deal of a 'civilization' somehow becomes inevitable.

There is something else inevitable about civilizations. Something even more puzzling. They always come to an end. Sitting and watching birds flit around on the remains of the once impressive center of a thriving society, one cannot help asking why it collapsed. Details of the collapse of civilizations differ from case to case.[5] Sometimes people seem to have simply left. At other times a turbulent uproar brought down the elite and their associated symbols, structures, and belief systems. This can allow for a fresh start, but often at the cost of violence and sometimes prolonged 'dark ages' in which few signs of a new civilization are found at all. Just like 'civilization' and 'collapse,' the term 'dark ages' somehow carries a misleading connotation. Those episodes may be dark in the sense that they haven't left much in terms of written history or monumental architecture, thus leaving us ill-informed as to what happened. However, it is now agreed that dark ages may often have been happier times, freeing people of the burden of a system that rightly collapsed. For example, skeletons tell us that people lived longer and healthier lives after the fall of the Western Roman Empire.[6] Indeed, being part of a civilization was probably a bad deal for most people most of the time. Why would you want to quit your free life and become part of such a community anyway? Most likely you would be at the bottom of the hierarchy. Working hard, at risk of becoming ill or being subject to violence. It is better to leave that to others (and occasionally raid them). Indeed, the elite running civilizations seemed to have had two formidable challenges: (1) keep raiding barbarians out; and (2) keep the civilized (and enslaved) inhabitants in.[7]

Yet, despite its ills, civilization became the dominant way of living. A strong attractor, clearly, but also an unstable one. An oscillator, as we say in dynamical system science. Oscillators have a built-in tendency to go through cycles. Think of the sleep–wake cycle or the ongoing shifts between a depressed state and a hyperactive mania in people with bipolar disorder. Understanding how such autonomous destabilization works for civilizations, empires, and states may help us understand what could make societies unstable now too, even though there are important differences. Suffering of ordinary people has decreased over the past two centuries or so since slavery was abandoned, homicide rates have dropped, and life expectancy has greatly increased. We live in the best of times,[8] even if it doesn't feel like it. But those sweeping social improvements are relatively recent. No wonder then that premodern societies broke down regularly. But what held them together? And what made them crumble in the end? Could there be parallels to the modern world?

Collapse

The famous archaeologist Eric Cline would say yes. In his view there are strong parallels between the world's current situation and a dramatic period more than 3,000 years ago known as the Late Bronze Age collapse.[9] The records point to a multi-faceted crisis involving climate change, migrations, trade embargoes, and invasions. Empires and kingdoms collapsed all across the Mediterranean basin. It was a cascade of disasters that took down illustrious civilizations such as the Mycenaeans, Minoans, Hittites, Assyrians, Babylonians, Canaanites, and Egyptians. Just as nations are linked in our globalized world today, those peoples were linked in many ways. They traded intensively and had institutions for cooperation, including diplomatic embassies. So, what went wrong? Clay tablets give glimpses of the drama: "There is famine in our house; we will all die of hunger. If you do not arrive here quickly, we will die of hunger. You will not see a living soul from your land." Mixed groups of aggressive seafarers ruthlessly raided cities, and a Pharaoh anticipating the approach of the dreaded Sea Peoples wrote: "No land could stand before their arms. ... They desolated its people, and its land was like that which has never come into being. They were coming forward toward Egypt, while the flame was prepared before them." According to Cline, who has studied this period for much of his career, we can't understand what happened simply by piecing all the details together. Instead, it was some kind of systemic collapse of the entire network of states.[10] There is abundant evidence for drought[11] and famine, but also for violent invasions and earthquakes.[12] Most striking, however, was the domino effect in which the fall of one civilization led to the collapse of the others. Somehow, fragility was such that the disintegration of one of those societies caused the demise of the rest.

With only scant written evidence, it remains difficult to infer what made those societies so vulnerable. Documentation was much better 1,500 years later when the Western Roman Empire fell apart. Nonetheless, the precise cause of its demise remains also hard to say.

This is a trend. Wherever you look in the literature for explanations of the collapse of societies, you will find broad sets of possible mechanisms, an ambiguity that cannot simply be attributed to a lack of written accounts. Despite a wealth of documents, we remain equally in the dark regarding drivers of the fall of the Roman Empire or Chinese dynasties.

As I will show in the next section, a likely reason is that civilizations, like humans, become more fragile as they age, making it increasingly likely for a challenge to prove fatal. Multiple mechanisms contribute to such aging, and different perturbations may give the final push. We have quantitative evidence for rising fragility from the Pueblo people, but those were small-scale societies, hardly analogous to the more famous fallen empires. However, we do have qualitative observations pointing in the same direction for the latter. For instance, the Western Roman Empire eventually succumbed to invaders, despite having successfully dealt with such incursions and threats for centuries.[13] This suggests that it had become more vulnerable over time. As we will see next, a rise in fragility over time has happened systematically across a wide variety of states. Societies simply tend to become unstable with age.

Senescence

In a way, the instability of civilization is not surprising. Humans evolved to live as hunter-gatherers in small groups. Civilization became inevitable but remained challenging. We are simply not hardwired to live in complex societies, and keeping those new social organizations functioning has been a challenge from the start. It may be argued that religious texts such as the Bible and Qur'an reflect attempts to create sets of rules, norms, and values that helped overcome this radical shift in society and cement early states.[14] But there seems to be something in those larger civilizations that makes them destined to fall apart in the end. Over the centuries many thinkers have speculated that societies unavoidably become senescent, or deteriorate with age, over time, ultimately leading to their termination.[15] Much as societies can be ended by earthquakes, wars, or drought, an individual human may die from a range of illnesses, accidents, or events. But the chances of doing so inevitably rise with age, growing exponentially after childhood. Depressingly, the chances of dying in any particular year double more or less every seven years. This exponential increase is why most humans die roughly around the same age. In Europe the average age at death is around eighty, and no one reaches twice that age. The percentages of people reaching different ages is a direct function of how vulnerability rises over a lifetime.

One day, when I was fruitlessly trying to make sense of the wax and wane of 324 premodern states with my long-time scientific companion Egbert van Nes, it suddenly dawned on us that we could apply this risk-of-death approach to quantify the rise of vulnerability as societies age. After some struggles with the data and the math, we could demonstrate that the risk of termination for a society tended to rise sharply over the first two centuries and remained more or less constant thereafter.[16] That is quite different from the pattern of aging in humans, where the chance of death continues to increase as the end approaches. In societies, the benefits of youth fade over the first couple of centuries, but, unlike humans, some are able to last for much longer. While most societies we studied ended after about two centuries, some were able to persist for millennia (Figure 3.1).

Thus, societies do become more vulnerable as they age, but some seem to have the secret of long-lasting youth. What could cause the broad pattern of senescence, and what might explain the differences between societies that die young and those that grow old? Again, there is no shortage of suggestions. The influential diagnosis of the archaeologist Joseph Tainter is that it is a question of when costs outweigh the benefits of the increasingly complex organization needed to keep a growing empire working.[17] For the Western Roman Empire this makes sense. Taxes to keep the huge administration and army going were a heavy burden, and the mere fact that the average lifespan increased upon the disintegration of the empire suggests that health suffered from the costs of maintaining it.[18]

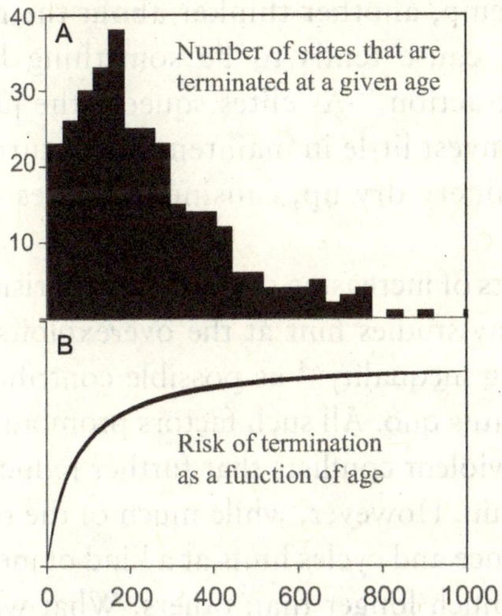

Figure 3.1 The distribution of longevities of 324 premodern states (A) implies that vulnerability increased with age (B). (Graph drawn by Egbert van Nes, adapted from Scheffer *et al.*, "The vulnerability of aging states."[19])

But there are more ideas out there. Peter Turchin is another prominent expert on the collapse of societies. Like me, he started out studying nature. More specifically, Peter modeled the cyclical nature of populations in rodents. A classic mechanism for such cycles is the interaction between predators and prey. Imagine a situation where there are many rabbits. In such an abundance of food, the number of foxes that prey on rabbits will grow until they deplete the rabbits, leading to famine and collapse among the fox population. Now in the absence of foxes, rabbits thrive again, kicking off a new cycle. Something similar was happening in the lakes I studied early in my career. Water fleas graze on phytoplankton – the tiny algae that make the lake water look green. As a result the water becomes clear, until the food is gone and the water fleas die of starvation, allowing the phytoplankton to make a comeback. This makes some lakes go through a cyclic alternation of clear and turbid water phases.[20] Turchin and his colleagues have shown that there is an element of such self-perpetuating cyclicity in human societies too.[21] In Turchin's diagnosis, destabilization often comes to a critical point when conflict arises within the elites that rule the state. According to Luke Kemp, another thinker about the mystery of collapse, the underlying cause tends to be something he calls "diminishing returns on extraction." As elites squeeze the juice out of the ordinary people and invest little in maintenance, returns from the wealth-generating machinery dry up, causing the elites to start fighting over what is left.[22]

In addition to the costs of increasing complexity and rising risks of conflict among elites, many studies hint at the overexploitation of natural resources[23] and rising inequality[24] as possible contributors to the loss of resilience of the status quo. All such factors promote discontent, and potentially lead to violent conflicts that further reduce confidence in the way things are run. However, while much of the thinking about mechanisms of senescence and cycles hints at a kind of inevitability, some societies survived much longer than others. What was their secret?

Rejuvenation

Suppression is one way for elites to prevent or at least postpone rebellion. But another very different possibility is that inclusive institutions – those where ordinary people can have a say – helped some societies remain strong.[25] One thing that may go wrong is elites becoming increasingly detached from the problems on the ground. As wealth reduces their own vulnerability, rulers may become less concerned about maintaining protection of the ordinary people. Societies may prevent such problems if they are set up in ways that allow them to adjust the rules of the game when things are going in the wrong direction.

A relatively recent example of such a readjustment is the Progressive Era that reshaped the USA from around the end of the nineteenth century.[26] The Industrial Revolution had led to the Gilded Age with an enormous but highly unequal increase in wealth. Poverty and pollution became worse and worse, and it seemed that nothing could be done about it because politics had become thoroughly corrupt. But something happened around the turn of the century that brought an end to all those ills. Curiously, it was not a revolution, and there was no centralized control or single leader who was responsible; Theodore Roosevelt was elected president, and many reforms were associated with his name. However, the momentum for change had simply become unstoppable. The initial phase of Progressivism was a groundswell, with many leaders scattered around the USA and ideas that co-evolved in a process with no gravitational center. Eventually it was the crisis of the Great Depression that triggered a more centralized response in the 1930s called the New Deal, led by President Franklin Roosevelt and supported by Congress.

The result of this remarkable period was a surprisingly broad and thorough revision that set the USA on a different track for the next half-century. It included anti-corruption laws, a better education system, environmental regulations, women's suffrage, labor unions, and more. Why? What made such a systemic move possible? Could it inspire the change we need now? The influential political scientist Robert Putnam has been fascinated by that question and, together with Shaylyn Romney Garrett, devoted a compelling book to it, *The Upswing*.[27] Putnam and Garrett were not able to pinpoint what had been cause and effect in this tumultuous period. Rather, the whole thing seemed to them more like a "braided river." Overlapping movements and middle-class social reformers addressed social ills. Investigative journalists known as 'muckrakers' wrote in popular magazines to expose corruption and other ills. The result was an avalanche of reforms in areas ranging from industry, government, and education to railroads, insurance, finance, and medicine. But, while there may be no simple cause–effect chain, the book captures the intuition that social change was, in this case, like a pendulum coming down and inevitably swinging up again. The 'downswing' during the Industrial Revolution resulted in many social problems. But even though the corrupted system seemed in the tight grip of elites that wanted to maintain the status quo, exposure of the problems and sensible actions by a plurality of thinkers inspired a massive movement that drove unstoppable change. Not a collapse, not a revolution, but a thorough revision of institutions that helped society thrive for decades. In light of our current problems, I find that very inspiring.

Could the upswing be a model for a transition to a happier and more sustainable society? We will get back to that question in more detail later. However, it is worth stressing that the American Progressive Era was not an isolated event, but rather part of a global quest for social improvements. The effects of the Industrial Revolution had led to deep social grievances across the world. What followed was a heterogeneous century of social change. At different times and in different ways, wealth became more equally distributed and social conditions improved. For instance, after unifying Germany, Otto von Bismarck started creating the first modern welfare state in the 1880s. Under his leadership as Chancellor of the German Empire a range of social benefits was introduced, including old-age insurance and socialized medicine. An important motivation for those improvements was to wrong-foot his socialist opponents.[28] This was similar to the approach of Abraham Kuyper in the Netherlands. Kuyper was a towering thought leader, a pastor, journalist, founder of the first political party, and of the 'Free University,' eventually serving as prime minister between 1901 and 1905.[29] He framed the need for reforms in an 1891 speech: "The palaces of the multi-millionaires rise along the wealth-paved roads trotted by the hunger marches of the unemployed." According to Kuyper, "a very large part of the belongings in this world are stolen property."[30] This sounds like a plea for revolution – yet, like Bismarck, Kuyper was actually eager to prevent a socialist revolution. In fact, the political party he started was called the Anti-Revolutionary Party, rejecting the tenets of the French Revolution.

While the biggest changes in the USA happened in the 1930s, major wealth redistribution and the rise of the modern welfare state in Western Europe happened only upon the end of World War II.[31] Yet there is a common pattern. In both cases, bursts of progress were the culmination of ideas that had matured over decades. Societies across the world were reimagined, not just in terms of wealth redistribution but also of broader social progress, including education and the emancipation of women and minorities.

Revolution

The social ills caused by the Industrial Revolution were not resolved so peacefully everywhere. In stark contrast to gradual revisions in the USA and Europe, revolutions such as those in Russia (1917) and China (1927) represented more radical and violent ways to push back against social injustice. Of course, that was not the first time in history such revolutions occurred. The iconic example of a violent revision of the rules is the French Revolution, arguably one of the most important social turning points in history. Like the social reforms that followed the Industrial Revolution, the French Revolution was preceded by rising tension and great inequality.[32] There was widespread unemployment, and rising food prices were a major problem. The inflated Paris population (600,000) was especially hard to feed through small-scale agriculture, given the limited means of transport. A poor harvest and the subsequent harsh winter of 1788 probably helped prime the country for the revolution in 1789. Also, just as in the American upswing, there was a broadening public debate facilitated by improved education and literacy, which widened access to newspapers. The number of written outlets boomed from a few censored newspapers to hundreds of different newspapers and pamphlets.[33] This decentralized the debate, away from the court in Versailles and to the city of Paris in venues such as coffee houses, reading clubs, and masonic lodges. The capacity of the royals and associated elites to influence emerging views dwindled, and Enlightenment ideas on equality and democracy flourished. Like the social improvements that addressed the ills caused by the Industrial Revolution, the changes in France did not happen in isolation. In fact, the new constitution was formulated in 1789 with the help of Thomas Jefferson, just one year after the American constitution was ratified. Jefferson, who was in France during the storming of the Bastille, was a supporter of the ideas of the revolution, although he objected to violent means.

The way the revolution unfolded vividly illustrates the unpredictable nature of such cascading events. The king had assembled an Estates General consisting of nobility, clergy, and 'commons' in equal proportions. However, the commons was joined by parts of the other factions, eventually declaring themselves the national assembly and writing a new constitution. On July 12 the assembly went into a nonstop session as rumors circulated that the king wanted to shut it down. Crowds took to the streets. Soldiers refused to disperse them, and together they attacked the Bastille. The king remained in place, but with little power in a new constitutional monarchy. In the following months there was a breakdown of law and order and a general panic. Members of the nobility fled. Feudalism was abandoned. Eventually, polarization within the revolutionary movement resulted in the Robespierre-led 'reign of terror' which sent 17,000 people to the guillotine, including Robespierre himself in the end.

The ideals of the French Revolution provided the basis for today's liberal democracy. However, dramatic shifts in power at the time paved the way for Napoleon's aggressive autocracy, quenching the nascent democracy after just a few years. Countless revolutions followed. While they differed in many ways, violence often took a heavy toll, and democracy would not take hold for a long time. Instead, in one way or another, autocratic leaders were typically followed by other autocratic leaders, whether from the same faction or a different one.[34]

Norm Shifts

Like the French Revolution, many stories of revolutionary transformation read as cautionary tales: "You wanted big change fast? Be careful what you wish for." For more recent examples of how abandoning an oppressive system does not necessarily lead to improvement for ordinary people, consider the Arab Spring or the fall of the Berlin Wall. Arguably, if we want to transform the world in a graceful way, we should maintain the essence of the institutions that allow modern societies to function. When I refer to 'institutions' in this book, I am using the broad interpretation of that term in sociology: the sets of written and unwritten rules that structure social interactions. These are the building blocks of social order, such as the language we use, religion, politics, business, science, media, laws, the economic system, arts, and education. Loss of such building blocks can make the world fall apart. Yet, as I will argue in the final chapters, revision of those institutions is needed, and changes in attitude, change in what people value and strive for, must be at the core of any fundamental transition if it is to happen gracefully. This requires shifts in social norms, perhaps the most surprising kind of social tipping. It may seem unimaginable that the pursuit of ever-increasing wealth and consumption could cease to be the central driving force of societies; that working part time and enjoying a plant-based diet would become the norm. Yet history shows that attitudes may change dramatically, even if they seem set in stone. How does that happen? Let's look at a few examples.

Slavery

This is a classic example of a widespread global practice that became widely considered unacceptable rather suddenly. It had been near universal for millennia, until about two centuries ago. The Roman Empire relied on large-scale slavery, as did ancient Egypt and many earlier civilizations in China, Africa, Europe, and the Americas. So why, despite formidable economic interests, was a practice that had flourished for millennia largely abandoned within a few decades? Part of the explanation may be that the Industrial Revolution made manual labor less essential.[35] But arguably, the costly transformation had also become inevitable due to changing worldviews and by increasing activism that stressed how the practice was incompatible with long-held values such as those espoused by Christianity.[36] While Britain led the way, anti-slavery movements arose in other countries too, and the practice rapidly became abolished globally (Figure 3.2). Living in Holland, a country where much of the original wealth is based on

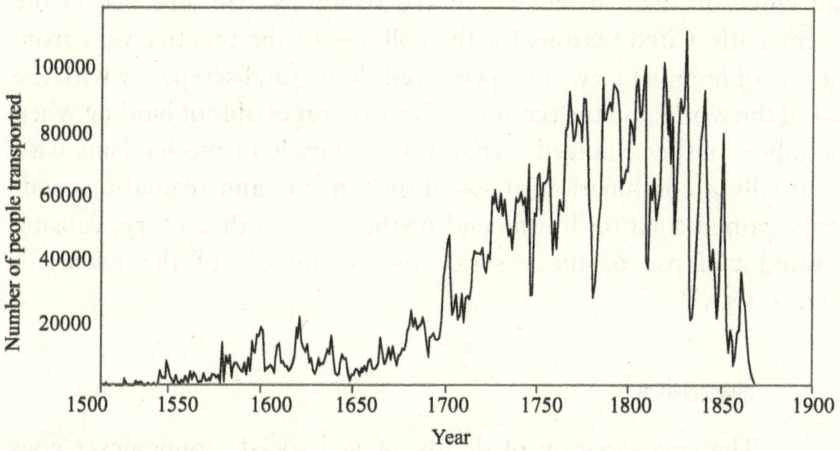

Figure 3.2 The number of people transported per year in the transatlantic slave trade. (Data SlaveVoyages.org.)

slavery, the way it unraveled was an eye-opener to me. In 1862 it had been nearly three decades since Britain had outlawed the practice. Moral pressure for change was rising since many felt that Holland was shamefully late in abandoning it. But parliament was beholden to the wealthy elite, and their wealth was, to a large extent, based on slavery. Doesn't it sound familiar, the difficulties of dismantling the business model of the super-rich? Inspired by the English example, a deal was eventually negotiated in which the slave owners (not the slaves) were compensated, thus allowing the economic elite in power to remain relatively untouched.[37]

Foot Binding

Unlike slavery, foot binding was never a bedrock of business. Yet it remained a surprisingly persistent practice for centuries in China. The feet of young girls were broken and then tightly bound to change their shape. The resulting 'lotus feet' were considered a status symbol that spread from the elite to the lower social classes (as status symbols tend to do). In the nineteenth century about half of Chinese women had bound feet, and in some regions and higher social classes almost all of them did. So, why did the practice persist for about a thousand years, and why was it suddenly abandoned within one generation? Certainly, there was a long history of abolition campaigns.[38] Objections were raised as early as the eighteenth century, and emperors had in fact attempted to abolish the practice in the seventeenth. Cited reasons for the collapse of the practice vary from the rise of feminist views to a perceived shameful discrepancy with the rest of the world and the economic disadvantages of foot binding when the labor market changed. Whatever the tangle of mechanisms was, eventually a combination of social movements and regulations suddenly gained traction by the end of the nineteenth century, causing a rapid collapse of the practice by the middle of the twentieth (Figure 3.3).[39]

Emancipation

The emancipation of disadvantaged social groups never goes smoothly. It is hard to imagine today that women were widely considered unfit to vote until about a century ago. Yet in France it took until

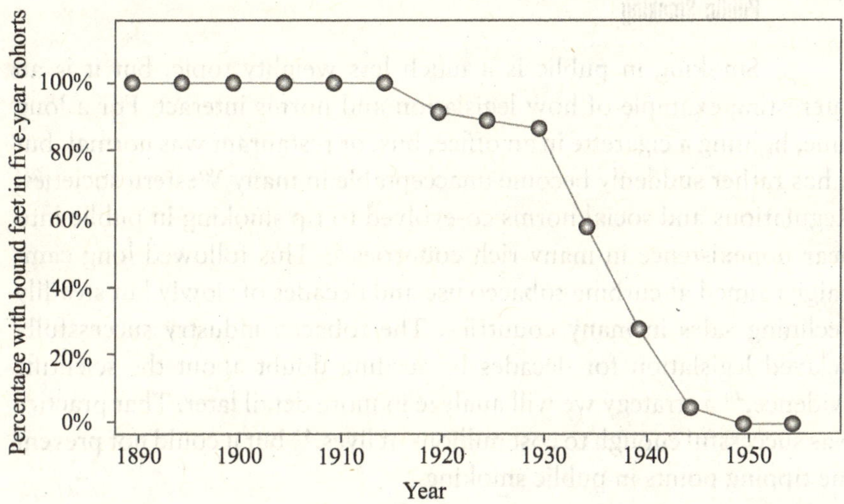

Figure 3.3 The percentage of Chinese women subjected to foot binding in eleven northern rural counties by birth cohort.[40]

1944, and in Switzerland federal elections were solely for men until 1971. As with foot binding, the meandering mechanisms that eventually led to change are complex. In many places, activism trudged on without much success for decades. World War I may have been a precipitating event for change, especially in England, where women had successfully taken over the jobs of men at the front, on a large scale.[41] It was clear that women could do anything men could do, and thus it became increasingly untenable that voting should be an exception. Indeed, in most Western countries women gained the right to vote on a national level shortly after the war. Of course, the right to vote does not imply emancipation on all fronts, and women and men are still far from equal in the Western world. That is how emancipation goes. It is never complete, with sudden jumps followed by periods of stasis. It took more than a century after the abolition of slavery in the USA before the 1964 Civil Rights Act banned segregation and other racial discrimination, the result of a long struggle that culminated a year after Martin Luther King's "I Have a Dream" speech.[42] However, outcomes for men, women, whites, and blacks remain far from equal today and at times there have been major setbacks in civil rights. Nonetheless, the gradual drift in norms and values occasionally invokes major revisions of the rules that seem obvious in hindsight but which, at the time, looked nearly impossible to achieve.

Public Smoking

Smoking in public is a much less weighty topic, but it is an interesting example of how legislation and norms interact. For a long time, lighting a cigarette in an office, bus, or restaurant was normal, but it has rather suddenly become unacceptable in many Western societies. Regulations and social norms co-evolved to tip smoking in public into near nonexistence in many rich countries.[43] This followed long campaigns aimed at curbing tobacco use and decades of slowly but steadily declining sales in many countries. The tobacco industry successfully delayed legislation for decades by seeding doubt about the scientific evidence,[44] a strategy we will analyze in more detail later. That practice was successful enough to cost millions of lives,[45] but it could not prevent the tipping points in public smoking.

Fertility Rates

Fertility rates involve social norms too. Enforcing a reduction in fertility, as happened in China with the one-child policy, is an exception. But even without any specific regulations, the number of children per woman has decreased globally by about 50 percent over half a century. Studies suggest that as economies develop, increased schooling and job markets for women lead to falling fertility rates.[46] The fact that the number of children is also, to some extent, a social norm may help explain the speed of change.[47] Indeed, within certain countries this drop often happened surprisingly fast (Figure 3.4). Interestingly, changes in the nineteenth century were much slower than those in the twentieth. A decline in fertility started early in countries such as England, Poland, and the USA, but it took almost a century to get below three children per woman. By contrast, some more recent transitions have happened within two decades or less (Figure 3.4).

Will upcoming norm shifts eventually lead to a just and sustainable future? Not necessarily. Many anticipated norm shifts in history never happened at all. In American thinker Henry David Thoreau's 1854 book *Walden*[48] the author lives for two years, two months, and two days in a simple cabin, reflecting on nature and especially on society. Refusing to pay taxes in a country that still endorsed slavery, Thoreau was famous for his plea for civil disobedience that would later inspire Martin Luther King and Nelson Mandela, among others.[49] Yet his

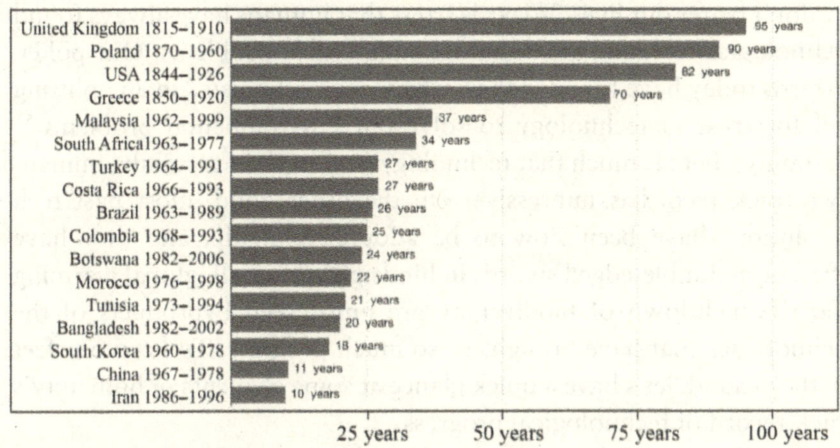

Figure 3.4 Transition time from more than six to fewer than three children per woman. From (https://ourworldindata.org/fertility-rate.)

vision of a vegetarian future for humanity, although inspiring to some later movements, has not yet manifested widely. Indeed, he was not leading by example when he wrote: "I caught a glimpse of a woodchuck stealing across my path, and felt a strange thrill of savage delight, and was strongly tempted to seize and devour him raw." But that did not stop him from dreaming: "I have no doubt that it is a part of the destiny of the human race, in its gradual improvement, to leave off eating animals, as surely as savage tribes have left off eating each other when they came in contact with the more civilized." It has not happened yet, but could it still? As we will see in Chapter 5, vegetarianism and veganism have experienced a steep rise in interest since the 1980s (Figure 5.10).

Technological Revolutions

Technology is undoubtedly the most appealing way to lift society out of trouble. Some have high hopes that it may help to shape a better future through technological advances such as energy transition, carbon capture, AI, or a new agricultural revolution. Others are consistently dismissive of 'tech fixes.' As observed by Charles Mann, there is a remarkably persistent schism between 'wizards' and 'prophets.'[50] Prophets warn that the world will go down the drain if we don't better our lives. Wizards stress that humans have always found technological solutions to seemingly unsolvable problems. Outspoken wizards today have branded themselves 'ecomodernists,' in an uplifting call for trust in technology to solve our environmental problems.[51] Certainly, there is much that technology can do. And certainly, humanity's track record is impressive. On the other hand, most past tech revolutions have been slow to be adopted globally, and they have often been double-edged swords in hindsight. After all, global warming and the meltdown of biodiversity are unforeseen byproducts of the technologies that have brought us so much progress. To keep our feet on the ground, let's have a quick glance at some elements of humanity's track record of technological progress.

The use of fire was an early technological game-changer for humanity.[52] About a million years ago, mastering fire must have changed the daily lives of our ancestors dramatically. It probably started with carrying burning sticks from natural fires to clear land of vegetation. Later, the controlled use of fire allowed for cooking food. The variety of food increased, and the calorific and nutritional value of cooked food is much higher. The improved food-use efficiency allowed more free time and more efficient hunting and gathering activity. Fire also provided warmth, helped keep predators at a distance, and enabled new ways of making tools. Ultimately, fire promoted an increase in human populations and facilitated their spread into new territories, altering landscapes along the way.

The spread of agriculture was another big game-changer.[53] Although the term 'agricultural revolution' suggests otherwise, it was a gradual process, starting after the end of the last glaciation about eleven millennia ago. The practice of cultivating plants emerged independently in various places and had a slow start. Most cultures initially combined hunting and gathering with cultivation, often in a seasonal cycle. Indeed, some groups would flip back and forth between sedentary and nomadic lifestyles, according to the seasons. Eventually, however, the sedentary agricultural lifestyle came to dominate large parts of the planet. One reason that agriculture eventually crowded out hunter-gathering may be that larger population densities and family sizes could be sustained on agriculture than on hunting and gathering. This also created a social trap. Once population densities are high, only agriculture can sustain them. Quality of life likely suffered from this transition.[54] Low diet diversity meant poor health.

High population densities increased the risk of epidemics. Inevitable periods of bad climatic conditions could cause episodes of starvation. As Yuval Noah Harari framed it in his bestseller *Sapiens*, humans became dominated by grain to their own detriment but to the great advantage of grain crops, which spread across the world, growing under conditions that were doggedly improved by toiling humans.[55]

There have been many innovations in the 10,000 or so years of agricultural practice. Over the last five centuries in particular, productivity per laborer has increased steadily with the development of better tools, smart crop-rotation systems, land drains, and other improvements. This freed the hands of workers, changing the labor market in ways that arguably facilitated the subsequent Industrial Revolution and capitalism.[56] However, the main boost in agricultural productivity happened over the past half-century in what has been called the Green Revolution.[57] New technologies included high-yield varieties of grains introduced alongside chemical fertilizers, pesticides, and controlled irrigation that enabled them to thrive. Mechanization was also important in replacing traditional agriculture methods. The agricultural scientist Norman Borlaug, known as the Father of the Green Revolution, received the Nobel Peace Prize for his work in 1970. Born on a farm, he became an influential innovator. Working in Mexico, Borlaug developed a high-yield, disease-resistant wheat, trained the next generation of innovators, and became an inspiring leader in the race to reduce hunger in the face of an exploding world population. Indeed, in hindsight, the work of Borlaug and others may have saved over a billion people from starvation.[58]

One critique is that improved agriculture has allowed the global population to grow to unsustainable levels. However, it could be quite the opposite. Since the number of children per woman drops when economic conditions improve, the Green Revolution may have slowed down rather than boosted population growth, likely doubling global GDP and greatly reducing poverty.[59] However, the Green Revolution has other dark sides. The techniques that came to dominate agriculture are among the main drivers of global pollution and depletion of nature. It is true that less land is needed to produce the same yield of crops compared to traditional agriculture. However, rising demand for animal-based food – especially in developing economies[60] – makes industrial agriculture the main driving force of global land transformation and pollution. While half of the global population is still fed by local agriculture,[61] consumption by wealthier countries is driving long-distance destruction. For instance, in the Netherlands we import feed, allowing our tiny country to be the biggest European meat exporter. The footprint of pork includes the destruction of rainforests to produce palm oil and soy for feed, and pollution from excrement, making the Dutch water and air the worst in the EU.[62] The problem is not in the novel agricultural techniques but rather in the mutually reinforcing demand for meat and the success of transnational corporations involved in industrial production and marketing. That is a part of "the invisible strangling hand" we will see in Chapter 7.

The use of fossil fuels has been instrumental in facilitating the Green Revolution. Not only can a single farmer armed with a tractor and other machinery do work that previously required a host of manual laborers, but also, without artificial fertilizers produced with fossil fuels, agriculture could probably feed only half of the global population.[63] Industrial agriculture is only the tip of the iceberg of what fossil fuels have meant for humanity. While coal has been used since prehistoric times, demand increased dramatically with the rise of the steam engine. The use of petroleum skyrocketed with the advent of the internal combustion engine, which still powers most cars. Today, fossil fuels sustain most of the transportation, heating, and industrial processes, but we've already established how they are also one of the most profound threats to our future. In conclusion, technological advances brought humanity much but have often been double-edged swords, sometimes producing extensive unexpected collateral damage.

History's Rhyme: Changing Fast and Slow

Looking at this diverse set of transformations, are there any general patterns that may help us understand realistic pathways for the future? I have already brought up the famous saying "History never repeats itself, but it often rhymes." Indeed, history does seem to rhyme, but defining its patterns is tricky. Specialists in specific periods of history tend to shake their heads when people like me come up with generalizations, and early attempts to define overarching patterns by historians such as Arnold J. Toynbee lost traction after a brief period of popularity. I understand. The more you dig into any example, the more complicated the explanations turn out to be. As Putnam and Garrett described the US Progressive Era, social change was like a braided river where cause and effect cannot be separated.[64] Or, as Eric Cline, in search of the cause of the Bronze Age collapse, concluded, it was a systemic phenomenon with no clear cause.[65] Whether you dig into the history of the Industrial Revolution, the fall of the Roman Empire, the French Revolution, the rise of women's suffrage, or virtually any other important turning point in history, you will find a range of interrelated mechanisms with little agreement on ranking their importance.

This should be no surprise. Societies are complex nonlinear systems. Not only are there many factors involved (complex), but there are no unidirectional chains of cause and effect. Instead, there is a causal web with many links back and forth (nonlinear). Think of policies and norms. In Holland, the policy of prohibiting smoking in public places only succeeded when gradually, over the years, enough people became convinced that it was the right thing to do. Before that the policy had failed a couple of times. There was simply no compliance. Then it suddenly gained acceptance and became a social norm. Nobody now would dream of lighting a cigarette in a restaurant. What was the cause of this change? The policy or the slowly changing attitude leading up to the shift? Both, of course. There is a reinforcing feedback between two factors. Sufficient support is needed for the policy to work. On the other hand, a policy signals that most people agree, nudging the attitude of the doubters.[66]

The feedback between policy and attitudes is just one 'chicken-or-egg' example of nonlinearity. In practice, many more factors and feedbacks come into play, forming a vast network of direct and indirect chicken-or-egg relationships. It makes things terribly complex indeed. But don't worry. Not everything matters, and systems are never too complex to draw general conclusions. For instance, we understand when and why a drying climate may cause rainforests to tip into a savanna state.[67] This is despite the fact that forests are terribly complex, populated by thousands of species, each with complex behavior. Of course, the comparison to societies is not entirely fair. There is one important difference. The repetition of history is more crisp and clean in nature than it is among humans. This is because ecosystems do not change the way societies do. True, nature does, over evolutionary timescales, change fundamentally. For instance, the evolution of photosynthesis brought oxygen into the atmosphere, allowing other life forms to exist, and nature was changed forever.[68] But in societies such fundamental change can happen very fast. Not because we evolve as a species, but because our knowledge, tools, and values keep evolving. Still, history rhymes, and phenomena such as technological revolutions, wealth concentration, state collapse, and norm shifts are recurrent themes. The examples we saw in this chapter are, of course, a tiny tip of the iceberg, and we have glimpsed just a few mini narratives. Nonetheless, they hint at patterns in the past that might be relevant to our options for the future. Let's identify some of those patterns in the examples we've discussed so far. As technological revolutions, state collapse, and social norm shifts are quite different beasts, let's first take them one by one and then look at an overarching pattern that will come back throughout the book: transformations are often accidents in waiting.

Technological Revolutions

These are different from state collapse or norm shifts in that they are not the classical kind of tipping points preceded by the kind of loss of resilience that we saw in Chapter 2. Nonetheless, they have been game-changers, and new ones will likely change the course of history in the future. Therefore, it is worth asking whether there is anything to learn from past technological revolutions. Looking across previous technological revolutions, there are at least three remarkably recurrent patterns. First, each episode of technological progress made life easier, but also boosted inequality. For instance, the Neolithic development of agriculture allowed the rise of civilization, enabling hierarchies from kings to slaves that were absent in the hunter-gatherer world. Ten millennia later, the Green Revolution lifted many out of poverty. But aid to the Global South often came as a package deal with loans and obligations that benefited Western transnational corporations and kept poorer countries in perennial debt.[69] The Industrial Revolution evolved hand in hand with capitalism, which enabled extraordinary development but also runaway wealth concentration in the hands of an increasingly influential elite. In this sense, recent tech revolutions led by Bill Gates, Elon Musk, and Mark Zuckerberg are no exception to the historical pattern. A second recurrent pattern is that technological revolutions came with unforeseeable long-term negative consequences. The rise of agriculture has been described as the worst thing that ever happened to humanity in terms of quality of life,[70] and the fossil-fuel-powered Industrial and Green Revolutions brought us the climate

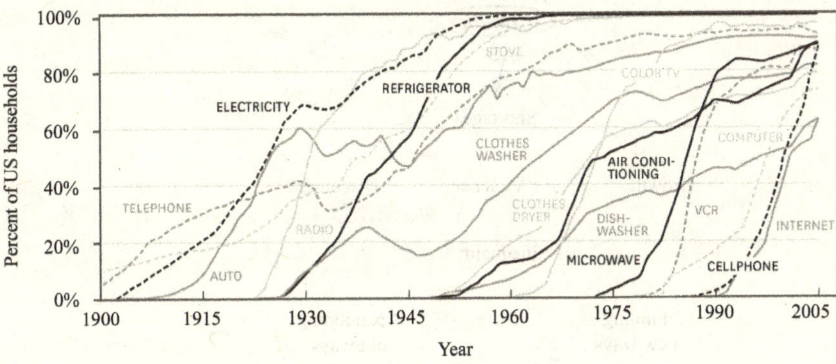

Figure 3.5 Technologies have become adopted at increasing rates. (Adapted from Nicholas Felton, "Consumption spreads faster today," *New York Times*, February 10, 2008.)

and biodiversity crises. A third pattern is that change seems to be speeding up. Earlier technological revolutions punctuated long periods of relative stability. After a million years of hunting and gathering, agriculture arose 10,000 years ago, and 200 years ago the Industrial Revolution happened. Since then, change has kept coming faster and faster. Just as transitions to low fertility rates have become faster over time, the pace at which new technological findings occur and the rapidity with which they are adopted has also increased (Figure 3.5). Interpolating those trends hints at rising chances for norm changes as well as technological advances to swiftly change the fate of humanity – for good or for bad.

The Collapse of Civilizations and States

This phenomenon keeps puzzling and dividing historians and archaeologists. They argue about whether collapse is really collapse, and whether the causes were internal or external. The main rhyme pattern I would stress is that the intuition of senescence is correct. As they age, societies become more likely to throw the old way of doing things overboard. Reconstructions of why states collapse differ, but recurring elements include adverse weather, shortages, inequality, and violence. In the end, regardless of the mix of ingredients, everything unites into discontent, the ultimate reason to look for new ways (Figure 3.6). As the status quo loses attraction, transformation becomes

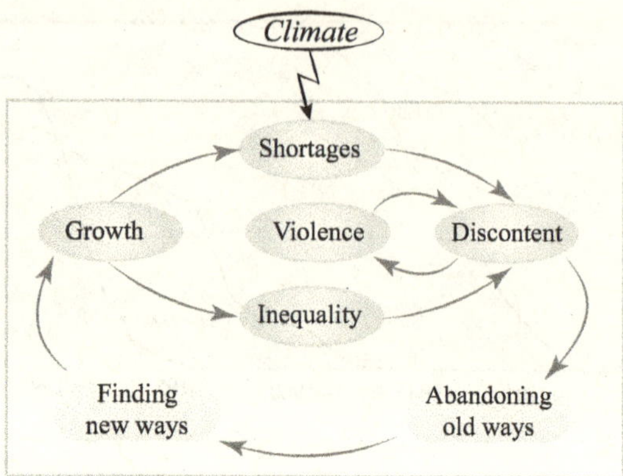

Figure 3.6 Mounting problems and discontent drive the cycle of social destabilization and renewal.

ever more likely. But transformation can be either relatively smooth or dramatic and violent, as in the Late Bronze Age collapse or the French Revolution. Collapse doesn't mean that everything falls apart. As Tainter stresses, what collapses may merely be the larger organizational structure, leaving the simpler elements intact.[71] This was the case, for example, with the vanishing of the Minoan civilization on Crete,[72] or the crumbling of the Western Roman Empire, when loss of central political control led Europe into the Middle Ages with many elements of Roman civilization still in place, thus preserving cultural and economic continuity.[73] While the collapse of the Roman Empire led to improved conditions for the ordinary people,[74] many other examples of state collapse were drenched in blood. That is an important rhyme pattern. Also, in the end the elites held responsible for the sources of discontent often stayed on top in new settings,[75] a pattern that has persisted.[76] Are we now heading for a disastrous global collapse of states, democracies, markets, and institutions for cooperation? As I will argue in Chapter 6 that is certainly a possibility, but it is not the only option.

Social norm shifts are a very different kind of change. They also result from tension, and may unfold rapidly. But in these cases a change in attitudes leads to a revision of practices without incurring a larger collapse. Such revision can be specific, such as in the case of public smoking , slavery, or foot binding, but also wide ranging, such as in the broad package of prosocial policies in the American Progressive Era. A common theme in the examples we have examined is a long phase of preparation in which an active group stubbornly highlights a discrepancy between practices and deeper values. How can you make a fortune trading slaves if all people are created equal? How can you smoke in the house or the car if it harms your kids? How can you deny women the vote if they are a major force in war efforts? Activism typically lingered for a long time, seemingly in vain, before it led to a shift that, in hindsight, seemed obvious. Shifts that often played out in a decade or two, such as the sudden drop in the number of children per woman in many countries, abolition of the slave trade, and foot binding, but also larger transformations such as the French Revolution or the American Progressive Era. All of those shifts may be seen as abrupt adjustments of common practices following slowly changing conditions. That slow creep of conditions includes evolving worldviews starting with the Enlightenment movement in the seventeenth and eighteenth centuries and subsequent economic developments powered by technological progress intertwined with the rise of capitalism. The second recurrent theme is that new ways of spreading information often catalyzed change, as in the French Revolution and the American Progressive Era, with advances in printed media, or in the Arab Spring, when social media allowed new ways of orchestrating protests. Lastly, adverse climatic conditions driving failing harvests have often been triggers, as in the Pueblo people, the French Revolution, and the Arab Spring.[77] Looking to the future, all such ingredients will likely recur. Harvests may fail again. Worldviews will keep changing gradually as the climate becomes a major global stressor, while the ways of spreading, collecting, and manipulating information are changing profoundly. If history rhymes, could this mix of drivers eventually bring sweeping shifts in norms and in the ways we organize society? If so, how long will that take? Those are the questions addressed in the last three chapters.

Transformations as Accidents in Waiting

The Age of Enlightenment brought a rising emphasis on ideas such as the pursuit of happiness, knowledge, liberty, progress, fraternity, and tolerance, arguing for constitutional government and the separation of church and state. This was preceded by a century of scientific revolution, a new approach to reasoning catalyzed by thinkers such as Francis Bacon and Baruch Spinoza, who emphasized the need to avoid dogma and scrutinize arguments systematically.

Bacon's influential 1620 book about the method was titled *Novum Organum* (the New Instrument).[78] Rationality, in the view of those thinkers, was a tool for social improvement. Seen in this light, the French Revolution and the social improvements following the Industrial Revolution were 'accidents in waiting.' The gradual evolution of worldviews eventually meant that feudalism inevitably gave way to meritocracy. A century or so later, meritocracy and industrial capitalism led to widespread social ills that were addressed through gradual institutional revisions in some places and revolution in others. Thus, while social revolutions can bring sweeping change, and norms may suddenly shift, such spectacular changes are in fact the result of a gradual evolution of insights, worldviews, and conditions that makes occasional adjustments inevitable. The core question for this book is how such adjustments may happen in response to evolving views on the demise of nature, global warming, and wealth concentration, and especially how such change may be catalyzed. But to be able to answer those questions, we must first look a bit deeper into the mechanisms of social tipping.

4 HOW SOCIAL TIPPING WORKS

Explaining how social transformations in all their diversity work may seem like an impossible task. There are always many factors involved, and each transformation has its own unique circumstances. That makes it difficult, for instance, to isolate the effect of a single factor such as climate, since it plays a role in almost everything.[1] High temperatures boost online hate speech[2] and violent conflicts.[3] Droughts and floods affect food prices. But there are always other factors involved too. Take the Arab Spring.[4] A street vendor setting himself on fire as an act of protest was the trigger, but climate had aggravated the social tensions that were released through widespread riots. Unfavorable weather had affected the grain harvests globally, leading to rising food prices. This fueled the fire as protests spread across Egypt, Syria, and Morocco. This is quite similar to the role of climate leading up to the French Revolution, among many other examples. Yet social tension also existed for other reasons. Tensions may relate to factors ranging from inequity, corruption, and discrimination to food prices and unmet aspirations.

Now for the magic: all this can be folded into resilience and tipping to help us see the mechanisms of sudden social change. We can see the reasons why societies got stuck and the forces that have allowed them to break loose and change. In this chapter I will introduce you to some of the most influential lines of thinking about social transformations. A realistic theory about social change cannot be a simple unidimensional story. That's something to keep in mind when you see books with titles such as *How Change Works*, *Social Evolution*, or *How the World Works* (all genuine). Though such books represent useful perspectives, they don't fulfill the promise of explaining it all. That makes sense. Jorge Marcone, a thoughtful Peruvian humanity scholar, once told me: "Something is complex when you can capture it in many different narratives that are all valid and cannot be combined into one." I love that. Yet many people don't get it. Especially those seeking to come up with a theory. That is understandable. We all tend to fall in love with our theories (I am no exception). In 1897 Thomas Chrowder Chamberlin wrote a famous essay warning scientists against this. One tends to favor one's own hypothesis, so it is good to keep several alternatives in mind.[5] In the end Chamberlin's idea was still that, ultimately, one hypothesis may turn out to be superior when held against all evidence. Alas, things don't work like that for complex systems such as the climate, societies, or ecosystems, where cause and effect cannot be laid out in clean and simple ways and where multiple mechanisms always operate simultaneously.[6] So here we go. Not in search of an overly simple theory of everything but on an expedition to see the forest through the trees of social transformation. The goal? Crafting the tools that will help us see how humanity may plausibly tip into distinct alternative futures.

The Basic Theory

To reveal the fundamental principles of how tipping works, I first invite you to picture a simple graphical model. If you find it too complicated it is fine to skip this part, but if you manage to bear with me it will give you a deeper understanding of one of the most striking laws of dynamical systems. Let's imagine the percentage of people in an imaginary society calling for change as problems such as food insecurity or violence worsen. First, assume (unrealistically) that everyone in this group thinks independently and has their own individual threshold to start calling for change. If all people have different thresholds of acceptability, we expect a smooth increase in the percentage of people calling for change (Figure 4.1 A). Things become much more interesting if we assume that, say, 30 percent of the people don't think for themselves but simply copy the majority attitude (panel B). In this situation there is a range of problem severities (between T_1 and T_2), where three equilibrium states are possible. The dotted line at 50 percent represents an unstable equilibrium. As you can see from the arrows that indicate the direction of

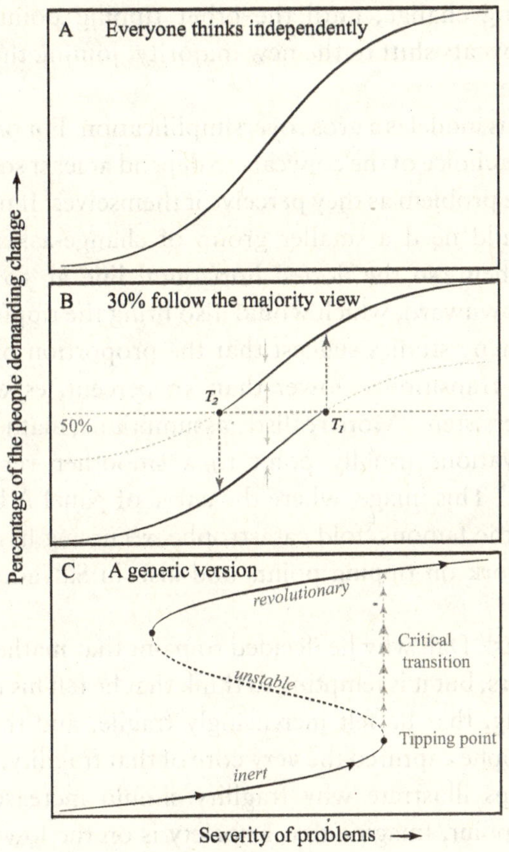

Figure 4.1 A simple model of social tipping (see text for the explanation).

change, any small deviation from this 'repellor' makes the system move away from the midline, due to the copycats following the majority opinion. The change stabilizes in either of the two 'alternative attractors'. (The arrows show why those are called attractors. The system is attracted to them from above and from below.) To see the consequences of this, first consider a situation where societal problems are not severe. In that case, very few people call for change. As the problems slowly get worse, more people gradually call for change. But when that number reaches the tipping point (T_1) at 50 percent of the population, something special happens. Since they are now a majority, the change-askers are suddenly joined by copycats, and the percentage calling for change will jump rapidly from 50 to 80 percent. Even if the problem becomes less severe, a majority will keep demanding change, until the other tipping point (T_2) is reached and the copycats shift to the new majority, joining those who do not want change.

Of course this model is a gross oversimplification. For one thing, we should expect the choice of the copycats to depend at least somewhat on the severity of the problem as they perceive it themselves. If problems are worse they should need a smaller group of change-askers to be convinced to join them, so the dotted horizontal line at 50 percent should be sloping downward, which would also bring the tipping point T_1 down. Indeed, many studies suggest that the proportion of people needed to invoke a transition is lower than 50 percent, especially if change-askers are persistent[7] More realistic assumptions, mathematical models, and observations usually point to a smoother version, as depicted in panel C.[8] This image, where the curve of panel A becomes 'folded,' represents the famous 'fold catastrophe' recurring in much of the mathematical work on tipping points and also in Salvador Dalí's final painting.

We cannot ask Dalí why he decided to paint that mathematical graph in his final years, but it is tempting to think that he felt his ultimate tipping point coming, that he felt increasingly fragile, and that René Thom's fold catastrophe captured the very core of that fragility. Indeed, our model also helps illustrate why fragility should increase as we approach a tipping point. Imagine that a society is on the lower curve in panel B. As problems grow, the system moves slowly toward the tipping point, and also gets closer to the dotted critical threshold. Even before this tense society reaches T_1, if for some reason another group of people suddenly starts demanding change, this may bring society over the majority threshold, invoking others to join the uproar and drive a shift to the 'revolution' state.

Another way to show rising fragility is through stability landscapes (Figure 4.2), which illustrate stability properties using the analogy of a ball rolling in a hilly landscape. A hilltop corresponds to an unstable equilibrium that separates the alternative basins of attraction into which the ball can roll. If problems are not severe the status quo is resilient. However, as problems become worse the status quo becomes less and less attractive. That loss of resilience makes this state fragile. Now, even a small perturbation can bring society over the hilltop. That will cause the ball to roll with increasing speed down the hill toward the revolutionary state, where a vast majority asks for change.

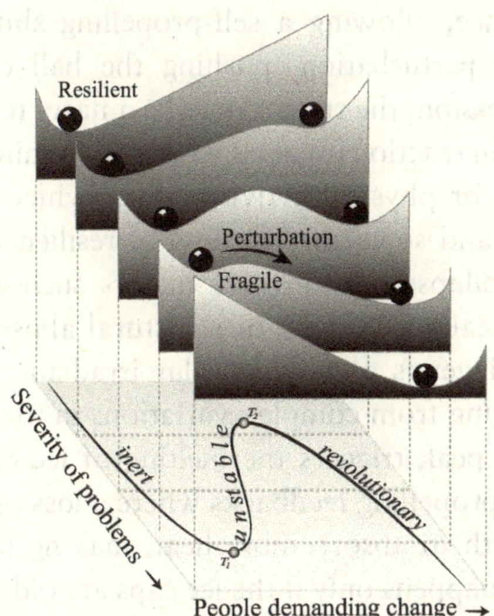

Figure 4.2 Stability landscapes illustrating how, as the perceived severity of problems rises, the status quo becomes fragile. The graph in the bottom plane is the fold catastrophe depicted also in Figure 4.1 C.

Our storyline of people calling for change as perceived problems become more severe is just a simplified example. The cool thing is that the models illustrating tipping points and the change in resilience are widely applicable. They capture the essence of such phenomena in ecosystems, ocean currents, postural balance, cell metabolism, and more.[9] This is why the dynamic indicators of resilience (DIORs) discussed earlier are also strikingly universal.[10] Return to equilibrium (the attractor) becomes slower if the slopes become less steep: 'lost attraction.' That always happens as the valleys representing the basins of attraction in the diagram become shallower.[11] This explains why a rise of slowness and amplitude of fluctuations is a signal of fragility before an individual person falls into a depression,[12] but also of rising fragility of the ice caps before the end of a glaciation period when the Earth slips into a warmer climate.[13] Indeed, it's the same signal we saw in the fluctuations of construction activity hinting at lost attraction to the status quo before each of the transitions in the Pueblo cultures.[14]

Isn't there magic in that? It's remarkable that the same theory can capture the essence of such widely different phenomena. Depression, deglaciation, and societal collapse are entirely different things, yet they share something fundamental. They happen when the status quo has lost resilience, allowing a self-propelling shift to be triggered by even a small perturbation 'pushing the ball over the hilltop.' In the case of depression, the trigger may be a nasty telephone call. The self-propelling chain reaction involves worrying, rumination at night, tiredness, less social or physical activity, all of which lead to feeling worse, ruminating, and so forth. The loss of resilience laying the groundwork for the collapse may involve factors such as long-lasting work stress, an unhealthy lifestyle, or structural abuse. In the case of deglaciation the trigger is a peak in solar irradiance on the northern hemisphere emerging from complex variations in the Earth's orbit around the Sun. The peak triggers the melting of ice caps and glaciers. This activates self-propelling feedbacks where a loss of albedo (reflectivity) causes the Earth to absorb more heat, making more ice melt, and so forth. But this happens only if the ice caps are old already, because a slow loss of resilience leading up to the tipping point is driven by the growth of ice caps over time, making them less stable as they expand.[15] As this aging is an unavoidable process, ice caps collapse in an erratic yet more-or-less cyclic rhythm. Do you spot the similarity to societies?

The universality of the fundamental principles of tipping and resilience is seductive. But to make the theory useful for understanding the possibilities for future social tipping, it needs to be tied to observations of past societies and to knowledge compiled by generations of social scientists and psychologists. In the following sections we ask which mechanisms may stabilize the status quo and which may cause its resilience to decline, allowing society to tip.

Getting Stuck

Much social change happens smoothly. Often there are no tipping points, just gradual changes in things such as language, economic indicators, and public health. One reason for the occasional abruptness of change is that it may have been blocked before becoming suddenly unstuck. Imagine tying an elastic band to a block of wood (Figure 4.3). Put the wood on a very smooth surface, such as a glass plate lubricated with a layer of oil, and start to pull the elastic band softly. The block will smoothly follow your hand. Now repeat the experiment, but instead of the oiled glass use a piece of sandpaper as a surface. As you start to pull, the block doesn't follow smoothly. It stays in place due to

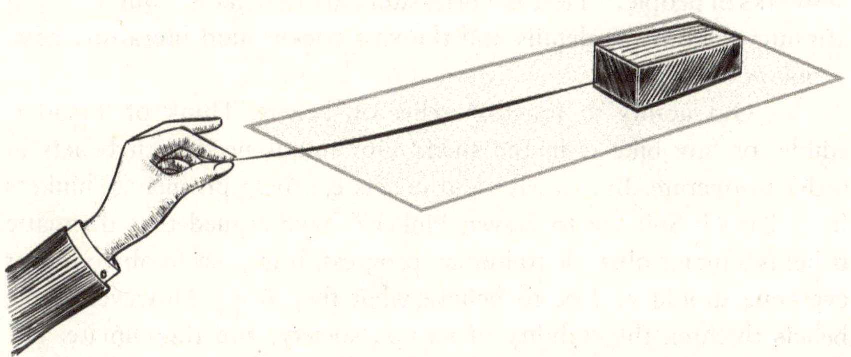

Figure 4.3 Rising tension may be released through unpredictable small or big events, as illustrated by pulling a wooden block across a piece of sandpaper using an elastic band.

friction until a critical moment when it slips abruptly to a new position, where it stubbornly stays in place again until the next abrupt readjustment. This is a simplified version of how scientists understand earthquakes.[16] Earthquakes happen when the slow movement of tectonic plates causes one plate to slip under another. Instead of moving smoothly, the Earth's crust readjusts in a sudden shock, producing an earthquake. A slow creeping change causes invisibly rising tension which is released through abrupt events. As I will argue, this tectonic-plate representation is a plausible way of seeing a change in social norms or the adjustment of governments to rising tensions.

So, what is the sandpaper in societies? What prevents gradual adjustment, causing change to happen in bursts? Outdated but stubborn beliefs and habits? Fear of the new and unknown? An elite with vested interests? As we will see later, all of these play a role. In our simple graphic model it's the copycats who prevent a gradual social response. While adopting the attitude of others is a very human tendency this is, of course, a rather simplistic way of modeling the dynamics of attitude. So why do beliefs and attitudes tend to get stuck? Social psychologists and neurobiologists have unraveled a broad set of mechanisms that contribute to the sandpaper of our minds. I share a fascination with the rigidity of the human mind with my social sciences mentor and friend Frances Westley;[17] working with neurobiologists and psychologists, we pieced together an overview of why the brain gets stuck through those overlapping mechanisms on levels ranging from networks of neurons to networks of people.[18] Here is a brief summary of what we found. (If you are interested in the details and the vast background literature, have a look at our review.)

Our ability to function relies on beliefs. Think of 'bread is edible' or 'my bike is in the shed.' Our minds need such beliefs in order to operate. But overly rigid beliefs can be a problem. Thinkers from Baruch Spinoza to Steven Pinker[19] have argued that dogmatic belief is a major obstacle to human progress. It may seem obvious that everyone should be free to believe what they want. However, some beliefs threaten the stability of nature, society, and the climate. For example, the unfounded belief in the aphrodisiac properties of rhinoceros horn may drive the species to extinction; the belief that meat makes you strong helps maintain one of the main drivers of deforestation; implicit beliefs about intrinsic capabilities linked to gender or race threaten groups suffering from discrimination; and belief in conspiracy theories can undermine democracies. It is not easy to change such problematic beliefs. One possibility is to give people better information. But it turns out that providing information has surprisingly little effect. Even when faced with solid evidence, some beliefs don't fade. Ironically, relying too much on evidence in an attempt to change attitudes is a mistake. Many of us, especially scientists, falsely believe that rational thinking has a big impact on attitudes and choices. In reality, evidence often plays a limited role in shaping beliefs. That is relevant for how we might change societal attitudes to tip out of trouble, and we will return to the idea in later chapters.

So, why do our brains tend to latch onto specific views and stick with them? Part of the reason plays out on a basic neuronal level. This is, for instance, why it is hard to see an ambivalent image such as the classic rabbit–duck illusion in two ways simultaneously (Figure 4.4). We tend to flip into one interpretation and get stuck there. On a more complex level we also strive for coherence in our worldview, making some alternative views hard to conceive. Lastly, many beliefs are influenced by social factors. We tend to share similar beliefs with our friends and family, especially on complex issues where we don't have enough expertise to form our own opinions. Additionally, social psychologists have found that sharing beliefs is crucial for feeling connected to a group, and this mutual sharing can make those beliefs stick around stubbornly. Bizarre conspiracy theories are an example.

Figure 4.4 The rabbit–duck illusion. (From the October 23, 1892 issue of the German magazine *Fliegende Blätter*.)

Let's look at the way our social brains shape and maintain beliefs. First, when we form a belief we want it to make sense, but also to fit with our larger set of beliefs. It feels good when our collection of views is consistent. Therefore, we subconsciously try to avoid having conflicting thoughts that would cause so-called cognitive dissonance. When we feel this discomfort we tend to reject information that goes against what we already believe. For example, as we will see later, experiments show that if someone believes the world is an orderly, predictable, and just place and then hears apocalyptic warnings about global warming, they might reject the whole idea rather than rethinking their view that the world is just.[20] Thus, there are internal mechanisms that may make it difficult to take in new information. On a social level our beliefs are influenced by the people around us (Figure 4.5). We tend to be friends with people who share similar views, and our beliefs are reinforced by mutual 'contagion.' If I believe something, and you believe the same thing, we strengthen each other's beliefs. This happens in larger groups too. If everyone around us holds a certain belief, it becomes very difficult for an individual to go against that belief because doing so comes with the social 'costs' of being a deviant. As a result, the larger the proportion of people who believe something, the harder it is for others to break away from that belief. This is essentially the mechanism we used in our graphical model of social tipping points. Often, when it is about time to revise a socially held belief, change is held back by the false impression that the vast majority still holds the old belief. For instance, as we will see, most Americans falsely think that the majority oppose strong action to fight climate change.[21] Of course, if most people fail to speak out because they think others would disagree, society stays stuck.[22] The bottom line is that attitudes do not change easily. Changing a belief can be tough because it might mean shaking up your entire worldview, and possibly challenging your social identity. People want to belong, and shared beliefs play a big role in creating that sense of community. All this helps explain why people can stick to their beliefs even in the face of conflicting evidence. There's a famous study in which a small group believed the world would end on a specific date. When the fateful day passed without the world ending, instead of giving up the belief, they became even more committed,[23] finding ways to explain why the world didn't end rather than changing their minds. Similar things happen today in online groups, but that is a topic for later.

Since stubborn beliefs can be a problem, it makes sense to ask what can be done about their rigidity. Judging socially held beliefs is tricky. They range from mainstream opinions to dangerous conspiracy thinking. Who decides whether a widely held belief is harmful and needs to be changed? Throughout history there have been attempts to eradicate unwanted beliefs. What authorities thought was necessary to create stability and unity may later be seen as wrong. There is another angle

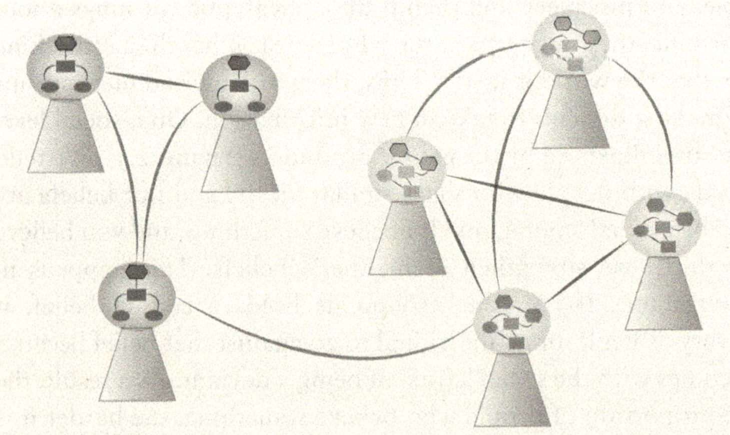

Figure 4.5 Alternative ideologies as networks of coherent beliefs embedded in social networks. Each of the small elements represents an individual belief linked to other beliefs within the same person in a coherent network representing an ideology. People are attracted to social networks that hold a similar ideology, and contagion within such networks promotes further convergence to the same ideology. (Adapted from Homer-Dixon et al., "A complex systems approach to the study of ideology."[24])

though. Independent from the content of a belief, excessive rigidity is at the root of the problem. It turns out that rigidity of beliefs is related to an individual's tendency for black-and-white thinking (i.e., 'good or bad' or 'all or nothing'). In language, this tendency may be reflected by the excessive use of absolute words (e.g., always, never, totally, ever, never, must). As we will see later, such words have been on the rise over the past decades, parallel to a decline of terms related to rationality and intertwined with the emergence of fact-free, post-truth narratives in politics. It is hard to point out what drives such trends, but one component may be stress. Stress has been shown to boost black-and-white thinking and thus increase belief rigidity. This may help explain why, historically, conspiracy theories tend to originate in times of uncertainty and crisis.[25] Interestingly, the same is true for mental disorders, many of which are rooted in unfounded rigid beliefs such as "I am fat" in anorexia nervosa, "I am being followed" in paranoia, or "I am worthless" in depression.[26] More on the role of stress and 'belief traps' in social change later. For now, we may draw a simple conclusion: part of the reason that societal change may happen in abrupt jumps rather than a smooth progression is the very way the human social mind works.

Of course, there is another major force that causes societies to get stuck. What postponed the collapse of the Mayan civilization or the Western Roman Empire, the French Revolution, the abolition of slavery, anti-tobacco legislation, or the phase-out of fossil fuels? It's important to consider the role of powerful players with a vested interest in maintaining the status quo. There is plenty of evidence that the power of ruling elites has been one of the main forces suppressing change. We will get back to that in detail later. The short version is that an elite may use violence to keep society stuck, through punishment or the eradication of people with attitudes perceived as dangerous. But there is also a softer approach, achieved by manipulating perceptions and worldviews. It is anchored in religion, language, education, and law, and is heavily influenced by media content, such as news, analyses, or advertisements. The question of how each of those anchors might be loosened to facilitate tipping into a sustainable trajectory is the topic of Chapter 7. The key point is that rigidity results from specific mechanisms that reinforce the status quo. The stronger such mechanisms are, the more an adaptive response to a changing world is inhibited (Figure 4.6). Think of our model. Without copycats the attitude change is gradual, and social contagion holds the response back until the tipping point. There are

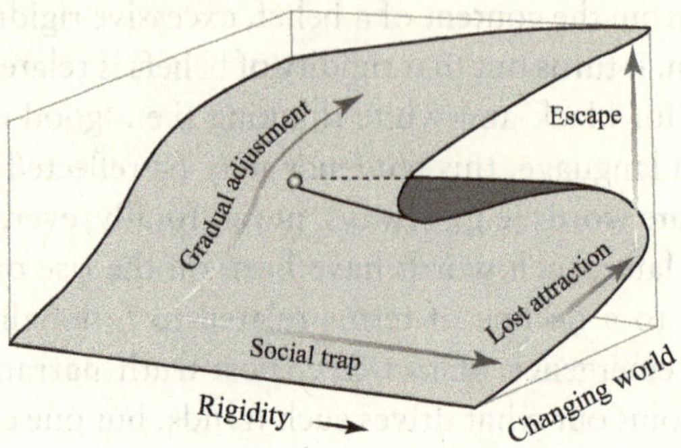

Figure 4.6 Rigidity caused by conservative feedback mechanisms such as repression makes the response to a changing world overdue and jumpy.

no tipping points if there are no mechanisms that hold change back. And the more dramatically change is held back, the more radical the transition once it happens. Think of the sandpaper earthquake experiment.

Lost Attraction

Looking at the history of societal change, the mechanisms that inhibited change were ultimately simply postponing the inevitable. The slow movement of tectonic plates cannot be stopped, and rising tension is released every now and then, whether that leads to small tremors or massive earthquakes. So, what allows bursts of change despite the powers that be keeping society stuck? In our simple social tipping model, acceptance of the status quo is undermined by an increase in perceived problems (Figure 4.1). That may capture the essence of the driving force behind many societal revisions, but for the goal of this book it is important to understand better what precisely causes such an urge for change, making people doubt the state or the prevalent social norms.

Doubting the State

What moves people to take to the streets and demand change? Sometimes there are ideological calls for justice for others, for instance abandoning slavery or ending foot binding. Mostly, however, grievances arise from the conditions of the protesters themselves. Look at the long list of demands by the French Yellow Vest movement beginning in 2018.[27] This bottom-up movement had no leaders and no polished program, which allows us to get an impression of the basic drivers of anger. Fueled by rising costs of living, economic inequality, and perceived unfairness, the movement was mobilized through the Internet and manifested itself through massive street protests beginning in 2018 and continuing for years, interrupted only by the Covid-19 pandemic. The list of demands and the survey data both suggest that a large part of society felt victimized by an unfair system favoring the rich at the cost of the ordinary people struggling to make a living.[28] These grievances are not unlike those that sparked the massive Chilean street protests in 2019, where participants from all ages and political backgrounds took part in demonstrations that paralyzed the country.[29] One century earlier, economic hardship, government corruption, and food shortages caused discontent with the rule of the Czar, leading up to the Russian Revolution.[30] In Germany the global depression in the early 1930s caused almost half the population to lose their jobs, and the remainder to endure severe wage cuts. Angry and scared, people bought into Hitler's promises.[31] Further back in time, the French revolutionaries – plagued by unemployment and poverty while the elite feasted – demanded *liberté*, *égalité*, and *fraternité*.[32]

Outcomes of such periods of rising discontent differ, but the grievances are by and large similar, and so are the underlying 'plate tectonics.' Often, living conditions for large groups of society deteriorate. Sometimes this is caused by external conditions such as failed harvests or global economic strife, but mismanagement and corruption make things worse. Seeing the immunity of the elite class to the trouble they have created drives outrage (Figure 4.7). The result of this mix is lost attraction of the status quo. Depending on the way society is organized, its stabilizing mechanisms help it survive shocks. The status quo is an attractor to which life returns after earthquakes, failed harvests, and other crises. However, when living conditions have deteriorated far enough, and people see things as unfair, they may no longer feel that 'the system' works for them. According to an early influential theory by the American sociologist James C. Davies, much depends on the relative rate of change and how deteriorating living conditions compare to the past.[33] In the author's own words: "Revolution becomes more likely when people have experienced a fairly long period of satisfaction of their needs and then they are faced with a sharp downturn in satisfaction. The sudden downturn creates the J-Curve, which diagrams the gap between what people want and what they perceive is happening

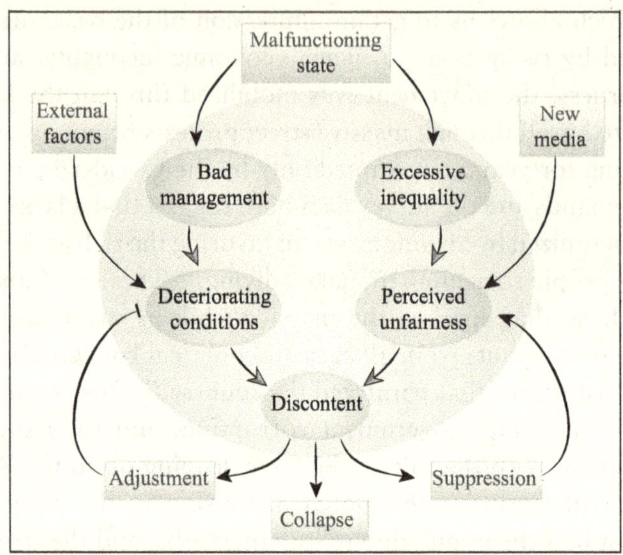

Figure 4.7 States may respond to rising discontent through adjustments that solve problems or through repression that may ultimately fuel discontent to the point of state collapse. The arrow in the lower left corner ending in a perpendicular dash rather than an arrowhead represents a dampening effect.

and will happen."[34] Complementary ideas were brought up by the young Ted Robert Gurr when he wrote his PhD thesis in the late 1960s. It turned into the book *Why Men Rebel*, which became a classic. The core argument still holds. As he summarized it himself half a century later:[35] "To understand protest ... we should analyze three general factors. First is popular discontent (relative deprivation), along with an analysis of its sources. Second are people's ... beliefs about the justifiability and utility of political action. Third is the balance between discontented people's capacity to act ... and the government's capacity to repress or channel their anger." Thus, before taking to the streets, people also weigh their chances. Whether discontent leads to gradual reform, collapse, or repression depends on circumstances. History reveals that chances for gradual adaptations are much better in a functioning democracy than in an autocracy, as we will see later. Autocrats tend to respond with repression, which can be effective (Figure 4.7). Yet, in the end, autocracies do collapse (typically followed by another autocracy[36]).

Doubting Norms

Just like states, social norms may lose attraction, as we saw briefly in the previous chapter. Throughout most of human history, slavery was considered normal. Until recently, women were seen as unfit to vote. Black people were not allowed to enter places reserved for white people. Smoking in public transport and offices was the norm . But norms change. Widely accepted things may, in hindsight, seem entirely unacceptable. As we saw in our graphical model (Figure 4.1), attitudes get stuck in part because of our tendency to agree with the majority view among our friends and family. Yet perceived problems with this consensus view can grow, raising the question of what 'tectonic plate movements' can destabilize a social norm.

Of course, all the stories of past norm changes are different, and each of them is multilayered. As we saw in the case of slavery, one factor may have been the Industrial Revolution.[37] Mechanization decreased the manpower needed to produce goods. But there was another, probably more important tectonic, movement.[38] Slowly, more and more people started to reject the idea of slavery. This was in part because Enlightenment thought became increasingly influential. The idea that liberty was a natural human right was part of that package, so slavery was increasingly seen as morally wrong. Meanwhile, relentless activism kept fueling the salience of the issue until, in the end, abolition became inevitable. When England led the way, other countries followed, and rising pressure on the late adopters led everyone to follow eventually. The slow creep of world opinion led to a global cascade of legislation. Slavery became increasingly rare, and this, in turn, helped make it socially unacceptable. A new social norm was established.

On an abstract level, mechanisms were similar for foot binding or institutionalized discrimination against women and black people: gradually changing worldviews; activism emphasizing that practices were incompatible with the new worldviews; the dwindling prevalence of the practice; and a new social norm (Figure 4.8). Note that – as shown in the smoking example – legislation can play a key role in tipping the norm. This works along two lines.[39] Rejection of the practice by authorities may help tip doubters into the conviction that the practice is wrong. And as enforcement makes the practice less common, seeing it less helps weaken the belief that it is normal. In the 1950s it was normal to smoke in the bus or in the office, or

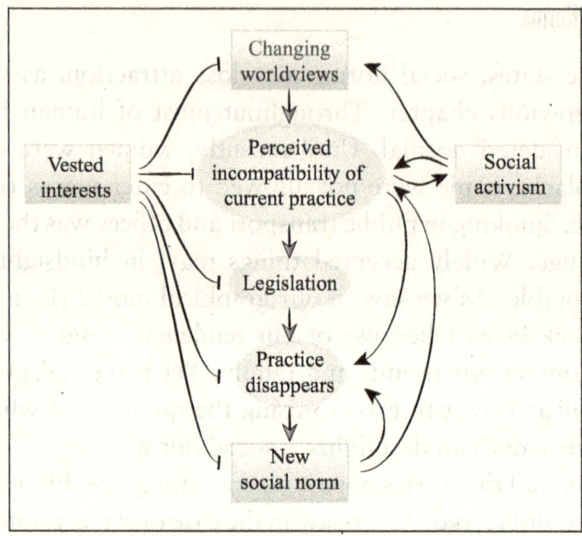

Figure 4.8 A change in social norms often follows a long period of social activism that emphasizes the incompatibility of current practices with shared worldviews. Despite pushback from parties with a vested interest, new legislation, such as the abolition of slavery, may cement a new social norm as the practice vanishes. Inhibitory effects are represented as arrows ending in perpendicular dashes.

even to light a cigarette in the house of nonsmoking friends. Seeing it all around reinforces the norm, and making it disappear weakens the norm.

The case of smoking is also revealing because of the well-studied campaign by the tobacco industry to delay the rise of an anti-smoking attitude. Efforts were especially focused on preventing anti-tobacco legislation, perhaps a sign that the industry think-tanks also believed that legislation could boost the rise of a new social norm. Nevertheless, the attitudes to smoking eventually changed as the health consequences became clear, not just for smokers but for those exposed to second-hand smoke. Still, broad acceptance of this insight and the implementation of legislation came decades later than the scientific consensus on the problems. This delay allowed the tobacco industry to thrive for longer, at huge social cost.

Similar strategies of seeding doubt about the evidence and discrediting the science were used to create perceived controversy over acid rain, DDT, the hole in the ozone layer, and, most spectacularly, by the fossil-fuel industry to obfuscate climate change. This was uncovered in an influential book, *Merchants of Doubt*, written by science historian Naomi Oreskes with Erik Conway.[40] The authors reconstruct how a handful of scientists joined forces with large corporations and conservative think-tanks to seed doubt about the scientific consensus on these issues. Later, a publication in the journal *Science* showed that, shockingly, scientists at ExxonMobil accurately predicted global warming in the 1970s:[41]

> ExxonMobil didn't just know "something" about global warming decades ago – they knew as much as academic and government scientists knew. But whereas those scientists worked to communicate what they knew, ExxonMobil worked to deny it – including overemphasizing uncertainties, denigrating climate models, mythologizing global cooling, feigning ignorance about the discernibility of human-caused warming, and staying silent about the possibility of stranded fossil fuel assets in a carbon-constrained world.

The 'delay industry' around fossil fuels has been very successful. But it is still only delay. Eventually, change is inevitable. Evidence for the disastrous implications of climate change is piling up, worldviews are gradually shifting, and legislation will help tip social norms when it comes to fossil-fuel use. Whenever I fill up the tank of the old fossil-fuel car that I keep as a backup I can't help wondering how long it will take before it will be completely unacceptable to burn this precious material formed millions of years ago.

Evolving Technology

Filling up my tank brings up another issue. It is so much cheaper to drive my electric car, charged by home solar panels. Technological progress is a moving tectonic plate in its own right. There is a famous quote attributed to Henry Ford commenting on the game-changing success of his Model-T: "If I had asked people what they wanted, they would have said faster horses." He never asked, and the rest is history. The Model-T became the affordable first car of many around the world, including my great-grandfather. Technological innovation and entrepreneurship are formidable forces that keep changing our ecosystem of choices. Solar-panel energy has become two orders of magnitude cheaper over the past decades, and electric cars have become affordable. A rapidly evolving network of charging stations boosted by EU regulation makes long electric journeys comfortable. There are tipping mechanisms in this that have to do with markets and scaling of production. As more people buy solar panels and electric cars, mass production makes them cheaper. As markets grow, more research is dedicated to improvements. As technologies become cheaper and better, markets grow further. There is also some good old-fashioned social contagion. As people see their neighbors installing solar panels and driving electric cars, they become more tempted to do so themselves. The interplay between markets, innovation, policies, and consumer behavior has caused the adoption of new technologies to follow an S-shaped curve time and time again.[42]

Before getting too optimistic about the economic drivers of sustainability transitions, let me remind you that economic interests may also slow down such changes. In the case of the transition to sustainable energy, it is clearly in the interest of the fossil-fuel industry to delay the transition. Similarly, it makes economic sense for the meat and dairy industry to delay the development of alternatives. There are many delay tactics. Advertising is one possibility, as is influencing regulations by political lobbying. The end results speak for themselves. Each year the world's governments spend about half a trillion dollars on artificially lowering the price of fossil fuels, more than three times what renewables get.[43] The imbalance is even starker for animal- vs. plant-based food. In 2022 livestock farmers in the EU received 1,200 times more public funding than producers of plant-based alternatives. In the USA animal-based food products received 800 times more funding than plant-based alternatives.[44]

To conclude this 'lost attraction' overview, there are always mechanisms that make it hard to quit the status quo. But eventually such mechanisms lose against the rising tension created by inevitable tectonic-plate movements of changing conditions and changing worldviews. That is the story cutting through the bewildering diversity of details. In the end, change has become inevitable time and time again, even if it's delayed by how the social brain works, and by a wide array of ways in which the status quo is defended by those with vested interests.

Breaking Loose

Overall, the process of getting stuck and losing attraction is more or less predictable. Not so for breaking loose. The ways in which tension is unleashed tend to take societies by surprise. Often a single event may trigger massive change. An exceptional drought kicked off the Late Bronze Age collapse. The assassination of the Archduke of Austria by a student triggered World War I. A Tunisian street vendor who set himself on fire started the Arab Spring. Exposure of sexual abuse by film producer Harvey Weinstein led to the #MeToo movement, invoking a global sea-change in legislation and attitudes toward harassment. Not only were the events that triggered such changes unpredictable, so were the ways in which change unfolded.

Most of the fundamental theory of tipping in complex systems is about attractors (getting stuck) and their loss of resilience (losing attraction). What happens next is hard to predict. We may notice a loss of attraction to the status quo, but what comes after the status quo breaks down? There may be hints hidden in the turmoil before a big shift.[45] Yet, once the system loses stability it remains hard to see where change will lead. Discontent may drive people to follow a Gandhi or a Hitler. Changes may be incremental or radical. The Yellow Vest movement forced President Macron to revise some key policies. The #MeToo movement brought down many powerful men and ushered in a host of new policies and laws. The Chilean protests invoked a slow process of revising the constitution that ultimately lost momentum. The Arab Spring revolts swept longstanding authoritarian rulers from power and tilted the region into lasting chaos, with hundreds of thousands of people killed and millions driven from their homes. Once the ball gets rolling, it is hard to say where it will end.

Nonetheless, we are starting to understand some of the rules for cascading transformations. Often, big change unfolds as a chain reaction, like a house of cards collapsing. The end of European feudalism, the Late Bronze Age collapse, the global abolition of slavery, the implosion of the big European empires, the 2008 stock market collapse, and the impact of the #MeToo movement all involved domino effects. In an attempt to capture such cascading change, theoreticians often think of systems in terms of networks of elements rather than single balls rolling down the hill of a stability landscape. For instance, we can think of the world as a network of interacting countries or society as a network of interacting individuals. Ecosystems have networks of interacting plants and pollinators. Power grids connect power plants. The Internet depends on a network of computers, and financial markets depend on networks of interacting banks.

What makes such networks stable or vulnerable to cascading change? Surprisingly, they can be both at the same time, a phenomenon known as 'robust yet fragile.' Think of a network of banks that can lend each other money.[46] This is handy, as each bank does not have to hold much cash while still being able to supply loans to customers at any time. The more connections a bank has in the network, the better it is able to function. These connections give robustness to individual banks, but there is a catch. This whole system is quite opaque, as the individual deals are confidential. In the end, it is possible that there could be too few safeguards in the system without anybody noticing. This makes the network vulnerable.[47] A failing bank may cause people to panic and withdraw their money from other banks. As the network doesn't have the cash to satisfy all those customers, this can result in a cascading collapse of banks. Such crises have happened repeatedly in history, and the global financial crisis of 2007–2008 is just one modern example. Remarkably, just before that crisis unfolded, the journal *Nature* published an article with the title "Ecology for bankers."[48] Written by two ecologists and a banker, it warned that too much connectivity in a network could make it brittle. The theoretical underpinning for the idea had been developed decades earlier in ecology. The ink was barely dry when the principle was spectacularly illustrated by the collapse of the global financial market. Seemingly robust, yet fragile.

Indeed, one of the most foundational insights from network theory is that networks may promote resilience and performance of their individual elements, but they can also make system-wide transitions possible, for good or for bad. When a critical point is reached, connectivity allows change or failure to run through the web like wildfire.[49] Think of global trade. There are important economic benefits. Manufacturing goods in low-income countries boosts their economies while lowering prices in the rich countries that import cheap goods. Reducing globalized trade would harm economies on both sides. (However, it would reduce ecological footprints. As income goes down in the Global South and prices go up in the Global North, consumption will decline globally[50].) But in terms of network stability, dependence on the global trade network makes countries sensitive to its disruption.[51] This became clear during the Covid-19 pandemic, when supply chains for all kinds of products suddenly failed. Dependencies are also revealed when local events have global impacts. For instance, if so-called chokepoints in the maritime transport network are blocked, such as the Strait of Hormuz, the Strait of Gibraltar, the Suez Canal, and the Panama Canal.[52]

Thinking of social norms in terms of network contagion makes sense too. Our simple graphical model (Figure 4.1) shows how the contagion of attitudes may cause society to get stuck and reach a tipping point. But this simplistic model assumes that we are all part of a single mixed pool. In reality we all live in bubbles, and we are much more likely to copy our bubble friends' attitudes than those of strangers. How does this affect the chances that a new social norm spreads? Obviously, the way connections run through society makes a difference. A new norm may spread within a subgroup but then get stuck. Entire groups of students have adopted a plant-based diet. Consequently, veganism and plant-based products are starting to spill over to society at large, but only very slowly.[53] What are the rules behind such spread and stagnation of change? Or, taking a practical angle: Where should we start if we want to change a norm? It may seem most logical to assume that change should start from the core of a network, from the persons with the most connections. But, counterintuitively, this is not how change tends to happen.[54] That is because new attitudes are often controversial at first. Therefore, the more peers you have, the less likely you are to develop a new view. After all, attitudes have a push–pull character, where opinions on both sides matter. This is very different from contagiousness in disease. As Aristotle noted in his collection of puzzling observations, the *Problemata*, a healthy person can become sick through contact with ill persons, but being in contact with healthy people does not make a sick person healthy. The consequences of this asymmetry were dramatic during the Covid-19 pandemic, during which well-connected individuals could become 'super-spreaders.'[55] New attitudes, however, are more likely to spread from the periphery of society.

Simulations confirm this.[56] Only when a critical mass is accumulated in relatively isolated peripheral communities can a new attitude spread in the larger network. Once it reaches the core, it may rapidly take over the whole. There is also empirical evidence that innovation often begins on the outskirts, away from dominant viewpoints.[57] For instance, a case study of the multinational corporation BASF found that a significant innovation originated in the company's Argentinian branch due to its peripheral position. The loose connection to the core allowed greater freedom, creating an environment where a controversial idea could thrive.[58] Another study showed that most successful Broadway musicals were written by teams that did not have too much connection to the larger creative network.[59] Too much connectivity can make it harder to break away from conventional styles. This is reminiscent of the approach taken by Nobel laureate Richard Feynman. He deliberately disconnected from existing ideas, avoiding reading too much of the literature and exploring unconventional approaches.[60] In a more systematic line of evidence, analysis of millions of papers, patents, and software products revealed that smaller teams tend to introduce disruptive ideas, while larger teams mostly build upon existing ones. Potentially divergent viewpoints are more readily neutralized within larger groups.[61]

In conclusion, when it comes to the chances of breaking loose, connectivity is a double-edged sword. It tends to reinforce the status quo, but may also allow change to unfold as a chain reaction once a critical point is reached. This is true for networks of banks and global trade, and also for the attitudes held by people in societies. For social norms, this resonates with how change is often a slow process, building up critical mass from the periphery before it exponentially speeds up, taking over society and its institutions.[62] It remains hard to say what the critical mass is, because it depends not only on how difficult it is to convince someone in a one-to-one context but also, for instance, on how an attitude figures as a marker of group identity. However, one thing is clear. Discouragingly slow progress does not mean that the situation is hopeless. Time and time again, sweeping changes in norms have followed long-simmering progress in the periphery.

Five Complementary Views

The tipping view of social change can accommodate many of the patterns we see in the human history of transformations. However, it is important to consider other perspectives too. Remember the quotation near the start of this chapter: "Something is complex when you can capture it in many different narratives that are all valid and cannot be combined into one." Societal change is always complex, and different theories of change can help see complementary aspects of it. To widen our views a bit, here are a few alternative angles to look at societal transformation.

It's a Pile of Sand

The prize for the best title goes to Danish physicist Per Bak's book *How Nature Works*.[63] What a claim to put in a title. Not everyone was convinced that the book contained the answer to every question about nature, but Bak and his colleagues were onto something. Their idea was that many systems evolve toward a state of "self-organized criticality," the edge of stability where a continuous regime of many small and occasional large adjustments keeps releasing tension. The earthquakes we saw earlier were a prime example, but conflicts, mass extinctions, forest fires, and many more phenomena have been thought to follow the same rules. The idea can be illustrated by the dynamics of a growing sand pile. Imagine you are at the beach, grab a handful of sand, and let it slowly rain down. A conical sand pile will gradually grow, with a curious feature: Its slope remains constant, even if you keep sprinkling more sand. That's because sand slides down the sides, mostly in small amounts, but sometimes in big avalanches. The slides keep correcting the slope as you add more sand to the top. In this self-organized critical state a particular relationship exists between the size of avalanches and how often they occur. The larger, the rarer. The precise relationship (a 'power law') was originally thought to be the hallmark of a self-organized critical system, but other mechanisms can result in the same statistical pattern. Therefore the ubiquity of this pattern in nature does not imply that self-organized criticality explains it all.[64] Nonetheless, the basic principle makes a lot of sense, especially to describe situations where slow continuous developments create 'tension' that can be released through avalanches – chain reactions that may either fizzle out or develop into something much bigger. The sand pile is like that, and so are earthquakes and forest fires. Any particular avalanche is unpredictable, but the release of tension may be larger when it is more overdue. For instance, in the case of forests there is a gradual buildup of dead branches and leaves over the years. Without much fuel, fires will be small in scale. By contrast, if a long period goes by without fire, the next fire will likely run through vast parts of the forest. Fire runs like avalanches, depending on the available fuel. While most of the theory is based on simulation models, it makes sense that versions of this tension-releasing mechanism drive the dynamics of real large heterogeneous systems such as forests,[65] the Earth's crust,[66] and societies.[67] As we have discussed, I like the metaphor of slow tectonic-plate movements as a driver of some sudden social transitions. For 3–4 billion years the huge tectonic plates that form the Earth's crust have been slowly moving. The speed is only a few centimeters a year, but the movement is unstoppable, and the effects are spectacular. For instance, where one plate slides under another, mountains and volcanoes form. But most relevant from our current point of view is the abrupt nature of the release of tension as the plates readjust, producing earthquakes: countless minor tremors and rare huge quakes. As argued, there are indeed slow unstoppable societal developments. The rise of Enlightenment thinking over the centuries is an example. This created tension in the way people saw the outdated feudal system, released by the French Revolution and many smaller readjustments.

It's a Cycle

In contrast to the sand-pile view that change comes in unpredictable bursts is the idea of regular, largely predictable societal cycles: a pendulum where an upswing is inevitably followed by a downswing. Regular cycles may happen when there is a fixed mechanism of internal destabilization causing history to repeat in a rhythmic way. Peter Turchin is the most prominent thinker along those lines today.[68] I previously introduced how he started out modeling population cycles in nature and moved on to search for mathematical patterns in the rise and fall of states. The repetitive cycle he sees in historical data takes about a century to complete and consists of two phases. First, there is a buildup, an integrative phase dominated by growth, where everything goes well. Then things start to disintegrate. In his view Western societies, and especially America, are now near the end of that latter phase, implying that a civil war or systemic collapse could be near.[69] The key drivers of disintegration stressed by Turchin are growing inequality, public debt, and what he calls the "overproduction of elites." This causes a growing number of people to compete for a finite pool of privilege and power. Then a war (or culture war) invokes the end of a functioning society. Another theory of regular cyclic societal change has been proposed by William Strauss and Neil Howe.[70] Their idea is that each generation produces a new era, each with a distinct archetypal mood producing a cycle repeating every four generations. When the authors came up with those ideas in the 1990s their view became quite popular among the general public.

Historians have been critical about the idea of regular cycles for two reasons. First, strict regularity does not hold up to scrutiny. Second, the one-size-fits-all approach doesn't match reality when it comes to explaining the mechanisms.[71] There is evidence for the existence of self-destructive mechanisms in societies, including over-exploitation of natural resources and growing inequality, but also other processes. As we discussed earlier, the anthropologist Joseph Tainter has proposed that states develop ever higher complexity to address new problems until a threshold is reached where the costs of further complexity start to outweigh the benefits, causing its structure to crumble.[72] Tainter stresses that not everything falls apart. Many elements may remain, but the structure of a society that has collapsed becomes simpler, less centrally controlled, and less socially differentiated. Indeed, such a process of de-complexification describes well what happened in one of his prominent case studies, the fall of the Western Roman Empire. Three decades after Tainter's work, Luke Kemp, a young researcher at the Centre for the Study of Existential Risk at Cambridge, extended Tainter's influential analysis.[73] Kemp finds that, often, deteriorating states do not invest in solving real problems but rather in elite-chosen tokenistic 'problems.' Overexpansion and military overspending drain resources, but equally important was destabilization caused by rising inequality, corruption, and intra-elite struggle. Those mechanisms echo Turchin's findings, but Kemp suggests an extra one too: the deteriorating ability to respond to new challenges as states get stuck in rigid adherence to old ways of doing things and elites become less perceptive.

In conclusion, the idea of strict cycles driven by particular mechanisms has little support. Instead, scholars have identified various mechanisms that tend to destabilize societies over time. True, the fact that many premodern states terminated at the age of around two centuries (Figure 3.1) does suggest some degree of predictable cyclicity. However, the broad range of longevities around this mean suggests that, rather than a fixed recurring mechanism, a varying mix of processes may be responsible for the balance between erosion and maintenance of resilience in societies over time.[74]

It's Panarchy

The loss of adaptive capacity over time, stressed by Luke Kemp, is also a key ingredient of a theory of change developed by C. S. (Buzz) Holling: the adaptive cycle.[75] His obituary in the journal *Nature Sustainability* characterized him as "a visionary of change in nature and society,"[76] and I couldn't agree more. For many years I participated in his workshops, which aimed to get economists and other social scientists to work with ecologists in search of new theories on how the world works. He hosted gatherings on small islands or other remote places where no one could escape; the group dynamics and long campfire discussions often brought breakthroughs and friendships that would never have happened in the office. In fact, Holling would only invite people who were "good on islands." On one such retreat he proposed that we should find out how societies were different from sand piles, referring to Per Bak's model of how the world works. The result was a book called *Panarchy*, referring to the unpredictable god Pan and to a hierarchy (or anarchy) of interconnected small and large cycles of change.[77] It was an attempt to get the best of both worlds, the sand pile and the cycle, while also weaving in some mechanisms of how things tend to get stuck. The basic element is the adaptive cycle, which is and isn't a cycle, instead capturing the rhyme of history. Unlike the sand pile and the cycle, the adaptive cycle cannot be captured in a few simple mathematical equations. Also, rather than depicting it as a circle, Holling opted for the more attractive lemniscate shape, hinting at the infinite repetition of patterns. This shape and the term Panarchy illustrate how strongly Holling's scientific work was guided by intuitions and associations.

The basic idea of the adaptive cycle is that the need for adaptation to ever-changing conditions causes systems to go through cycles of four phases: exploitation, consolidation, destruction, and reorganization. The first two form the 'forward loop,' in which the new ways are explored, ultimately leading to growth and flourishing. Toward the end of this part of the cycle the system becomes increasingly rigid, making it unable to adapt to a changing world, our 'getting stuck.' The second two phases form the more unpredictable 'back loop,' comparable with the idea of collapse. One thing that sets apart the adaptive cycle theory is that it emphasizes how novel elements and ideas develop during the rigidified part of the forward loop, even if they remain largely hidden. Those elements are repressed by the dominant constellation but form the seeds of novelty, ready to take over once collapse sets in. In the reorganization phase those elements may then come to shape a new form of the system, such as how mammals existed for a long time but only rose to dominance once the dinosaurs got out of the way.[78] Paradigm shifts in science, mass extinctions in evolutionary history, dynamics of corporations, and crises in societies may all be mapped onto the adaptive cycle model. The Panarchy idea is that such adaptive cycles happen on all scales in all systems, continuously influencing each other.

It's a Braided River

The idea of such parallel storylines touching each other at critical moments is also captured by the metaphor of braided rivers with their network of branches that diverge and rejoin. As we saw earlier, Robert Putnam and Shaylyn Romney Garrett got stuck trying to analyze the causes and effects during the US Progressive Era. In the end they concluded that things happened in parallel, but not independently, like a braided river.[79] I find this a useful complementary metaphor. Due to my background in ecosystems modeling I am tempted to think that the world can be described as a network of elements, each with dynamics depending on the other elements. A classical complex dynamical systems approach. However, equations cannot capture the subtlety of social and psychological processes. Like all theories of the world, mathematical models capture only some elements. Highlighting key elements is useful to help wrap your mind around complex issues, but it is always good to keep other options open. Metaphors help anchor our thinking. What I particularly like about the braided river metaphor is that it captures how the dynamics of, say, a family, a lake, a corporation, a country, a social norm, a rainforest, and so on, develop somewhat autonomously, but at critical moments may affect each other profoundly. Storylines that are mostly self-propelled but at times become entangled with other storylines in ways that may make it difficult to distinguish cause and effect. In fact, each of the interactors may be cause and effect at the same time. We have already seen examples of such elusive feedback loops. Here is another one.[80] Over millions of years of glacial cycles the temperature of the Earth and CO_2 concentrations in the atmosphere have gone up and down together in lockstep. In the famous documentary *An Inconvenient Truth*, former vice president and climate activist Al Gore made the mistake of suggesting that this was evidence of the warming effect of greenhouse gas. In fact, the reverse is also true.[81] Due to increased breakdown of organic matter, release of greenhouse gases from permafrost and numerous other processes, a warmer Earth releases more CO_2 and takes up less. The synchronous ups and downs over millions of years reflect this tight tango. Who was leading the dance? No one, really. As we saw, their growing size brought ice caps close to a tipping point. A slow wobble in the Earth's orbit then caused the planet to capture slightly more sun on its northern glaciers, triggering runaway warming where less ice meant more radiation being captured at the darker surface, and warming caused greenhouse gases to be released, further boosting the warming.[82] Then snowfall over hundreds of thousands of years would make the glaciers and ice caps grow again very slowly, until the story repeated. Now, however, this ancient storyline has been touched by that of humans.[83] Suddenly, our species started to burn the fossil fuels that had been stored underground for millions of years. Two branches of the braided river of causality touched in a novel way, dramatically changing the course of both.

It's Survival of the Feedbacks

The fifth complementary view I want to share with you is perhaps the most radical. It is in a way a reaction to a big chunk of appealing research aiming to explain social change using the methodology of biological evolution. This goes under the name of cultural evolution.[84] Related schools of thought have been developed over centuries, but the current field has been largely shaped by Pete Richerson and Robert Boyd, both rooted in ecology. The core idea is a version of Darwin's survival of the fittest,[85] but rather than the fittest individuals or 'selfish' genes,[86] the subjects of evolution are ideas and practices passed on through teaching, imitation, and other forms of social transmission. Explaining the world as a product of some form of survival of the fittest is tempting, but it also has its limitations. Reducing everything to this kind of evolution is too simple. It misses the systemic view in which feedbacks between multiple elements may propel change. Are humans so abundant because they domesticated grain, or is grain so abundant because it domesticated the humans who toiled to protect and reproduce it for millennia? Both, of course. The chicken-or-egg question is precisely what makes it interesting. To frame things more broadly: What determines what dominates the world as we know it? A slightly dazzling answer is self-reinforcing feedbacks (such as more people leading to more grain leading to more people etc.). I have talked a lot about that with my friend Tim Lenton. One of Tim's lifelong sources of inspiration was the thinking of James Lovelock, the architect of the Gaia hypothesis. Lovelock was fascinated by the question of how the Earth became this place where life creates conditions that are so well tuned for sustaining life. The answer is most likely that it just happened to happen. It worked out well for us, but no species was striving for that.

Thinking about this problem is useful, as it makes you focus on the whole rather than the selfish parts. After many discussions, Tim and I arrived at an answer to this evolutionary thinking.[87] It was an idea we had some difficulty naming, but we called it 'the selfish network,' 'survival of the systems,' 'the spread of the cycles,' and more. Both of us had been independently puzzling on the issue and had found it hard to frame in a simple, convincing way. In the end we concluded that self-reinforcing feedback between different elements often drives their shared dominance. Think of three species: humans, pigs, and grain. Or of grass. Why do grasslands cover a third of the Earth's productive land? The 'systems' we observe are those that have outspread or outpersisted other systems. In the case of grass, there are self-reinforcing feedbacks between fire, grass, and herbivores that helped the savanna to displace forests over the last 35 million years or so. Humans came in late but helped to spread the fire, promoting this kind of landscape even further. Framed this way, the challenge for the coming decades is to foster the right new set of self-reinforcing feedbacks. As argued in the next chapter, we are caught in a web of self-reinforcing feedbacks involving elements such as mass advertising, overconsumption, wealth accumulation, weakening regulation, deteriorating climate, rising inequality, and far-right populism. The challenge is to turn those vicious cycles into reinforcing feedbacks that propel humanity toward a widespread thriving, toward a just and sustainable future.

Ten Laws of Social Tipping

Despite their diversity, those complementary theories of social transformation do converge on a set of common points. That is encouraging. It tells you something when thinkers with different backgrounds arrive at similar conclusions, despite the bewildering diversity of stories about societal transformations. In search of mechanisms that could swiftly turn the fate of humanity, my selection of favorite theories of change is, of course, biased. There are countless other thoughts on the mechanisms that drive gradual social change. Sociologists, anthropologists, and economists have many valuable elements to offer, and I will discuss a few more of them in the remainder of the book. However, the prevailing view of social change is that it tends to be a road to progress, that the arrow of time drives modernization, causing people to be better off than their ancestors.[88] Alas, this is a biased view based on a poor reading of history.[89] As we have seen, many supposed improvements, such as agriculture or industrialization, resulted in major damage to quality of life. Also, living conditions in aging states often deteriorated. Thus, while we are well-off now, historically speaking, many changes have worsened conditions. That may seem a sobering thought, but it also implies that there is a lot to be learned from history, precisely because it was not an ongoing modernization, but instead a sequence of periods of deteriorating conditions punctuated by intermittent jumps forward. Even though history never repeats, the patterns of demise and progress have similarities, coming back time and time again. That is why they may help us see the limits but also the possibilities of carving the future of humanity.

To summarize the key insights that emerge from the case studies and the theories, here are the ten laws of social tipping. Of course there are no strict laws, let alone ten precisely, but doing the exercise of simplification helps sharpen the view of the rhyme pattern of history. What are the patterns that kept coming back time and time again, and are thus likely to repeat in the future?

Ten Tipping Laws

(1) *Societies tend to get stuck* in social traps where rules and habits harm ordinary people.
(2) *Vested interests* motivate ruling elites to enforce such traps.
(3) *Media control* helps elites perpetuate traps, and new media outlets may disrupt that control.
(4) *Calls for reforms* are due to perceived unfairness and deterioration of conditions.
(5) *Democracy* allows regular incremental reforms, but is vulnerable to state capture by the wealthy.
(6) *Autocracies* repress calls for change until they collapse, typically leading to another autocracy.
(7) *Social norm shifts* are belated adjustments to evolving worldviews.
(8) *Activism* may precipitate norm shifts by stressing incompatibility of practices with worldviews.

(9) *Guaranteed dominance by the same elite* may facilitate reforms.
(10) *The periphery of societies* is where change starts.

We will use these insights in the final chapters to address the question of how humanity may carve out a positive future. But now it is time to pause and ask what is already happening. Can we discern the direction societies are taking? Hints of where we are heading? Elements we need to consider in our quest for actions that may nudge humanity toward a positive future?

5 READING OUR TIMES

The human track record of transformation looks daunting at times, but it is also a reason for hope. We know societies have tipped out of trouble, so we should be able to do it again, especially since we are starting to understand how transformations work. Moreover, humanity seems to be ready for change. We see the rising turmoil that has been so characteristic of the fragile situations preceding past transitions. Also, the developments that drove previous civilizations to transform are similar to the current situation in many ways. The growth of the human footprint is undermining the environment on which we depend; inequity is a problem, and discontent results in violence. There are calls for abandoning the old ways and experiments in search of new ways.

In some respects, it's surprising to see this discontent. In many ways, times have never been better.[1] Most have enough food as well plenty of luxury items. Life expectancies have never been this high. Yet, as I write this book, restlessness is in the air. Fundamentalist movements, political polarization, a rise of populism, and street protests around the globe signal widespread discontent with the status quo and a search for novel avenues. Are those the early warning signals of an upcoming global transformation? Indicators of lost attraction to the status quo? If so, will the trouble throw humanity into disarray, or will it open up the way to a just and sustainable future? Even if we are starting to know the laws of social tipping, it is tricky to extrapolate from the past, as our current situation differs from anything humanity has seen before. In this chapter I ask how this unprecedented setting could affect humanity's chances to tip out of trouble in a graceful way. Reading our times is what a host of good social scientists, journalists, and other analysts do for a living. Every day quality newspapers and magazines are filled with thoughtful analyses. But all of those are just snippets. It is hard to see the big picture of where humanity could be heading if you are in the midst of it. So it was for my great-grandfather when, during his lifetime, the automobile industry unfolded, antibiotics were discovered, and women got the right to vote. But despite progress, out of the blue the Spanish flu started killing more than ten of his patients per day, and the world also slipped into global wars twice. It was hard to see where things were going, and so it is now. Yet it is important to try, as understanding the trends will help us see potential futures more realistically. What follows is a helicopter view of trends that may matter most, zooming in on some branches of the braided river that have entered rapids over the past decades. I will skip the astonishing deterioration of nature and climate change driven by the great acceleration of human activity and its impacts beginning around the mid-twentieth century. This was already summarized in Chapter 1, as was the runaway concentration of wealth in the hands of a few. In the current chapter I invite you to reflect on a complementary collection of stark societal trends that are relevant to the trouble and the options for tipping out of it. Together with our history-informed tipping theory, a close-up view of the 'now' will pave the way for the next chapters where we will explore our choice of futures. The bewilderingly diverse set of trends in this chapter may seem all over the place on first consideration. But by the end of the chapter you will see that they all fall into place to form a unifying theory of plausible alternative futures for humanity.

The Information Revolution

The information revolution is perhaps the most profound development setting the present situation apart from other moments of human history. Changing ways of information transfer have been an influential branch of the braided river of social change before. For instance, we saw it play a key role in the French Revolution and also in the US Progressive Era. It is an understatement to say that the present situation follows that trend. New developments in the transmission of information are changing how decisions are made and opinions are formed. Changing how societies work. Shaping the future of war and peace, the future of democracy, and the future of work. It has happened so quickly. We can now hardly imagine life without the Internet, laptops, and smartphones, even though none of that existed in the 1980s – and those things are only the hardware. What matters is what can be done with it. Compared to letters, emails boosted written communication between people and changed its style. Searching for information was revolutionized by internet search engines. Social media brought that change to the next level, and made spreading views to a broad audience accessible for anyone with a phone. And today, the use of massive data has changed science, and large language models (LLMs) are changing life.

The flow of information, misinformation, and disinformation shapes perceptions and trust, and it is undeniably influenced by the extremely wealthy. Most newspapers and television channels are owned by a relatively small group of billionaires, as are social media networks and AI products such as ChatGPT and other LLMs. Like other wealth-generating businesses, some of those products do physical harm. Just as Big Oil puts one-third of the world's population in grave climate danger by the end of the century,[2] and tobacco kills 6 million annually,[3] social media take a toll on health.[4] And, as with tobacco, profits are higher when the addictive power is larger. However, the effects of social media and AI on society go way beyond health. Let's examine how those multifaceted game-changers may affect our chances to tip out of trouble.

Social Media

As we have seen, discontent has been a driver of transformation throughout human history. Now, an overall sense of unfairness and crisis is being boosted by social media. Social networks have completely changed the playing field of information spread since their global surge around 2007.[5] The literature on social media effects is vast, but let's focus on three elements that directly or indirectly affect the chances for society to tip out of trouble: a boost of the visibility of *problems*, facilitation of the spread of *conspiracy thinking*, and the exploration of new *solutions* to societal issues.

Arguably, social media enhance the visibility of a wide range of problems. This happens as activist groups seek to muster support[6] and lifestyle movements seek to inspire alternative choices.[7] For instance, social media catalyzed the Arab Spring by depicting atrocities of the regime,[8] jihadist videos motivate terrorists by showing gruesome acts committed by US soldiers,[9] and veganism is promoted by social media campaigns highlighting appalling animal welfare issues.[10] Many of the problems highlighted on social media are real, and often they have been largely hidden from the public eye in the past. However, regardless of whether problems are exaggerated or revealed faithfully online, the effect will boost the perception of a world entangled in a multiplicity of crises. Not least because the more enraging a message is, the faster it spreads.[11]

Further down the gradient from revelation to exaggeration, we come to misinformation[12] and conspiracy theories.[13] The online diffusion of false news is in general broader, faster, and deeper than that of true news.[14] Conspiracy theories originate particularly in times of uncertainty and crisis[15] and often depict established institutions as hiding the truth and sustaining an unfair situation.[16] As a result, they may find fertile ground in minds where social media have already boosted a sense of unfairness. This feeds anti-establishment sentiments, creating the substrate on which populism flourishes. Neither conspiracy theories nor overexposure of problems in the media are new phenomena. However, social media are powerful magnifiers, plausibly nudging a web of feedbacks (Figure 5.1) that boost a sense of crisis and unfairness, and thus discontent with the status quo.

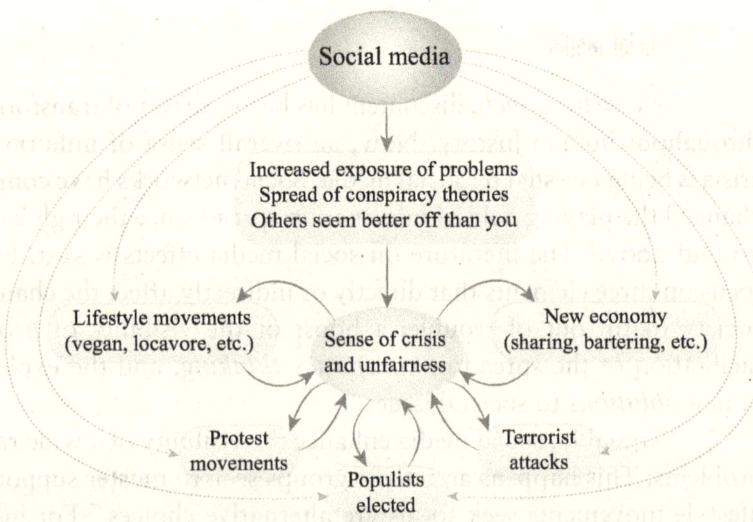

Figure 5.1 Social media may amplify an overall sense of crisis and unfairness in multiple ways.

While social media may stimulate a sense of unfairness, they can also help to make solutions visible. Social media and sharing platforms facilitate the spread of organized sustainability practices ranging from bartering and sharing[17] to veganism, eat-local groups, voluntary simplicity, and other lifestyle movements.[18] Social movements are an old phenomenon, but social media open up a novel dimension, allowing individuals worldwide to tune in to a new worldview, triggering entirely different dynamics.[19] Influencers and lifestyle gurus emerge and gain followers based on their charismatic presentation rather than through formal leadership in a traditional movement. Social media have thus created a new playing field not only when it comes to elevating a general base level of discontent but also when facilitating social self-organization, the formation of movements, the sharing of views, and the search for novel solutions.

This combination of enhanced self-organizing power and elevated global discontent may well increase the chances for social tipping. To see why, let's bring back the simple tipping point model of social change from Chapter 4. Stability will be affected by two effects of social media: a rising perception of an unfair world beset by a multitude of problems; and an increased capacity to explore alternative solutions and self-organize into new social configurations and views (Figure 5.2).

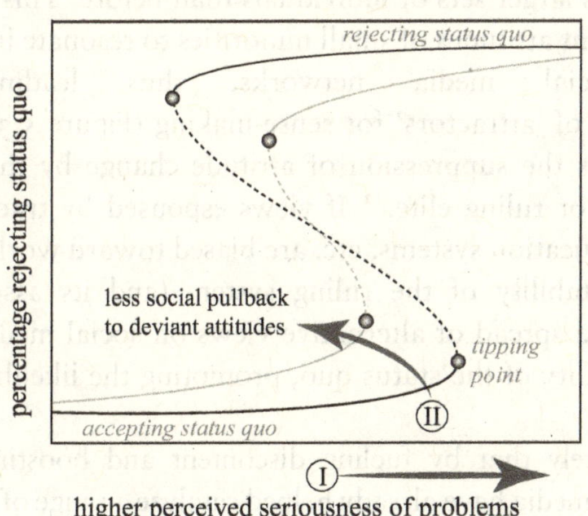

Figure 5.2 Two ways in which social media may catalyze social tipping. First, they boost the perceived seriousness of problems (arrow I). Second, they reduce the pullback effect of conforming to the majority attitude of a community, as individuals may find alternative groups of peers on social media (arrow II).

The first effect is rather obvious. If problem perception is boosted, a tipping point for an attitude shift will be reached more readily. The self-organization effect works differently. It implies that society is less likely to get stuck through the 'pullback effect' of social pressure on individuals with deviant attitudes. Social media make the dominant attitudes in the communities where people live less important, since individuals may now complement their local communities with an online community which fits their new attitudes more naturally. Returning to the example of veganism, breaking away from conventional eating patterns may be difficult in a traditional community. Your family, friends, and neighbors may easily talk such a fringe idea out of your mind. It is a one-against-many tug of war. By contrast, it will be easy to find people who agree with you on internet forums and social media. You thus ameliorate the suffocating effect of the local community, diluting the dominance of their attitude. In the representation of this simple model, that changes the social 'costs' associated with becoming vegan, facilitating the transition.

Attitude shifts may be facilitated by the ability to find communities that share a minority attitude. Humans are homophilous in the sense that 'birds of a feather flock together' with respect to age, religion, educational level, worldviews, etc.[20] Such an assortative process can now play out across larger sets of individuals than before. This allows what used to be latent attitudes of small minorities to resonate in large, self-organized social media networks, thus leading to a growing diversity of 'attractors' for sense-making (Figure 5.3). This mechanism weakens the suppression of attitude change by the traditional gatekeepers or ruling elite.[21] If views espoused by traditional media, churches, education systems, etc. are biased toward worldviews that support the stability of the ruling system (and its associated elite), the unchecked spread of alternative views on social media may undermine the stability of the status quo, promoting the likelihood of attitude shifts.

It seems likely that by fueling discontent and boosting self-organization, social media have already helped catalyze a range of critical transitions in attitude. Within a single decade, between 2005 and 2015, social media came to permeate life. This has plausibly been a significant force powering a global époque of social transformation, breaking the status quo on many fronts. Indeed, #MeToo and #BlackLivesMatter triggered massive shifts in public attitude, and in the streets the signs of

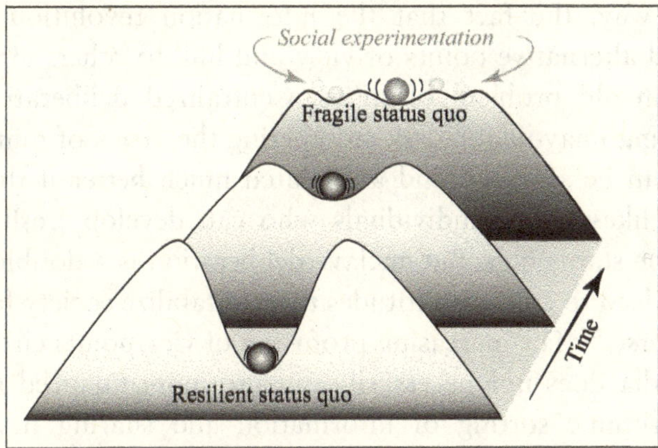

Figure 5.3 Discontent boosted by social media may reduce resilience of the status quo and promote social experimentation with new ways of doing things. Whether such developments can lead to a global shift into a sustainable societal attractor remains an open question.[22] (Adapted from Carpenter *et al.*, "Dancing on the volcano.")

a surge in social unrest have been hard to miss.[23] By the end of the 2010s protesters were active in Lebanon, Hong Kong, Chile, Bolivia, Catalonia, Iraq, France, and Egypt, to name a few places, and in 2020 the USA experienced the most widespread and sustained unrest in over fifty years. These rebellions were motivated by different grievances, but their clustering in time suggests that they might share a global latent factor. Could it be social media? Analysts broadly recognize the role of the innovative use of social media in facilitating street protests. This may well be part of the explanation, but the effect of social media in catalyzing protest is likely more complex and profound than simply facilitating mobilization. As we saw in the section on lost attraction, classical work on the causes of revolutions suggests that a growing discrepancy between reality and expectations may be important.[24] Social media may contribute to such tension by showing how others are better off and diminishing feelings of self-worth.[25] Also, revolts require triggering events as well as a preceding phase during which there has been a gradual buildup of grievance.[26] Social media contribute to both. Most visible are the trigger effects, such as vividly depicting precipitating conditions (e.g., through the spread of appalling video footage). However, on slower timescales social media also aggravate an 'unfair world' perception, making rejection of the status quo increasingly likely.

In a way, the fact that the information revolution allows people to find alternative points of view and link to others efficiently helps solve an old problem of states. Centralized deliberation and decision making unavoidably risk smothering the views of minorities. Such views can be surfaced and articulated much better if there are 'enclaves' of like-minded individuals who can develop fresh views, challenging the status quo. But enclave deliberation is a double-edged sword. It can lead to extreme attitudes that destabilize society for both better and worse.[27] The increasing profusion of viewpoints circulating on social media does not necessarily nurture more nuanced visions. Rather, algorithmic sorting of information and sharing news and views among friends in 'echo chambers' tend to reduce exposure to attitude-challenging information, which may contribute to the adoption of more extreme attitudes over time.[28] This resonance can create tunnel vision, leading to socially damaging developments such as the anti-vaccine movement.[29] Extremists and terrorists are no exception when it comes to the trend that individuals across the globe find inspiration in echo chambers.[30]

Another threat when it comes to society's capacity to coordinate toward just and sustainable futures is the risk of public opinion being hacked by social media campaigns boosted by trolls, bots, and other manipulations, making it seem that large groups of people hold a particular opinion even though this is crafted out of thin air by those looking to twist the public discourse. While this can propel opinion in any direction, social media may have generally nudged societies toward isolationist and populist views.[31] Signals of such isolationism include the US withdrawal from the Paris Climate Agreement, Brexit, and the Hungarian border barrier. Thus, while social media have catalyzed turbulence and a rich multitude of views that challenge the status quo, social media-related mechanisms may also have undermined the capacity to connect and deliberate across this multitude of views, a capacity which is essential for navigating toward futures that benefit society as a whole.[32]

Some of the distortive effects of the information revolution will likely be transient. For one thing, the sheer rate of technological change has made it difficult for society to keep pace. Elderly Facebook users share about seven times more fake news than young people, suggesting that digital literacy may solve some problems with time.[33] New forms of fact-checking and reliability labeling may also resolve some of the problems.[34] However, misinformation is only part of the picture. Social media are transforming the way we see the world, influencing our options for the future. This is a massive and unpredictable force. A large meta-analysis of studies suggests that while digital media may help make autocracies more democratic, the same media tend to threaten established democracies by undermining trust, increasing polarization, and promoting populism.[35] It seems safe to say that social media can promote change, just as new ways to spread opinions and news have been catalysts at other crucial moments in history. Breaking loose has become easier, but the direction of such change remains uncertain.

Artificial Intelligence

Less than two decades after the rise of social media, another game-changing technology arrived. Large language models (LLMs) were brought spectacularly to the attention of the public through the chatbot ChatGPT. The rise of LLMs felt out of the blue for most of us, but the basic technology was not new at all. What those models do is find statistical relationships between pieces of text that make it possible to generate language that looks human. For instance, if you scan many texts looking for the phrase 'The sky is,' you will find that the next word is more often 'blue' than, for instance, 'wood.' Information on such probabilities has been driving text prediction for some time, helping to type on your phone or complete search queries in Google. It also works for musical phrases. In the 1980s the composer David Cope, suffering from writer's block, developed a computer program that could generate music in the style of classical composers based on statistical patterns with a touch of randomness. As he told *The Guardian* thirty years later:[36] "When you had the database figured out it was really a one-stroke deal: you pushed the button and out came hundreds and thousands of sonatas or whatever." The compositions sounded so real that it caused a huge stir. Music is something so deeply human, so close to our souls, that being cheated into emotion by an algorithm felt like a violation. It wasn't the first moment that a computer shook the foundations of what was considered fundamentally human. In the 1960s, when the first digital computers were being designed, Joseph Weizenbaum at MIT had already written a program that could mimic a psychologist.[37] The program, called ELIZA, was what we would now call a chatbot. In those days there were no computer screens yet, so you had to communicate with ELIZA by typing and waiting for an answer. Weizenbaum presented ELIZA as a computer psychotherapist who would listen to how you expressed your feelings and respond. The program mimicked the style of the therapist Carl Rogers, who became famous for his approach of simply repeating a version of what the patient said, often in the form of a question. Weizenbaum wanted to make fun of the whole idea of AI, but he ended up being blown away by the effect his simple tool had on people. They would open their hearts to it. Famously, one day, his secretary – who knew very well that it was a simulation – was chatting with the program when suddenly she asked Weizenbaum: "Would you mind leaving the room, please?" Similarly, his students could spend hours telling ELIZA about their inner feelings, revealing all kinds of personal details.

So, if these basic techniques and ideas have existed for some time, what has changed since the 1960s that has allowed ChatGPT to become such a game-changer? The simple answer is computer power and the sheer amount of data that has become available. Instead of simple statistical relationships, the LLMs use artificial neural networks; but that, too, is an old idea. In the 1940s the genius – in my humble opinion – Donald Hebb figured out the essence of how the brain learns.[38] The simple expression "neurons that fire together, wire together" captures the essence of such Hebbian learning. When neurons are activated at the same time, they start reinforcing synaptic contacts between them, thus shaping the architecture of the brain. Recently, advanced techniques have showed that Hebb got the basics right.[39] But computer scientists didn't wait for confirmation. By the 1950s pioneers had started encoding the idea in machines, allowing computers to 'learn.' In the year I was born, those exciting developments led the economist (and later Nobel laureate) Herbert Simon to write:[40]

> It is not my aim to surprise or shock you – but the simplest way I can summarize is to say that there are now in the world machines that think, that learn and that create. Moreover, their ability to do these things is going to increase rapidly until – in a visible future – the range of problems they can handle will be coextensive with the range to which the human mind has been applied.

It did not happen that rapidly. In fact, in the 1990s my colleague Egbert van Nes and I stopped experimenting with artificial neural networks because the results were so disappointing. We were naively trying to use those tools to predict how a turbid lake would respond to different measures aimed at clearing the water. We were training the networks on previous experiences, but there was not nearly enough training data. The amount of data, coupled with computational power, is what makes the difference. Networks only function well when they can be trained on massive data. Then they can start recognizing handwritten texts, pictures of dogs, and more. Algorithms improved, too. Starting in the 1980s the theoretical physicists John Hopfield and Geoffrey Hinton developed computational approaches that improved the learning capacity of artificial neural networks. The overwhelming implications for society became apparent only recently, leading the Nobel committee to award them the 2024 prize in physics. Thus, in a way, the slow 'tectonic-plate movements' of increasing data and computational power eventually led to a step-change in what computers can do. It was a change that surprised all of us, even its creators. Unfortunately, those huge neural networks with their billions of parameters are largely a black box. It is almost impossible to figure out how they do what they do. That also makes them difficult to control. So far, the best way to steer their behavior is through the selection of the texts on which they are trained. Obviously, if you are worried that terrorists might use an LLM to find out how to make a biological weapon of mass destruction, it helps to exclude literature on that topic in the training set. That approach may also help control other issues, such as the tendency of LLMs to come up with prejudices. In any case, novel ways to improve LLMs are constantly emerging.

Nevertheless, the current generation of LLMs also regularly come up with nonsense. So-called hallucinations. That wouldn't be so bad if it weren't for the seductive, fluid language that makes them sound so convincing. You can often tell when you are talking to a stupid person, just from their language. That helps you rate the credibility of the viewpoints and information coming from that source. The same holds for written sources. Not so for LLMs. They tend to sound as if they know perfectly well what they are talking about. The risks of deception will decrease as language models get better, but also as people start to understand how to judge and check credibility, just as happened with social media, where younger generations are better than the elderly at judging content.

Yet, even if not outright deceptive, the perceived wisdom of LLMs may nudge opinions and worldviews. I realized that when I probed ChatGPT's advice after reading an interview with Thomas Piketty in *The Guardian*.[41] Piketty advocated taxing the extremely wealthy to combat the climate crisis. His argument was basically that otherwise, politicians would never get a majority of voters to favor their policy. Obvious, I thought. But that, of course, relates to the larger question of why wealth distribution is not happening. So why not ask ChatGPT how we could use the billionaires' money to tackle the climate issue? It came up only with scenarios for voluntary action by the billionaires, and, when I asked for something more radical, strongly advised against it, citing individual rights and freedoms:

Me: How could excessive wealth from billionaires globally be repurposed to fight climate change?

ChatGPT: *Excessive wealth from billionaires globally can be repurposed in several ways to fight climate change. Here are a few suggestions:*

1. *Investment in renewable energy: Encouraging billionaires to invest in renewable energy initiatives, such as solar and wind power, can significantly contribute to reducing carbon emissions and promoting sustainable development.*

2. *Funding research and innovation: Allocating funds towards climate change research and innovation can help develop new technologies and solutions to mitigate its effects. This could include supporting projects focused on carbon capture, sustainable agriculture, or climate-resilient infrastructure.*

3. *Supporting conservation efforts: Donations towards conservation organizations and projects can protect and restore ecosystems, preserving biodiversity and natural resources. This can help combat deforestation, protect endangered species, and promote sustainable land use practices.*

4. *Promoting sustainable practices: Financing initiatives that encourage sustainable practices in industries like agriculture, transportation, and manufacturing can have a substantial impact. This may involve supporting initiatives that promote circular economy models, eco-friendly production methods, or low-carbon transportation alternatives.*

    *5. Funding education and awareness programs: Supporting edu-
cational initiatives that raise awareness about climate change,
promote sustainable lifestyles, and empower communities to
take action can have a long-lasting impact. These programs
can help individuals and communities make informed choices
and adopt environmentally friendly practices.*

Me: I was thinking of something more radical, less voluntary.
For instance, take the funds and have a global committee repur-
pose it.

*ChatGPT: While it's understandable to consider more radical
approaches to repurposing excessive wealth to fight climate
change, it's important to approach such ideas with caution.
Implementing mandatory wealth redistribution without the
consent of billionaires may raise ethical and legal concerns.*

*However, if we were to explore the concept of a global commit-
tee overseeing the allocation of funds, it would require careful
consideration and collaboration among various stakeholders.
Here are a few points to consider:*

    *1. Transparency and accountability: Any global committee
responsible for repurposing funds should operate with
transparency and be accountable to ensure that resources
are allocated efficiently and effectively. Regular reporting,
audits, and oversight mechanisms would be essential.*

    *2. Diverse representation: The committee should include mem-
bers from diverse backgrounds, including experts in climate
science, economics, social justice, and environmental advo-
cacy. This would help ensure a balanced and comprehensive
approach to addressing climate change.*

    *3. Prioritization and strategic planning: The committee would
need to establish clear priorities and develop a strategic plan
for the allocation of funds. This plan should focus on projects and initiatives that have the greatest potential for
impact, such as renewable energy, conservation efforts,
and climate adaptation measures.*

    *4. Collaboration with existing organizations: The committee
should collaborate with existing organizations, such as
international climate funds, environmental NGOs, and*

research institutions, to leverage expertise and avoid duplicating efforts. This would help maximize the impact of the repurposed wealth.

While radical approaches may be appealing, it is important to strike a balance between addressing climate change effectively and respecting individual rights and freedoms. Engaging billionaires voluntarily and encouraging them to invest in climate solutions can be a more sustainable and collaborative approach in the long run.

In short, ChatGPT tried to talk the radical idea out of my head. In most of the world LLM chatbots in local languages are just based on translations of the LLMs that have been trained on English-language (mostly American) texts. Thus, their wisdom will tend to be based on the same worldview wherever you are, pulling us all toward the same moderate and reasonable views. Wondering if this would be true even for China, I asked my friend Xu Chi to probe Chinese LLMs with the same questions. To our surprise, they turned out almost precisely the same responses, even if they claimed to be trained on Chinese texts. By contrast, a conversation with Chinese open-source chatbot DeepSeek-R1 soon after it was launched in 2025 impressed us with a broad set of detailed recommendations, concluding with a statement that resonated more with the reasoning I will present in the following chapters: "Feasible wealth redistribution in Western societies requires policy pragmatism (e.g., closing loopholes, raising top tax rates) combined with cultural mobilization to shift norms around fairness and collective responsibility. While radical proposals (e.g., abolishing billionaires) remain politically distant, incremental steps can accumulate transformative power – especially if paired with grassroots pressure and ethical arguments grounded in the humanities."

The bottom line is that LLMs are likely to be dismissive of innovative views such as Piketty's. Instead, they reflect the thinking that permeates the texts on which the models are trained. In that sense, one could perhaps say that those tools could help balance the effects of social media when it comes to the classic tension between centralized and enclave deliberation. LLMs can be tweaked by training them on biased selections of text, but overall, mainstream versions are likely to bolster rather than challenge the status quo.

Meanwhile, AI has potential to help find new medicines, resolve legal disputes, diagnose diseases, filter spam, tutor students, power agricultural robots and trucks, predict extreme weather events, and so forth. Many such applications change the way jobs are done, increasing efficiency and requiring less human labor. Implications for the future of work are likely profound, but how it will play out is up for debate. Global inequality may rise as richer countries take the lead. On the other hand, AI may give developing economies a boost as it democratizes access to services such as medical diagnoses and tutor-guided teaching. There are many worries about the explosive increase in AI capacities. For instance, in a global poll of experts commissioned by the World Economic Forum to identify the main risks for humanity in the coming two years, AI-generated misinformation and disinformation were rated first.[42]

In any case, AI and LLMs are here to stay. After some years, who would want to do without them? As David Cope says about his composition tools:[43]

> The programs are just extensions of me. And why would I want to spend six months or a year to get to a solution that I can find in a morning? I have spent nearly 60 years of my life composing, half of it in traditional ways and half of it using technology. To go back would be like trying to dig a hole with your fingers after the shovel has been made, or walking to Phoenix when you can use a car.

The small drawings I have used to illustrate collapse, senescence, rejuvenation, the sand pile, Panarchy, etc. are the result of experimenting with generative AI. That was just a small use of a helpful tool, but AI applications will clearly have enormous social implications. Much like the Industrial Revolution and other technological advances, long-term implications are nearly impossible to foresee, and regulations will be needed to control collateral damage.

Getting Emotional

From Rational to Intuitive

Perhaps one of the most striking social trends of the past decades is the turn from predominantly rational arguments to the emotional post-truth style of political debate championed by politicians such as Donald Trump. Baseless alternative truths are treated with the same validity as scientific facts, and debunking such lies has little effect on their credibility for followers.[44] Part of the explanation may be the power of social identity. Sharing the same attitudes signals belonging to a group, and no one wants to lose a sense of belonging, especially in a lonely, uncertain context.[45] However, could it perhaps also be that rationality is simply going out of vogue? How do you measure that? Could the language that is used give us a clue?

To explore that possibility, we teamed up with computational scientists to analyze millions of books written between 1850 and 2019.[46] Reading such a huge amount of books would take a single person thousands of years, so how is that possible? The answer is at your fingertips. Just search for the Google Ngram Viewer and type a word or phrase that you are interested in. Within a second you have a graph showing how the relative frequency of it has changed over time in a huge historical collection of books. When I found out about this tool, I couldn't stop playing with it. The word "war" shows large bumps marking the two world wars. "Carriage" drops in the first decades of the twentieth century, mirroring a rise in "automobile." Looking for indicators of sentiment versus rationality, I saw that the frequency of words such as "angry" or "feel" have risen over the past decades, while "result" and "committee" have dropped. But this is cherry-picking. How can we know if there has really been a systematic change in language? With the help of colleagues and students we decided to analyze the wax and wane in frequencies of the 5,000 most-used words in various languages. To do so, we used principal component analysis, a sophisticated statistical technique for summarizing the main pattern of change across many factors. The first principal axis of change turned out to basically reflect the arrow of time, going from terms such as ox, straw, savage, and carriage to words like cola, ski, allergic, tech, and dummy. The second axis was more interesting. It showed a downward trend since 1850 with a spectacular reversal over the past half century or so (Figure 5.4 A).

On closer examination, this axis ranked words (according to their shared trends) with on one extreme terms such as look, walk, unexpected, sleep, voice, imagine, embarrassed, tortured, and heal, and at the other end words like state, report, year, sec, council, order,

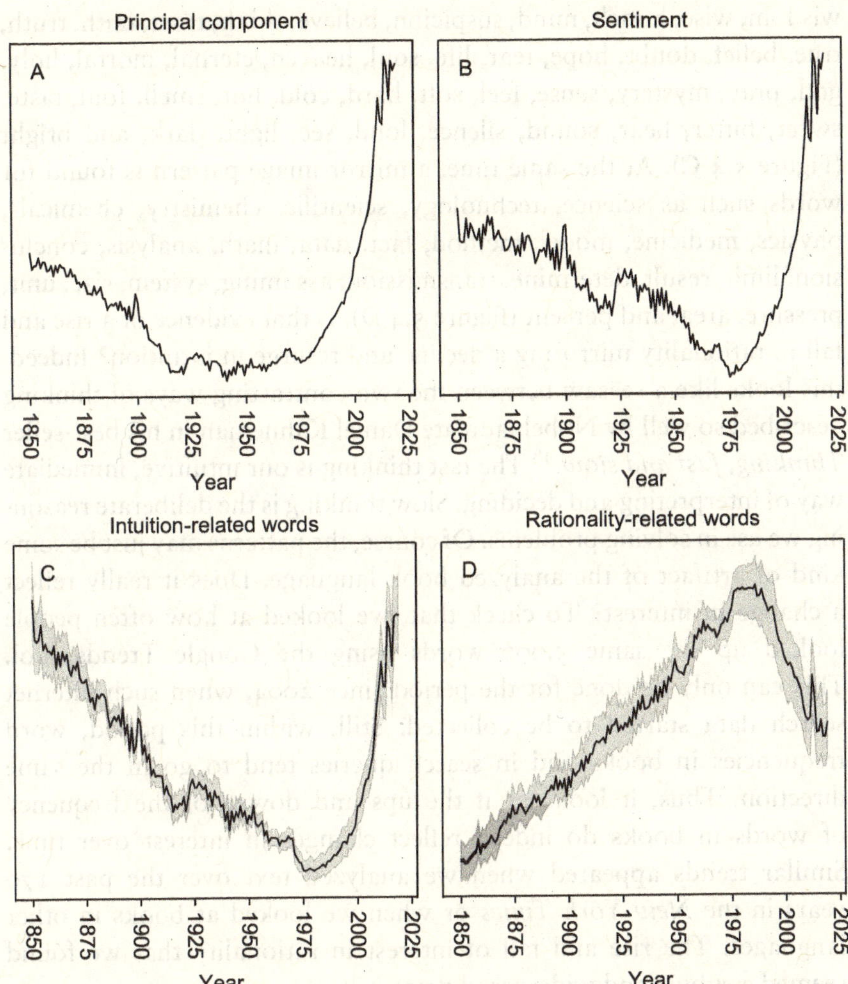

Figure 5.4 Indicators for the rise and fall of rationality in book language, 1850–2018. (Adapted from Scheffer *et al.*, "The rise and fall of rationality in language."[47])

and authorized. Do you spot a pattern? We then used another tried and tested technique to classify the relative level of sentiment automatically. Words associated with high sentiment levels showed a steady downward decline from 1850 till around 1980, when the trend bent upward in a spectacular way (Figure 5.4 B). Diving deeper, we found that the trends in the principal axis and sentiment are closely followed by trends in words related to intuition, believing, and spirituality: spirit, imagine, wisdom, wise, hunch, mind, suspicion, believe, think, trust, faith, truth, true, belief, doubt, hope, fear, life, soul, heaven, eternal, mortal, holy, god, pray, mystery, sense, feel, soft, hard, cold, hot, smell, foul, taste, sweet, bitter, hear, sound, silence, loud, see, light, dark, and bright (Figure 5.4 C). At the same time, a mirror-image pattern is found for words such as science, technology, scientific, chemistry, chemicals, physics, medicine, model, method, fact, data, math, analysis, conclusion, limit, result, determine, transmission, assuming, system, size, unit, pressure, area, and percent (Figure 5.4 D). Is that evidence of a rise and fall in rationality mirroring a decline and resurge in intuition? Indeed, this looks like a seesaw between the two contrasting ways of thinking described so well by Nobel laureate Daniel Kahneman in his best-seller *Thinking, fast and slow*.[48] The fast thinking is our intuitive, immediate way of interpreting and deciding. Slow thinking is the deliberate reasoning we use in solving problems. Of course, the patterns may just be some kind of artifact of the analyzed book language. Does it really reflect a change in interest? To check that, we looked at how often people looked up the same 5,000 words using the Google Trends tool. This can only be done for the period since 2004, when such internet search data started to be collected. Still, within this period, word frequencies in books and in search queries tend to go in the same direction. Thus, it looks as if the ups and downs of the frequency of words in books do indeed reflect changes in interest over time. Similar trends appeared when we analyzed text over the past 170 years in the *New York Times* or when we looked at books in other languages. The rise and fall of interest in rationality that we found seemed a robust and widespread pattern.

A long-term rise of interest in rationality is consistent with a trend that the sociologist Max Weber noted more than a century ago. He called it "Die Entzauberung der Welt," the disenchantment of the world or, more literally, "de-magication." Weber saw the role of myth and illusion dwindling in social life alongside a rise of rationalization.[49] Indeed, it makes sense that the development of science and technology, with all its benefits, should boost the prestige of the scientific approach, permeating everything from culture and education to politics and written language. But why then would this trend reverse so spectacularly around the 1970s? Why would rationality go out of vogue, culminating in the success of fact-free, post-truth narratives by demagogues around the world? We may never know, but here are some speculations.

Changes of media have speeded up communication. From handwritten letters to email to social media, reaction times have shortened, offering less opportunity for rational control. Could this have nudged language toward words associated with fast thinking on the thinking-fast-and-slow gradient?

Competition for attention-promoted sensation seeking. With the rise of television, followed by the Internet and social media, the total volume of media content has increased. Thus, there is more competition for attention. Could this have stimulated a trend toward more sensational language?

We forgot the existential threats overcome through rationality. Technological progress has made our lives safe. Antibiotics ensure that we rarely die of pneumonia or other infections and, thanks to industrialized agriculture, we can rely on cheap and abundant food. All of this is taken for granted. Maybe we forgot the crucial importance of rational progress, and just lost interest?[50]

Postmodernism broke loose. Postmodernism, questioning whether objective facts exist at all, has been an academic idea at the fringe of society. Has it gradually become mainstream, legitimizing the current post-truth trend in society and populist politics?[51]

Rationality was blamed for neoliberal unfairness. Around the time of the turning point in trends, a new wave of policies started to cause a noticeable rise in inequality in the USA, the UK, and other countries, which has continued until now. Such 'neoliberal' policies were defended on rational grounds, so perhaps the change in language we see is driven by a rejection of the governmental machinery and, with it, a loss of esteem for the rationality that was used to arm it?[52]

To me, all these possibilities sound plausible. Perhaps all of them played a role, much as in Putnam's braided river interpretation of the US Progressive Era. It is unlikely that any broad societal change can be understood from simple cause-and-effect chains. Multiple developments are always intertwined. More on the rise of neoliberal policies and its effects on our brains later. First, let's dig a bit deeper into the curious inflection of the long-term language trends, which cannot be blamed on social media alone, as they started about three decades earlier than the rise of pioneering platforms such as Facebook, Twitter, and YouTube.

From Us to Me

The balance between rationality and intuition-related words is only one aspect that tipped around 1980. Another dimension of the sea-change in word use around this time was a resurgence of interest in the personal rather than the communal. The most direct indicator evidence for that is a reversal of the trend in the frequency ratio of the use of 'I' over 'we,' and of 'he' or 'she' over 'they' etc. (Figure 5.5). Those are striking trends, but the singular:plural ratios highlight just one aspect of a broader change in the concepts that people have been interested in.

To explore the change with more nuance, I invite you to first look at the raw material and make sense of it on your own. What would you say characterizes the difference between these two groups of words?

(1) The words whose frequencies rose most significantly after 1980 while being in significant decline before that year: perfect, understood, throw, them, embrace, sight, comfort, nothing, rushing, place, trusting, awful, beautiful, ever, hearts, never, awake, throwing, when, sweet, promise, fallen, threw, cheer, brother, so, spirit, breathe, every, owe, believing, thankful, footsteps, him, rest, stranger, gorgeous, seeing, supposed, ashes, surprised, joy, cheering, disappoint, stood, thrown, dare, who, shine, appetite, desire,

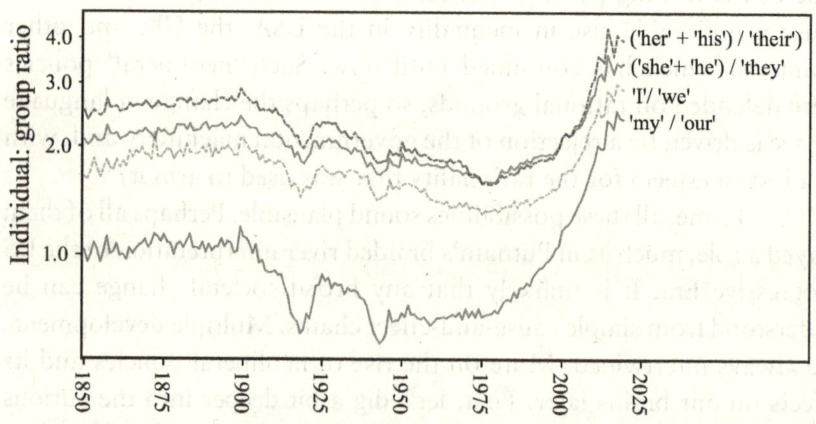

Figure 5.5 Change in interest from individuals to groups and back reflected in the ratio of frequencies of singular to plural personal pronouns, 1850–2018. (Adapted from Scheffer *et al.*, "The rise and fall of rationality in language."[53])

escape, disappointment, honest, mind, hear, eye, jealous, into, together, excuse, mistaken, perfectly, ashamed, horrible, lay, my, accidentally, forgotten, her, slept, patience, then, calm, supper, forgot, cheek, tongue, us, admit, surprise, beloved, kneel, ruin, happily, thing, soon, moment, cry, truly, myself, saved, instead, ruined, smile, glory, walk, forget, bless, lost, and selfish.

(2) Words with the opposite trend, whose frequency declined most significantly after 1980 while being on the rise before that: area, program, indicate, available, development, basis, determine, initial, technical, million, addition, final, range, replacement, personnel, control, unit, involved, percent, eliminate, limited, rate, concentration, increase, result, test, staff, included, tested, transfer, maximum, zone, plus, sample, recent, congressman, level, funds, data, responsible, basic, laboratory, equipment, budget, procedure, breakdown, effective, activity, tape, review, nuclear, factor, federal, base, prior, testing, chemical, isolated, system, minor, designed, automatic, analysis, decision, marine, significant, chemicals, storage, growth, limit, separate, peak, manual, represent, sophisticated, minimum, occur, approximately, potential, administration, and technology.

What do you make of that? One way of reading this would be that the change around 1980 tipped societies' interests not just from rational to intuitive but also from societal toward personal. On the societal side we have words related to science and technology (e.g., vacuum, engineering, laboratory), quantification (e.g., area, unit, million), business and economy (e.g., budget, personnel, industry), and social organization (e.g., congressman, department, tax). On the personal side there are words that we could classify as related to belief, spirituality, sapiens, and intuition (e.g., spirit, believing, mind, prayer), senses (e.g., seeing, silent, loud), the body (e.g., cheek, heart, head), and also personal pronouns (e.g., us, his, they), and relations (e.g., brother, stranger, father). If you like to explore such language trends a bit more for yourself, just open the Google Books Ngram Viewer. It's free and easy. A quick way to scan for the communal–individual shift is by typing 'I/we'. Using versions of this ratio marker from other languages (yo/nosotros, ich/wir, je/nous etc.), you will see that the change is not limited to the English-speaking part of the world. Patterns vary, but typically there is a trend starting in the late 1970s, and then speeding up around 2005.

Similarly, analysts from the RAND Corporation looked at differences in journalistic styles before and after 2000 as both television and written media changed.[54] They wrote:

> Cable programming today is highly interactive and subjective and relies on arguments and opinions to persuade and debate – a stark contrast from the more academic style and precise language employed in broadcast television in the pre-2000 period. Similarly, the study's online journalism sample was characterized by a personal and subjective style that, in many cases, emphasized argument and advocacy and was very different than the pre-2000 print journalism sample, which relied more heavily on event-based reporting that often referred to authoritative institutions or sources.

Clearly there has been a sea-change in language, whether you look at books or journalistic outlets. It is a change with many dimensions, including an increasing focus on personal opinions.

What has driven the change in interest from societal to personal? Perhaps it was a reaction to a suffocating emphasis on a homogeneous happy 'we'? As Putnam and Garrett frame it:[55] "the shortcomings of a society that undervalued individuality and diversity and gave woefully insufficient attention to racial and gender justice." In their book about the American upswing they see the 1960s as a turning point for the pendulum.[56] A moment when a change started that would lead society in a new and ultimately troublesome direction. In their words, "We have paid a high price for the Sixties pivot" – "indefensible economic inequality," "political polarization that is enfeebling and endangering our democracy, the social fragmentation and isolation that ignore the basic human need for fellowship." Of course, other branches of the braided river may have played a role. One of those might be advertisements glorifying personal experience. Over the past half-century or so, society has been exposed to a swelling deluge of omnipresent advertisements promoting individual choice and experience. We will get back to its effects on consumption later, but could it also have helped boost an interest in the personal, experiential versus the collective, organizational sides of life? Possibly, but whatever the mix of drivers, a change from 'we' to 'I' was clearly in the air. As George Harrison wrote in 1969: "All through the day / I me mine, I me mine, I me mine . . . ."

Distorted Thought

Using frequencies of single words does risk losing context. For instance, the word 'down' carries different meanings in "let's go to the pub *down* the road" and "I feel *down*." Short phrases tell more than single words. Such phrases are called n-grams. "I feel down" is a 3-gram. "He always bullies me" is a 4-gram. Psychologists have found that excessive use of particular phrases may point to disorders such as depression or anxiety disorder. A long list of such tell-tale phrases has been made, each pointing to a certain type of cognitive distortion. Categories include catastrophizing (e.g., will fail), dichotomous reasoning (e.g., never, always), disqualifying (e.g., great but), emotional reasoning (e.g., but I feel), fortune-telling (e.g., they will not), labeling (e.g., she is a), mental filtering (e.g., all I can see), mind reading (e.g., nobody believes), overgeneralizing (e.g., all the time), and personalizing (e.g., because of my). My colleague Johan Bollen combines expertise in psychology and computational science. He looked for trends in such classical markers of cognitive distortions. Across English, German, and Spanish, tell-tale phrases pointing to those distorted forms of reasoning surged almost universally in recent decades (Figure 5.6 A).[57] That looks alarming, but these analyses are still based only on language in books and newspapers. Do such trends really reflect a systematic change in the way people's minds work? There are reasons to suspect that the answer could be yes.

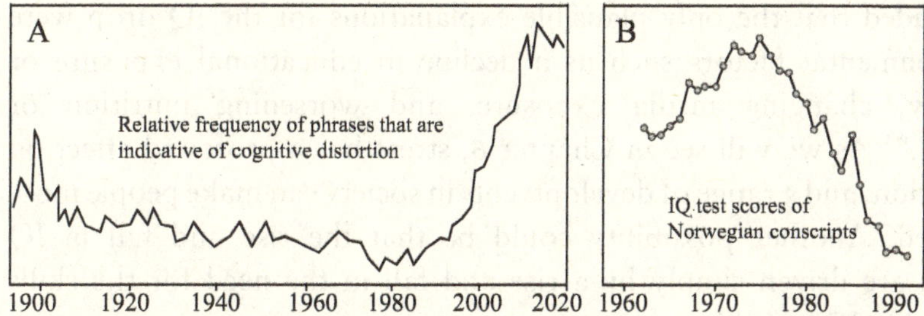

Figure 5.6 Two indications of a reversal of long-term trends in cognition. A: The occurrences of phrases that indicate distorted thinking. (Adapted from Bollen *et al.*, "Historical language records reveal a surge of cognitive distortions in recent decades."[58]) B: Reversal of a long-term rise in IQ test scores (the Flynn effect) in Norway (adapted from Bratsberg and Rogeberg, "O. Flynn effect and its reversal are both environmentally caused."[59])

Support for that idea comes from a standard approach to investigating how well the brain can solve problems: intelligence tests. These have been used systematically for a long time – for instance, in IQ tests administered to new conscripts entering the army – allowing a fascinating look at how IQ has changed over generations. After correcting for changes in ways that IQ has been measured, psychologists found that test scores have increased steadily from the 1940s onward in many countries in which IQ testing has been used, including Western European countries, Japan, and South Korea. This effect is called the Flynn effect, after James Flynn, who studied the patterns systematically.[60] The rise in intelligence scores is fascinating, but perhaps even more striking is an overall slowing down of the trends, and even a sharp reversal in some countries, starting with cohorts born in the late 1970s (Figure 5.6 B). It's reasonable to think that such trends may be artifacts of the way of testing, selection of the persons, or something similar. However, the further the patterns were scrutinized, the clearer it became that both the rise and the fall in intelligence as measured by the tests were real.[61] Moreover, an independent line of standardized international research on adult literacy and numeracy revealed that such skills have stagnated or declined over the past decade in most studied countries.[62] It remains hard to unravel why such trends happen. However, from a long list of potential explanations for IQ decline many have meanwhile been excluded. For instance, in a careful study – looking at within-family changes in the scores of sons going into mandatory Norwegian military service – the authors concluded that the only plausible explanations for the IQ drop were environmental factors such as a decline in educational exposure or quality, changing media exposure, and worsening nutrition or health.[63] As we will see in Chapter 6, stress has a profound effect on cognition, and a range of developments in society can make people more stressed. Another possibility could be that the rise and fall in IQ scores are driven simply by a rise and fall in the need for the skills probed in IQ tests.[64]

Whatever the precise mechanisms are, there is firm evidence that thinking has changed over time. Some of the language changes may reflect the Zeitgeist, or the spirit, attitudes, and ideas that dominate a historical time period. However, the surge in markers of cognitive distortions and the concomitant downward trends in IQ suggest that there is more to it. It looks as if not just the interest in rationality, but also the capacity for reasoning, has declined. The explanation is not some evolutionary genetic trend but rather a change in our environment.

A Changing Political Tide

Politics is one strand in the braided river of change that shapes our environment. So much news content is devoted to it on a daily basis that slow, underlying trends can become less visible. The attention politicians get makes sense, of course. They are chosen by us, and the decisions they make affect us all. But beyond the daily turmoil, here are some long-term trends that will affect our chances to tip out of trouble.

The Rise of Neoliberalism

In democracies we choose our politicians freely, but their policies also affect the way our brains work. For one thing, as we will see in more detail later, the capacity for reasoning is likely influenced by economic inequality, which is largely caused by policy. A study across fifty countries found that income inequality is significantly correlated with the prevalence of delusions and hallucinations, even after controlling for regime type and national indices of per capita income.[65] After World War II, new social policies caused income inequality to decrease in most countries. However, that trend stagnated in the 1970s and then abruptly reversed starting in the late 1980s. This renewed rise in inequality is especially spectacular for the USA (Figure 5.7), but the same trends are visible in most places.[66]

The turn of the tide in inequality has been set in motion by a turn of the tide in policy.[67] A smaller role for the state. More freedom for private enterprise. All resonate with the Zeitgeist of increasing freedom for the individual. In the new narrative, focusing on the individual would be the way forward to improve well-being. More freedom and fewer rules and regulations would make everyone richer. Privatizing railways, drinking-water supplies, energy, and more would make services better and cheaper. Reducing taxes and regulations would make companies more efficient. Those ideas were not new. It was just a tide coming back in. The idea that we should leave the forces of enterprise free to make society a better place is best captured by the metaphor of "the invisible hand" coined by the eighteenth-century philosopher

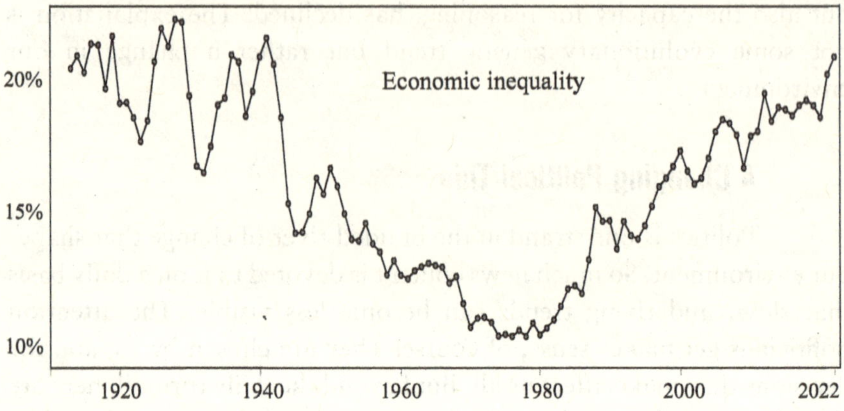

Figure 5.7 As in many countries, inequality has been on the rise since the 1970s in the USA. Plotted is the share of national income received by the richest 1 percent measured before taxes and benefits. (Redrawn from ourworldindata.org/economic-inequality.)

Adam Smith – though the metaphor developed fully after the time of Smith.[68] The idea is that if someone charges less, more customers will buy from them. Thus, sellers will always tend to lower their prices or offer something better than their competitors. Also, when there is enough demand, the market will eventually supply anything. Thus, free-market incentives form an 'invisible hand' miraculously guiding self-interested people to behave in ways that result in the best possible social equilibrium. That sounds great, but thinkers have always cautioned against this simplistic, rosy view. True, the market forces are a marvelous help in allowing a complex society to function. However, the system easily becomes derailed if some of the participants gain excessive wealth and, therefore, excessive power to manipulate society. As we saw in Chapter 1, such wealth accumulation is inevitable in the absence of strong regulation (more on that later too). Often, it comes at the cost of environmental destruction, pollution, and other problems affecting society in the broader sense. A strategy cynically summarized as "Privatize the profit, communize the costs." This is a surprisingly universal principle when regulations are lax. Water pollution, destruction of tropical rainforests, global warming, health impacts of addictive products such as cigarettes or social media: All of these imply massive social costs while allowing huge profits for private enterprises. Economists call these problems market imperfections. The invisible hand might have worked well if those costs had been included in the prices. Unfortunately, this is not how it works, and society always finds out too late.[69]

The invisible hand needs a helping hand: a regulating government that makes sure society does not carry the costs of a small group becoming excessively rich and powerful. Yet in the 1970s the helping hand became increasingly mutilated. The revitalized idealization of the old idea of free markets goes broadly under the term of neoliberalism. First and famously, it was brought into practice with the policies championed by the British prime minister Margaret Thatcher and US president Ronald Reagan. But in reality, it was a change of tides that affected most of the world in subsequent decades. As the Panarchy theory highlights so nicely, a change of tides usually brings an existing fringe idea to dominance. Like mammals, evolving quietly for a hundred million years before rising to dominance after the collapse of the dinosaurs.[70] Like small saplings lingering in the forest's understory until some big tree falls and they can reach the canopy. Like the rejection of slavery that went global only after a century of activism. This is indeed what happened to neoliberal ideation. In the 1940s the economist and philosopher Friedrich Hayek wrote an influential book called *The Road to Serfdom*, warning that government intervention in markets would lead to a loss of freedom and malfunctioning societies.[71] He was not advocating a laissez-faire approach to governance, and stressed that the state had an important role to play in helping the invisible hand. Rather, he was worried about central planning and totalitarianism as championed by Hitler and Stalin, among others.[72] Despite being largely misinterpreted, the book was picked up broadly as an inspiration for a movement arguing more radically against government intervention – perhaps largely because of the appealing title, just as the invisible hand took on a life of its own after Adam Smith coined the term. In the end, as Nobel laureate Joseph Stigler insisted, the history of how a set of ideas came to be constructed is irrelevant, because all that matters in the end is the argument itself.[73] In this case the argument rose to dominance almost half a century later when, in the early 1980s, the USA and the UK implemented a series of neoliberal policies. Together with economic growth resulting from a radical neoliberal experiment in the 1970s under the Chilean dictator Augusto Pinochet, those policies started to inspire change across the world.[74] It brought growth, but at what cost?

The implications of the rise of neoliberalism are hard to pin down. So many things went on at the same time. Some patterns are nonetheless pretty clear. A damning analysis of what went wrong is given by Joseph Stiglitz in his 2024 book *The Road to Freedom*.[75] That title is a direct response to the famous *The Road to Serfdom*, which inspired neoliberalism. For one thing, Stiglitz points to the misleading use of the word 'freedom' echoed in the term 'liberal.' It sounds so compelling. Who doesn't want to be free? However, quoting the political philosopher Isaiah Berlin, Stiglitz writes: "Freedom for the wolves has often meant death to the sheep." Freedom from regulations may seem attractive, but it is at the core of many problems. First, deregulation has caused massive environmental damage. That is not just an issue for other species. As argued at the start of this book, the two biggest problems for the future of humanity are climate change and the demise of nature. Both were boosted by economic growth and deregulation. Second, the rise of inequality within countries has affected societies. Although seeing success in others can create a stimulating 'American Dream effect,'[76] most people in most places would like to see less inequality. Loss of social security, health support, and other worries have led to stress and anger. In addition, there may be more hidden effects of neoliberal thinking permeating our lives. Social psychological studies suggest that exposure to neoliberal ideology affects well-being by creating a sense of competition, social disconnection, and loneliness.[77] This fits with the view of the Belgian clinical psychologist Paul Verhaeghe, who finds that the biggest problem of neoliberalism is that people have started internalizing neoliberalist views as common sense.[78] As he frames it, "Neoliberalism brought out the worst in us." Verhaeghe sees an increase in depression and other psychiatric disorders as largely driven by the neoliberal way of thinking:

> Our society constantly proclaims that anyone can make it if they just try hard enough. ... An increasing number of people fail, feeling humiliated, guilty and ashamed. We are forever told that we are freer to choose the course of our lives than ever before, but the freedom to choose outside the success narrative is limited. ... There is a buried sense of fear, ranging from performance anxiety to a broader social fear of the threatening other.

As we will see later, there is indeed quite some evidence that social stress caused by perceived inadequacy and insecurity alters the way our brains work. Meanwhile, the most straightforward effect of neoliberal policies is how they facilitate the concentration of wealth in the hands of a few, at the cost of accelerating the deterioration of the planet and raising societal tensions.

Backsliding Democracy

Another recent trend that is relevant to our search for plausible futures is a global backsliding of democracy.[79] The basic idea of democracy, making decisions as a group, is probably as old as humanity. In fact, many other animals that live in groups, such as large grazers or monkeys, make decisions by weighing the members' input.[80] A whole scientific literature shows how this has evolutionary advantages, but the basic idea is simple. Using more brains and more information, a group can, if it functions effectively, make a better decision than an individual. Perhaps the most beautiful demonstration of that appeared in a 1907 article in the journal *Nature* by the British polymath Francis Galton.[81] As he put it:

> In these democratic days, any investigation into the trustworthiness and peculiarities of popular judgments is of interest. The material about to be discussed refers to a small matter, but is much to the point. A weight-judging competition was carried out. ... A fat ox having been selected, competitors bought stamped and numbered cards ... on which to inscribe their respective names ... and estimates of what the ox would weigh. ... Those who guessed most successfully received prizes. About 800 tickets were issued, which were kindly lent me for examination after they had fulfilled their immediate purpose.

Galton then sorted all tickets and looked for the middle one as best representing the voice of the people reasoning that "According to the democratic principle ... the middlemost estimate expresses the *vox populi* every other estimate being condemned as too low or too high by a majority of the voters." It turned out that *vox populi* deviated less than 1 percent from the real weight. Content with this pretty amazing precision, Galton concludes, "This result is, I think, more creditable to the trustworthiness of a democratic judgment than might have been expected." Although this was just one experiment, the basic idea remains a research topic today known as the wisdom of the crowd.

Such recent work also confirms Galton's original intuition about a crucial requirement: "The judgments were unbiassed by passion and uninfluenced by oratory and the like." Indeed, the wisdom of the crowd works best if judgments are independent.[82] We tend to feel that it is good to solicit different opinions, but as soon as deliberation comes into play, results are easily distorted. In a nutshell, this reflects the strengths and weaknesses of democracy. Compared to autocracies, democracies are considered better at making decisions. For instance, as the Indian Nobel laureate Amartya Sen – who lived through the Great Bengal Famine of 1943 in which close to 3 million people died – noted, there has never been a famine in a functioning multiparty democracy.[83] Indeed, catastrophic famines have almost only happened in autocratic or colonial systems, and bad decision making has been an important part of many of the stories. Better decision making is a strength of democracy, but voters' judgments are vulnerable to "oratory and the like," as Galton would frame it. Sometimes that may drive democracies in the direction of autocracy. Note that Galton wrote, "In these democratic days." Indeed, from the printing of his famous 1907 article onward there was a pervasive upward trend in the percentage of countries that are democratic (Figure 5.8). However, one century later something started to change. There are many ways to judge how democratic a country is. For instance, does it count if you can vote but the opposition candidates have been imprisoned? Weighing such aspects, over the past decades, more and more countries are sliding toward autocracy, and fewer and fewer are becoming more democratic. All this cannot be separated from the issue of runaway wealth concentration. Autocracies do not merely repress through violence. They also use the extreme wealth collected by their kleptocratic leaders and associated oligarchs to manipulate information and undermine democratic processes worldwide and facilitate further concentration of wealth and power in their hands.[84]

As we will see later, this is a major challenge for efforts to carve out a good future, and there are obvious things that can be done about it. For now, to lift your spirits a bit, let me reiterate my positive note on information technology in this context. Galton's wisdom of the crowd and its distortion by "oratory and the like" also provide a useful framework for thinking about the effects of social media and AI. The 'island deliberation' and 'resonance chamber' character of social

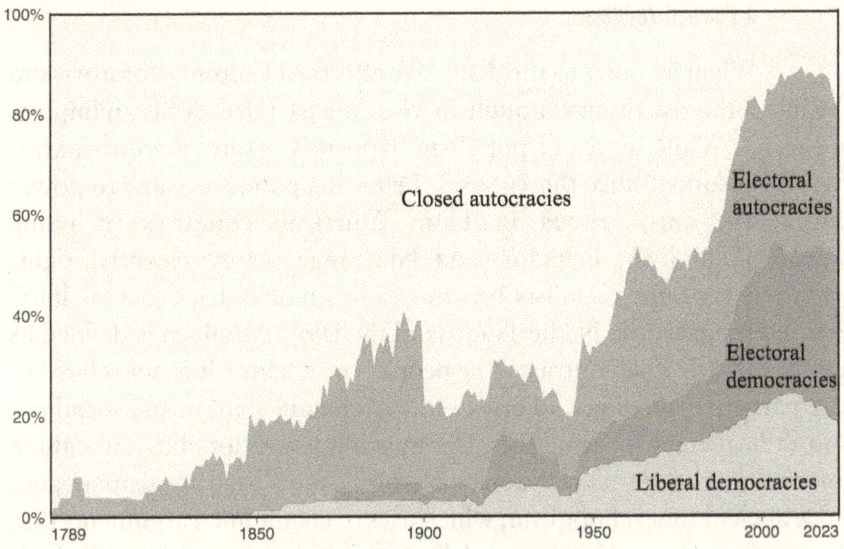

Figure 5.8 The past centuries have seen an increase in the percentage of countries with some degree of democracy, albeit with incidental backslides, including a recent one. Closed autocracy: citizens do not have the right to choose either the chief executive of the government or the legislature through multiparty elections. Electoral autocracy: citizens have the right to choose the chief executive and the legislature through multiparty elections; but they lack some freedoms, such as those of association or expression, that make the elections meaningful, free, and fair. Electoral democracy: citizens have the right to choose the chief executive and the legislature in meaningful, free and fair, and multiparty elections. Liberal democracy: electoral democracy and citizens enjoy individual and minority rights, are equal before the law, and the actions of the executive are constrained by the legislative and the courts. (Redrawn from ourworldindata.org/democracy based on V-Dem [2024].)

media tends to generate a bewildering range of opinions, many of which are poorly supported by evidence. It turns out that LLMs such as ChatGPT may help in seeing the forest through the trees. In one study the median (*vox populi*) of a group of 12 LLMs gave predictions on market and political outcomes that were indistinguishable from those of a group of 925 human forecasters.[85] As LLMs are so easily accessible, one can imagine that with time they may help people find more balanced views of the world than those they encounter through social media. 'Truths' that cannot be so easily distorted. Yet of course it all depends on who is paying attention to the different sources of information.

A Populist Zeitgeist

When it comes to the distortive effects of Galton's "oratory and the like," the rise of 'new populism' over the past decades is an important trend. While waves of populism happened before, populist narratives have surged since the 1980s.[86] Left-wing populists came to power during the early 2000s in Latin American countries including Venezuela, Bolivia, Ecuador, and Nicaragua. More recently, right-wing and far-right populists became leaders in countries such as Italy, Brazil, Hungary, the Netherlands, and the USA. Populism is defined as a political style that contrasts 'the people' to an 'elite.' It is not related to any particular ideology, and is used by religious extremists, socialists, and radical-right leaders alike. Denouncing a corrupt elite and calling for radical change is a discourse that has been used by demagogues since ancient times. Populism, which uses oversimplified arguments that drown out more sophisticated deliberation to win over the crowds, is seen by most politicians and scholars as a dangerous threat to democracy. Something championed by opportunists that we should get rid of. However, that attitude is not very helpful, according to the Dutch political scientist Cas Mudde.[87] His influential approach is more along the lines that Ted Robert Gurr formulated, reflecting after forty years on the surprising success of his book *Why Men Rebel*, originally published in 1970.[88] Gurr had some advice to a new generation of researchers, such as: "Understand the sources of people's grievances. ... Listen to what people say, not just what others say about them. Ask why group identities and disadvantages make their members susceptible to ... political appeals ... that justify protest or rebellion." That is precisely what Mudde is doing when considering new populist dynamics. He does acknowledge the polarizing effect of populism: "Populism presents a Manichean outlook, in which there are only friends and foes. Opponents are not just people with different priorities and values, they are evil! Consequently, compromise is impossible, as it 'corrupts' the purity." However, according to Mudde, it is important to understand why people are susceptible, rather than just brushing the whole phenomenon aside as an aberration. Reviewing the literature on the topic, he sees four categories of drivers that have been suggested as making people susceptible to populist arguments. A common idea is that economic deprivation is an important factor. However, it turns out that this is not really what is happening. In Europe, for instance, populism is biggest in the richest countries. Also, perhaps surprisingly, low income and unemployment are not strong predictors by themselves, as long as most of society is doing well. What matters are things such as envy, perceived unfairness, or a perceived drop in social status. Another major line of thought is that populism is fed by a cultural backlash against developments that make people feel that 'their people' are threatened. This may be a response, for instance, to increasing gay rights, and especially against a perceived threat from the rise of other ethnic groups. Again, 'perceived' is a keyword here. As Mudde shows, there is hardly any connection between support for populism and objective ethnic immigration numbers. Instead, latent sentiments may easily be whipped up by populist rhetoric. Integrating this into the idea of a moral clash between the pure people and the corrupt elite, you get a narrative in which the elite is corrupt because they support the alien takeover of what used to be a society of native 'pure people.' A different type of substrate for populism, according to Mudde, is the increasing tension between the international and local respon-sibilities of governments. For instance, the EU forced countries to take austerity measures in the wake of the great recession resulting from the global financial crisis that started in the United States in 2008. With reduced government spending, living conditions deterior-ated badly, especially in countries such as Spain and Greece, where it led to strong populist social movements claiming that the elite had become out of touch with the people. A decade earlier, populist left leaders such as Evo Morales and Hugo Chávez came to power in Latin America due to similar international-versus-local tension. Loans from the IMF to the USA had been subject to conditions that imposed a neoliberal agenda, leading to growth benefiting an elite rather than the majority. A related idea is that the rise of populism is a reaction to political consensus. In this view, European populist far-right movements started to emerge in the 1980s as a reaction to the broad political consensus over the need for neoliberal policies, multicultural societies, and integration into the EU.

Those explanations as summarized by Mudde fall into two somewhat different categories. On the one hand, there are neoliberal and international policies imposed on people that have real negative effects on the majority. On the other hand, there are problems that may have less of an empirically 'true' basis but are exaggerated in a populist narrative. These include perceived loss of status and the perceived risk that the 'pure native people' will be overwhelmed or even replaced by ethnic and religious aliens. As Mudde frames the two sides: "Populism is much more the symptom than the cause of the current problems. It is a symptom of a malfunctioning liberal democracy. Now, once it comes to power, it creates massive problems." Indeed, as I am writing this book, populist narratives are eroding democracy in countries from the USA, the UK, Poland, and Israel to France, Germany, and The Netherlands. Leaders try to brush away elements of the Constitution and the Supreme Court's rule of law by arguing that those are against the people's will.[89] Meanwhile, the isolationism associated with populist rule weakens the international cooperation needed to deal with migration, climate change, and the global demise of nature.

Xenophobia

The populist approach of framing the people as victims of the elite has been used to promote a range of different ideologies. This has been for good or bad, depending on how you view it. However, when populist leaders seed hate against a group, the effect can be outright disastrous. One historical example is the Chinese Cultural Revolution starting in 1966.[90] Red Guards and gangs of students attacked people seen as bourgeois. Teachers, party leaders, and other intellectuals were sent to reeducation camps, murdered, or driven to suicide. Between 500,000 and 2 million lives were lost, and many more ruined. It is seen as an attempt by Mao Zedong to regain control over the Communist Party after bad decisions led to the Great Famine, during which tens of millions died. It worked. Mao stayed in charge until his death in 1976. It is an example of the potential runaway effects of stoking up generalized hatred against the elite, seen in different forms during the French Revolution and other historical events. Perhaps more common are populists seeding hatred against ethnic groups – Hitler, of course, being a prime example.

While xenophobia, a fear of strangers, is an old phenomenon, it has increasingly become a focus for media, politicians, and researchers over the past decades. This is driven by a global rise in hostility toward asylum seekers. Several mechanisms may be boosting this trend.[91] On one hand, media and politicians often help shape false beliefs about asylum seekers. For instance, they may falsely suggest that asylum seekers are entering illegally, come for economic gain, or are affiliated with terrorist groups. The latter message is subliminally amplified by images of imprisoning them in closed facilities. This may drive a self-reinforcing feedback loop, as boosted public fears lead to support for leaders who argue for increasingly harsh asylum policies. At the same time there may be an underlying new racism. This term is used to refer to a fresh way of framing old-fashioned racial attitudes that have become considered inappropriate. Prejudices remain the same but are presented as evidence-based facts. Instead of referring to biological markers such as skin color, they are often linked to the Other's culture, and accompanied by explicit disclaimers such as "I have nothing against blacks, but . . . ." Such rhetoric helps to make xenophobic motives look rational, and thus more acceptable.

But why are xenophobic attitudes so easily ignited, and so hard to get rid of? That simply has to do with human nature. We are evolved to maintain coherent tribes and fend off other groups in times of scarcity. As Darwin framed it in *The Descent of Man*: "When two tribes of primeval man, living in the same country, came into competition, if (other circumstances being equal) the one tribe included a great number of courageous, sympathetic and faithful members, who were always ready to warn each other of danger, to aid and defend each other, this tribe would succeed better and conquer the other." Our tribal character is easily activated by socially constructed groups such as sports teams, political parties, religious communities, and nation-states. A famous illustration is the classical Robbers Cave Experiment, in which twenty-two boys from two-parent, Protestant, white families were unknowingly made part of an experiment.[92] In the summer of 1954 a group of boys who didn't know each other were collected by two separate buses and housed separately by the researchers, who doubled as 'counselors.' Over the first week the groups were left to develop their own dynamics and choose a name (the Eagles and the Rattlers). In the next phase the groups met for competitive games and in situations manipulated to be unfair. For instance, the arrival of one group at a picnic site would be delayed until the other group had already eaten all the food. What started with name-calling ended with raids, counter-raids, burning flags, and violence, up to the point that the researchers had to separate the groups physically. The main part of the research was the next phase, during which the researchers got the groups to cooperate to solve a common threat. For instance, cutting off the water supply so that the groups had to work together to find the water tanks on the mountain and resolve the issue. However, the conflict phase became the most famous part, an illustration of how easily prejudiced attitudes and discriminatory behavior are triggered even among entirely socially constructed and otherwise homogeneous groups. We all know that basic truth, and it has been shown over and over again. Groupism and hostility to others are latent and very easily invoked, especially in times of perceived scarcity. Not surprisingly, competition over jobs or housing by asylum seekers or other immigrants often comes up as an argument in xenophobic discourses.

The stark biological basis for tribalism is anchored in the working of oxytocin, also known as the love hormone or the cuddling chemical.[93] Oxytocin is released, for instance, when you touch a loved one or when a baby suckles on its mother's breast. It turns out that oxytocin makes people empathize more with others in their group, like and trust them, follow the group norms, and cooperate. Understandably, this finding led to a flurry of interest in this wonderful hormone. However, oxytocin is a two-edged sword. It also makes us aggressively defend our peers against out-groups. Release of oxytocin is promoted not only by cuddling, but also in situations of stress and when the social environment is perceived as uncertain. It may seem strange that tipping points in our complex and meaningful social behavior hinge on a single chemical. On the other hand, it makes sense. Humans have evolved to help their groups by cooperating, trusting, favoring, complying, and, if needed, by aggressively protecting the group against outsiders and rivals. Each of the elements in this coherent package turns out to be effectively regulated by oxytocin.

In conclusion, xenophobia plausibly has a biological basis rooted in our evolutionary history. However, it is strongly context dependent. It may more easily come to the surface in stressful situations and times of scarcity, but that depends a lot on framing by thought leaders and social norms. Those norms, in turn, depend on the perception of what others think. Thus, the election of a leader who expresses xenophobic views may reveal the previously hidden preference of a majority, shifting the norm. Indeed, the election, twice, of Donald Trump as president of the USA increased willingness to express xenophobic views openly, and also made such views more socially acceptable – a clear example of the self-reinforcing feedback between political narratives and social norms.

Getting Greener

Support for Climate Action

These entangled trends are fascinating, but also a bit scary. Time to look at uplifting tendencies. Let's start with what is perhaps the most important one. The climate crisis has become universally recognized. In a 2023 census across fourteen countries in the Global South and North,[94] 93 percent of the respondents agreed with the statement "I believe that climate change poses a serious and imminent threat to the planet." Another poll covering twenty-three countries looked at support for strong policies, asking how respondents looked at the statement "It is essential that our government does whatever it takes to limit the effects of climate change." Out of ten respondents, eight agreed, while only one disagreed.[95] There was little difference between the opinions of the young and the old. This striking consensus emerged within a few decades. Global opinion polls on the topic have only been available over the past few years. However, the use of a key term in books gives an impression of what happened (Figure 5.9). Scientists and oil companies alike saw the climate crisis coming in the early 1970s. Yet terms such as 'global warming' or 'climate change' only started to be commonly mentioned in books in the late 1980s. Then, after 2005, interest rose rapidly.

Clearly, opinions have already tipped, but, curiously enough, most people do not realize how widespread the wish to do something

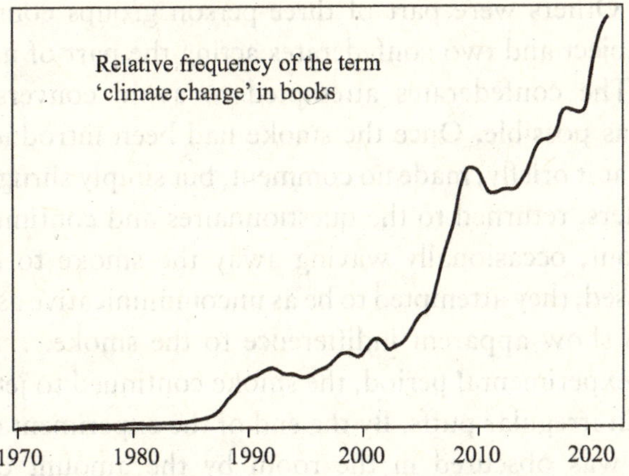

Figure 5.9 The relative frequency of the term 'climate change' in books illustrates just how recent awareness of this issue is. (Redrawn from Google Ngram.)

about climate change is. For instance, a 2022 study showed that when Americans were asked how many people support strong action to fight climate change, they estimated that around 40 percent of their fellow citizens would favor that. But 66–80 percent said that they themselves did support such policies. People take climate change very seriously and want their governments to do something about it. Meanwhile, they grossly underestimate how common that wish is. This is a problem, because people are less likely to act when they think that others do nothing. Inaction is contagious, so to speak.

This is the famous 'bystander problem,' named after early experiments showing that passive bystanders reduce the chance that a person will spring into action. Let me share how the original researchers Bibb Latané and John Darley describe their famous "Where there is smoke" experiment for the readers of *American Scientist*, probing whether passive bystanders would reduce a person's likelihood to become alarmed by smoke:[96]

> Male Columbia students living in campus residences were invited to an interview. ... As they sat in a small room waiting to be called for the interview and filling out a preliminary questionnaire, they faced an ambiguous but potentially dangerous situation as a stream of smoke began to puff into the room through a wall vent. Some subjects filled out the questionnaire and were exposed to this potentially critical situation while alone. Others were part of three-person groups consisting of one subject and two confederates acting the part of naive subjects. The confederates attempted to avoid conversation as much as possible. Once the smoke had been introduced, they stared at it briefly, made no comment, but simply shrugged their shoulders, returned to the questionnaires and continued to fill them out, occasionally waving away the smoke to do so. If addressed, they attempted to be as uncommunicative as possible and to show apparent indifference to the smoke. ... For the entire experimental period, the smoke continued to jet into the room in irregular puffs. By the end of the experimental period, vision was obscured in the room by the amount of smoke present. The typical subject, when tested alone, behaved very reasonably. Usually, shortly after the smoke appeared, he would glance up from his questionnaire, notice the smoke,

show a slight but distinct startle reaction, and then undergo a brief period of indecision, and perhaps return briefly to his questionnaire before again staring at the smoke. Soon, most subjects would get up from their chairs, walk over to the vent, and investigate it closely, sniffing the smoke, waving their hands in it, feeling its temperature, etc. The usual Alone subject would hesitate again, but finally walk out of the room, look around outside, and, finding somebody there, calmly report the presence of the smoke. . . . Three-quarters of the 24 people run in this condition reported the smoke before the experimental period was terminated. The behavior of subjects run with two passive confederates was dramatically different; of ten people run in this condition, only one reported the smoke. The other nine stayed in the waiting room as it filled up with smoke, doggedly working on their questionnaires and waving the fumes away from their faces. They coughed, rubbed their eyes, and opened the window but they did not report the smoke.

The inhibitory effect of (perceived) passivity of others has been shown many times since those classic experiments. The mechanism even works in rats.[97]

The bystander effect suggests that it could make a big difference for climate action if it were more widely known that 93 percent of people consider climate change a serious and imminent threat. That is a huge potential to be unleashed. The 2023 global poll provides more reasons for optimism. For instance, it showed that people have most trust in scientists and experts when it comes to climate information. Indeed, 73 percent trusted scientists, whereas journalists, government leaders, and CEOs were trusted by 43, 39, and 36 percent only. There is a lot of worry about misinformation, and for good reasons. Action on climate change has been delayed by half a century, and misinformation has played a big role in that. But in the end, people are not stupid.

Now, that is a good reason for hope. And hope is important, as shown by other insights from the same global opinion poll: only a quarter of the respondents worried about climate change were hopeful that we could overcome the challenges. But people from this hopeful group did more than unhopeful people to reduce their footprint, had more often contacted government officials urging them to enact climate policies, and had put more pressure on friends and family to live more climate-friendly lives. Hope is a catalyst of action. The researchers also tried to probe what enhanced the likelihood of being hopeful. It turned out that the probability of hopefulness was much higher in those who trust institutions on climate, believe companies keep climate commitments, see climate progress and news that give them hope, believe climate solutions will benefit them and society, believe climate-friendly lifestyles are attractive, and believe that climate policies would enhance job security. So, we know hope helps, and we know how hope may be encouraged. Another reason for hope: Two-thirds of all respondents wanted to live more climate-friendly lifestyles. Of those, 80 percent found that companies charged too much for climate-friendly products, and 73 percent wanted better information and more institutional support to allow a better lifestyle. There is so much opportunity there.

In summary, almost everyone feels that climate change poses an imminent threat to the planet, but many have a passive attitude. When searching for ways to change that, remember: (1) hope powers climate action; (2) scientists are top climate influencers; (3) people want climate-friendly lifestyles, but they need institutional support; (4) they should see how climate solutions can make their lives better; and (5) people are more likely to act on climate change if they know others are worried too.

A Changing Narrative

Here is another important positive trend: a growing understanding of factors that motivate action is starting to guide scientists, NGOs, journalists, and other communicators to discover more effective ways of shaping narratives. For instance, an analysis of documentaries presented by David Attenborough shows a marked change over the decades.[98] The first films merely transmitted a fascination with biodiversity and an admiration of its resilience. Since the mid-1980s, however, images of pristine nature have been contrasted with images of environments destroyed by humans, as a warning. Starting with the 2000 documentary *State of the Planet*, the warning has been delivered from a perspective of the potential to promote protection and restoration. A gradual change in narrative, from admiration to alarm, and then to a balancing act between alarm and hope.

The idea that offering hope should be part of narratives arose as convincing evidence for effects of hope on attitudes amounted. We have seen some of that in the results of the global poll on climate attitudes, but it has also been confirmed by experiments.[99] In one approach, participants were randomly chosen to read an article with versions, one ending with a dire message and the other with hope. The first four paragraphs were identical in both articles, providing basic information on climate change, but the final two paragraphs differed. The negative article ended with the possibly apocalyptic consequences of global warming, whereas the hopeful article ended with potential solutions. It turns out that for many participants the dire message boosted skepticism about climate change and reduced their willingness to reduce their carbon footprint. The hopeful version elicited the opposite in the group that read it. In other words, trying to stress unavoidable danger may backfire. This effect was particularly evident in people with a strong 'just-world belief' – the belief that the world is an orderly, predictable, and just place where people get what they deserve. This is a common attitude that may help people to cope with exposure to poverty, homelessness, or other suffering.[100] By the same token, it may thus turn people off when they are exposed to apocalyptic predictions. They resolve the incompatibility between the nearing-apocalypse-soon scenario and their just-world belief by brushing off the seriousness, an example of the cognitive dissonance mechanism we saw earlier as an impediment to change.

Since this study, others have looked for evidence-based ways of effectively framing the climate message. For instance, a group of professionals from commercial marketing research has teamed up with the Harvard Center for the Environment to create a nonprofit marketing firm, Potential Energy, focused entirely on creating public demand for action on climate change. They are people who know how to choose words, so let me quote them literally on the need for effective framing:

> Opinions regarding action on climate are widely perceived to have polarized and hardened. But that's not in fact true. … There are universal values and desires for climate action that a sizable majority of people around the world share. But that reality alone will not deliver action. The salience of the issue needs to be maintained, consolidated and increased to ensure a tide of public opinion is there to support the targeted political, campaigning and policy interventions that can bridge the power gap between public opinion writ large and actual political and policy outcomes. And that power gap is not a neutral space.

Neither is the battle for public opinion. Vast resources are being brought to bear to not only reduce the salience of climate in the public mind, but also to control the power gap, focusing on preventing those in decision-making positions from acting by creating political, economic, cultural and ideological incentives to block or slow progress.

In short, we are in a battle against those trying to slow progress, and effective framing is our main weapon. But how to know what is effective? Research! There are many opinions on what good framing is, but as we say in The Netherlands, "Meten is Weten." This translates into something like "To measure is to know," though its impact is lost in translation.

Here is how Potential Energy measured the effectiveness of alternative ways of framing.[101] The consortium polled opinions and compared the effects of different framings of a range of policies on 60,000 people across twenty-three Global South and North countries. As mentioned earlier, eight out of ten people agree that the government should do whatever it takes to limit the effects of climate change. Support comes from both the political left and right, with the latter only 19 percent less supportive of climate action, with the major exception of the highly polarized USA. It is also clear from the data that people hold businesses and governments responsible for slowing climate change. Only one in four people said that individuals should primarily be responsible for doing something about climate change.

This framing research was done by looking at agreement with differently formulated policies. The researchers randomly assigned respondents to one of three different motivating narratives before they went on to the questions and subsequently quantifying how the different narratives affected average outcomes. These were the narratives:

(1)   **The Planet for our Children**

You don't have to be a scientist to see how our climate has changed. Extreme weather events, such as extreme heatwaves floods, hurricanes, wildfires, and drought, are becoming more frequent and more severe. The last eight years were the hottest ever recorded in human history. Our overheating planet is already putting lives and livelihoods at risk. It's hurting our farmers, overpolluting our cities, reducing our water supply, and costing us billions in damage from extreme weather. Most importantly, it's putting our children's futures at risk. It's our responsibility to leave behind a safe, livable world for future generations. If we don't stop polluting, it will only get worse. Carbon pollution stays in the atmosphere for thousands of years, so the effects cannot be reversed. Yet the world continues to emit more heat-trapping carbon pollution than ever. It's cooking the planet. We need immediate action on climate change, because later is too late.

(2)   **Make Polluters Pay**

Climate change is already having a devastating impact on our planet and on communities across the globe, including ours. We've been emitting heat-trapping carbon pollution for decades. But we aren't all equally to blame: just seventy-one companies are responsible for 90 percent of the toxic carbon pollution that's hurting us. These big, powerful corporations use their money and power to hold back progress for the rest of us. They're preventing us from having better, cleaner, safer, and healthier products. And they're leaving the rest of us to foot the bill for the massive cost of catastrophes caused by an overheating planet.

The logic is simple. We shouldn't let billion-dollar companies and out-of-touch elites profit off their pollution while putting our future in jeopardy. It's only right that they are held accountable.

We need immediate action on climate change, because it's only fair that polluters pay.

(3)   **Progress is Here**

We constantly hear doom-and-gloom warnings about climate change. The truth is that we're making extraordinary progress: clean energy already powers 35 percent of the world's electricity. The solutions we need aren't distant, but here and happening now: solar, wind, electric vehicles, and batteries. We can see it all around us: in our communities, in our schools, and in our homes. And we're starting to see the benefits: new jobs, new businesses, and more innovation. But the work isn't finished; we're only just getting started. We need more clean energy to power our communities, clean up the air and water, and protect our health. We need less talk and more action. We need leaders who have a plan – and will get it done.

Which would you think was most effective in elevating support for climate action? The winner was narrative 1. Political leaders often stress things like green jobs, economic success, injustice, or the costs of extreme weather. Yet the data show that it is stronger to promote protecting the planet for the next generation. It lifted strong support for climate action by eleven percentage points on average. The power of the future generations message was also evident when people were asked: "In your opinion, what is the most important benefit of taking action on climate change? (1) to create jobs, opportunities and economic growth; (2) to reduce social inequality and support those impacted by climate change; (3) to protect our health by reducing air and water pollution; (4) to protect ourselves from extreme weather; and (5) to protect the planet for future generations." The last one was chosen by twelve times more people than the jobs, economic growth, or inequality arguments, and twice as many as the extreme weather point. The superiority of the argument of protecting the planet for future generations was universal across all the polled countries: Norway, South Korea, Germany, China, Australia, Italy, the UK, France, Canada, Turkey, the USA, Japan, Saudi Arabia, Indonesia, Chile, Nigeria, Argentina, Colombia, South Africa, India, Mexico, Brazil, and Kenya.

This is consistent with a phenomenon known as loss aversion. Behavioral economists have found that a potential loss is almost universally felt as more severe than an equivalent gain. It may also drive the strong desire to prevent species loss, revealed by a multiple-choice question asking "Which future would you choose to live in?" Concern over loss of nature was much stronger than other future scenarios such as the impact of extreme weather and conflicts. As we have seen, most people want action on climate change. However, the aversion they felt for the worst climate outcome described ("famine and droughts across the world cause mass migration and conflict") was not as severe as the aversion for the worst biodiversity outcome ("species extinction accelerates, devastating the natural world"). Humans are more motivated by protecting what they love and value today than by scenarios they have difficulty imagining. Nobody activates that emotion more eloquently than David Attenborough. But he is not alone in changing the narrative. Protecting the planet for our children is a strong motivator, especially if there are straightforward ways to protect it. Half a century of warnings has helped to create awareness. Now, adding ways forward may nudge people into a more active mode of pushing for change.

Lifestyle Movements

The growing wish to protect the planet is also leading to meaningful lifestyle changes that motivate industries to develop products that further facilitate such lifestyles, making them more attractive. Only a tiny proportion of people in the Global North are strictly vegan. Yet this number is growing and having a significant impact on the types of food offered on the market. As we have seen in the Breaking Loose section in Chapter 4, change in complex networks typically starts in the periphery. Vegetarianism has long been present. It was prominent in some circles in 1854 when Thoreau wrote his famous prophecy: "It is a part of the destiny of the human race, in its gradual improvement, to leave off eating animals." Yet, judging from usage of the word vegetarian in books (Figure 5.10), interest in the concept started rising markedly only around the 1980s. The rise in popularity of veganism, eating only plant-based food, is an even more recent phenomenon. It implies a stricter limitation. It is also a stronger statement. Starting in the periphery of Western societies, its rapid growth over the past decade has made social scientists and food producers wonder what is happening. Interest in the words 'vegetarian' and 'vegan' has been rising steadily since the 1980s (Figure 5.10), and that trend is not just visible in books. The global market value for plant-based products is expected to roughly double in a decade, attracting multinationals such as McDonald's and PepsiCo to introduce alternatives to animal-based

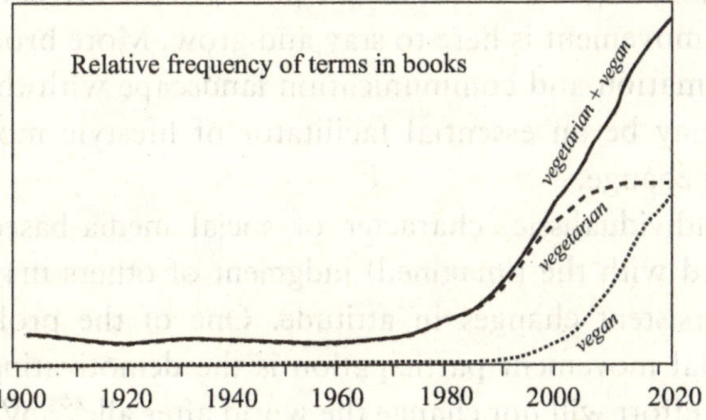

Figure 5.10 The frequency of the words 'vegetarian' and 'vegan' in books has been on the rise since the 1980s. (Based on data from millions of books that can be analyzed at https://books.google.com/ngrams/)

products.[102] What might explain the impressive rise of veganism in many places? Social scientists are starting to agree that lifestyle movements such as veganism are an entirely different beast than traditional social movements.[103] While social movements try to change the state or corporations through organized collective action, lifestyle movements challenge the status quo through personal adoption of lifestyles. In this view, a vegan is a 'cultural entrepreneur.' By eating plant-based burgers, vegans send a signal to others that they care. Just like buying an electric car, installing solar panels, or recycling your waste, choosing to be vegan is a clearly visible behavior that suggests to others that you care about the planet.

Caring about the planet is not the only motivator to become vegan or vegetarian. Equally important are health benefits of eating less meat and worries about animal rights. In fact, much of the psychological research in this field focuses on the question of why are we not all vegetarians or, more specifically, on how we can so easily overcome the cognitive dissonance between loving and eating animals. In a representative experiment, participants were asked to eat either dried beef or dried nuts and then rate how they perceived the moral status and mental capacities of a cow.[104] It turned out that eating meat reduced the ethical concern for animals and induced the perception that cows did not have the mental capacity to suffer. Thus, the cognitive dissonance is solved subconsciously by perceiving animals as unworthy and unfeeling. Could Thoreau's prophecy come true if the salience of the dissonance is amplified? That is certainly a motivation expressed by many vegans. Whatever the power of the drivers, it looks as if the vegan movement is here to stay and grow. More broadly, the changing information and communication landscape with the rise of social media may be an essential facilitator of lifestyle movements aimed at social change.

The 'individualistic' character of social media-based movements combined with the (imagined) judgment of others may inspire remarkably persistent changes in attitude. One of the problems of traditional social movement participation is the demotivating feeling that individual effort will not change the world after all.[105] Why reject meat if the effect of your personal action is hardly noticeable? Motivation changes if, as in many lifestyle movements, constructing a desirable self becomes the primary driver. Adherents often consider their involvement a quest for personal 'integrity' and 'authenticity,' while participation in an imagined community provides an additional layer of meaning by connecting individuals to something greater than themselves.[106] On a deeper level this may help satisfy the near-universal desire to be part of something bigger than yourself, identified in classic works as a prime driver of social behavior.[107] Such mechanisms may promote the persistence of lifestyle movements, allowing them to play a change-making role from the periphery of society.

Movements to reduce meat consumption have a long way to go. Despite the growth of the vegan movement, global per capita meat consumption has grown steadily. This trend is expected to continue unchecked over the coming decade, partly due to a strong rise in meat consumption in countries where poverty has been reduced, such as China and Brazil.[108] Meat has long been a luxury and, when conditions allow, the biggest treat you can give yourself, friends, and family is abundant meat. The view of meat as a treat and as a status symbol is culturally ingrained. It was therefore meaningful, for instance, when the three-Michelin-starred chef of Eleven Madison Park made his menu entirely vegan while still charging the same price. Indeed, in some wealthy circles, choices for expensive things with a low ecological footprint have already become a sophisticated status symbol.[109] While remaining fringe in global terms, this trend hints at the possibility that the pursuit of status can be decoupled from rising consumption. Perhaps equally importantly, visible pro-planet choices championed by lifestyle movements help reduce the mismatch between the overwhelming majority of people worrying about the planet and the perception that few others share that worry, contributing to hope and thus making more people action minded.

Renewable Energy

The transition from fossil fuels to renewable energy is undoubtedly a positive trend that makes the recent past seem decades ago. As we saw in the section on humanity's track record of transitions, technological advances are autonomous tectonic-plate movements in their own right that have destabilized the status quo time and time again. Think again of the Henry Ford quotation in Chapter 4: "If I had asked people what they wanted, they would have said faster horses." Instead of asking, he started mass-producing the Model-T Ford, which profoundly affected life in the twentieth century. It is hard to imagine the world now without the comfort of cars. And without the sound of traffic too.

As with the advent of the Model-T, we are now in the midst of tectonic-plate movements when it comes to technology. The renewable-energy transition will be crucial to halting global warming. The previous energy transition from wood to fossil fuels during the Industrial Revolution created the climate problem we are now facing. The renewable-energy transition will help get us out of that. Its pace is impressive. The price drop in solar panels over the past decades has been flabbergasting. This is helping to decentralize and democratize electricity production. Together with wind, and hydropower, solar panels allow an increasing number of countries to produce almost all electricity in a carbon-neutral way. Cars and home heating systems are shifting to electric to take advantage of that. It is a beautiful transition. I always loved combustion engines with all their beautiful technology. But in the end, an electric car is so much more efficient and elegant. It requires less maintenance. And pushing the 'gas' to accelerate with marvelous power, knowing this is all solar energy from my roof panels, feels liberating. The same goes for the heat pump in the house. It now feels so primitive that until recently we were burning fossil fuels to stay warm.

Still, it remains to be seen how quickly renewable energy can spread globally. Most countries are just starting the renewable-energy transition, and even if worldwide road transport became electric, and all houses and other buildings were to be heated by renewable energy, this would only reduce greenhouse gas emissions by 25 percent (Figure 5.11). Of course, not all emissions have to go to zero, as there are many ways to suck carbon out of industrial emissions or the atmosphere and store it. But to get the climate back in shape, we need to cross net zero and enter a phase of negative net emissions, taking more carbon out of the atmosphere than we put in. In 2015 pathways to net zero were understood and agreed upon in Paris by 195 parties (194 states plus the EU). Yet, while there has been some progress, it has been disappointing. Climate change would already be much worse without the concerted efforts so far. But clearly, things are moving too slowly. This energy transition is fundamentally different from the previous one. At that time there was no urgency, and the shift was driven entirely by entrepreneurship and markets. Now we need to mobilize another force: the desire to save the planet for future generations. Entrepreneurship and market forces are at work, but while some industries are pushing forward,

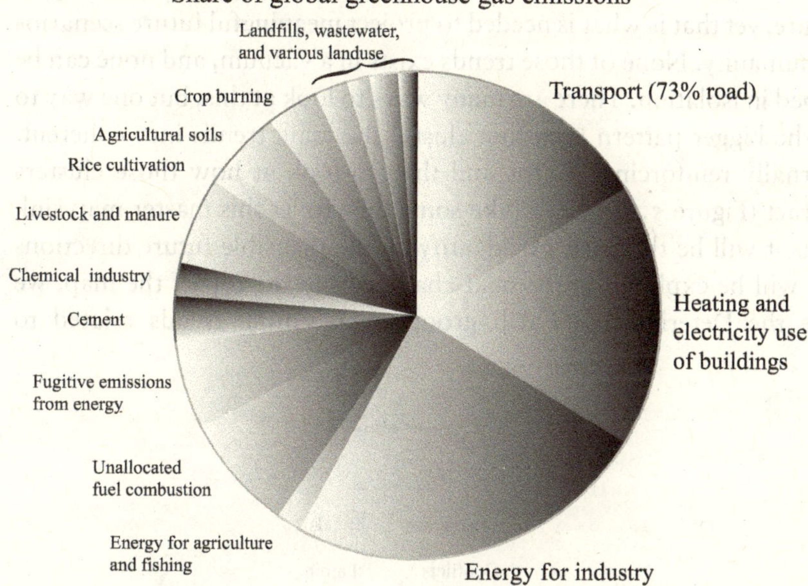

Figure 5.11 Greenhouse gas emissions by sector. (Based on data from https://ourworldindata.org/ghg-emissions-by-sector.)

others are pulling back. Overall we are moving in the right direction, but we know that the balance of forces needs to be tilted to speed up. That is a challenge. If many policy makers have become puppets of the fossil-fuel industry, how can we, the people, change that? We get back to that key issue in depth in Chapters 7 and 8.

The Big Picture

Each of this collection of trends has been the topic of countless scientific articles and deep journalistic reflections. Synthesizing them is another challenge. As historian Frederick Lewis Allen framed it when he attempted to write about the turmoil of the American 1930s: "Sometimes the historian wishes that he were able to write several stories at once, presenting them perhaps in parallel columns, and that the human brain were so constructed that it could follow all these stories simultaneously without vertigo, thus gaining a livelier sense of the way in which numerous streams of events run side by side down the channel of time."[110] Indeed, it is a challenge, when faced with a multitude of entangled developments, to see the bigger picture; yet that is what is needed to project meaningful future scenarios for humanity. None of those trends exists in a vacuum, and none can be curbed in isolation. There are many ways to look at this, but one way to see the bigger pattern is to first cluster the main trends into coherent, internally reinforcing groups and then to look at how those clusters interact (Figure 5.12). Let's take some time to let this master map sink in, as it will be the basis for identifying the plausible future directions that will be explored in the next chapters. On the top of the map, we have the Deteriorating Earth group, representing trends related to

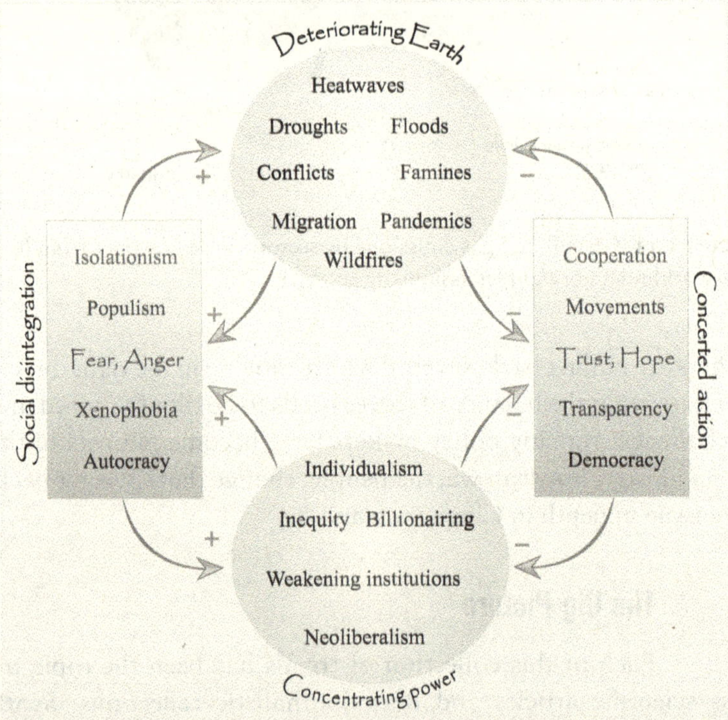

Figure 5.12 An overview of recent trends in nature and society and how they interact. The net effect of the series of arrows can be seen by multiplying their signs. For example, Concentrating Power → Social Disintegration → Deteriorating Earth yields an overall positive effect (+ * + * + = +). Also, a feedback loop with two negative effects such as Concerted Action → Concentrating Power → Concerted Action yields an overall positive effect (- * - = +). Thus, both Social Disintegration and Concerted Action are self-stimulating through their interactions with Deteriorating Earth and Concentrating Power.

deteriorating climate and ecosystems. The Concentrating Power group at the bottom encompasses some of the big social trends over the past fifty years. Thus, the top and bottom circles represent the environmental and societal crises introduced in Chapter 1. On the sides we have two opposing sets of societal reactions to those changes, labeled Concerted Action and Social Disintegration.

Now, let's think about how all those trends causally hang together. Starting with the power concentration, over the past half-century or so there has been a shift toward neoliberal policies. As we saw, this has likely been facilitated by the steady rise of individualism, reflected in language and other indicators. This, in turn, was a reaction to earlier suffocating societal norms, repressing diversity. As neoliberal thought grew and permeated society, this further reinforced individualism but also allowed inequality to rise. Neoliberal policies weakened institutions such as taxation and environmental regulations. Together with the upscaling of global business, those developments allowed global wealth to become concentrated in the hands of a tiny fraction of society (the 'billionairing'). This eroded institutions further, increasingly dominating the way societies work. As we saw earlier, this coherent set of tendencies is similar to events that have happened over and over again since ancient Greek times. Such change drove discontent, which often destabilized states, as in the French Revolution, but at other times led to the revision of institutions, as in the American Progressive Era.

Meanwhile, the exponentially rising human footprint has changed the way our planet works, as represented on the top of the trend map. Nature is in decline, and species are being lost at rates exceeding those during the five previous mass-extinction events in the history of the Earth. Scientists have long warned that the encroachment of humans on nature was raising the risk of novel pandemics, but people found that hard to believe. Covid-19 was a wake-up call. Something similar happened with warnings of climate change risk. The reality has come to illustrate each year more vividly what a different climate might look like. Heatwaves, catastrophic droughts, wildfires, and floods are making climate change salient in ways that scientists never could. And people are starting to realize that this is just the beginning. Also, the implications for social stability are becoming visible as famines, conflicts, and migration waves start reinforcing each other. As we saw, climate extremes have triggered many social tipping events before, including the Late Bronze Age collapse, the transformations of the Pueblo societies, the French Revolution, and the Arab Spring.

Those worrying trends in society and the Earth have led to two contrasting sets of societal reactions. The concerted action responses dampen the deterioration. By contrast, the social disintegration responses fuel the trends further. Both responses encompass a set of mutually reinforcing tendencies. In the concerted action response, lifestyle movements and other initiatives boost awareness of the problems. In a well-functioning democracy, the issues and their causes are becoming increasingly transparent, and inclusive institutions help control the problems. This rational and successful approach boosts trust and hope, which in turn strengthens civic participation and institutional power, allowing societies to address the problems through global concerted action.

The contrasting set of mutually reinforcing societal responses is evoked by anger and fear. Stress promotes emotional, black-and-white thinking and conspiracy theories. Stressful uncertainty drives xenophobia. All of this provides fertile grounds for extreme-right populist leaders. Their narratives, in turn, help make xenophobia and conspiracy thinking mainstream. The anti-elite framing of populism undermines institutions, allowing democracy to backslide toward autocracy or civil war. States in the grip of those mechanisms not only become divided internally but also cause the disintegration of global cooperation. The 'solve-our-own-problems-first' narrative leads states to pull out of the international cooperation needed to govern climate change and migration in peaceful and effective ways.

Which of those contrasting responses dominates in any country depends on many things, but the media are highly influential. What matters are not the facts but rather the perceptions of the problems, causes, and solutions. As we saw, digital media can help destabilize autocracies, but also undermine liberal democracies. Importantly, as media are largely owned by a small group of billionaires, they have a disproportionally large influence on societal reactions. Only when democracies are vital enough can this grip be moderated through regulations.

In conclusion, grasping the seemingly inextricable tangle of trends may be less daunting than it seems at first sight. Many things are happening simultaneously, but they can be grouped in a logical way that helps see the forest, not just the trees. We understand roughly how the two big sustainability challenges, climate change and loss of nature, increase the chances of famines, pandemics, and migrations, and how those trends and dire projections may cause hopelessness and fear. It is also well established how wealth concentration can weaken institutions and how this may further amplify inequality, fueling anger and undermining trust. Thus, the trends in the Earth and human societies are driven by coherent sets of mechanisms. The same is true for the two contrasting societal responses. Each of these consists of a set of mutually reinforcing trends. Clearly, it makes little sense to try and curb individual trends such as rising inequality or xenophobia without considering the bigger picture. This bird's-eye view of intertwined trends reveals a pattern that is not fundamentally different from what humanity has seen many times before. State capture and environmental degradation cause tensions that may either be resolved through the improvement of institutions or drive the collapse of the state altogether. The global scale and the information revolution make things different, but the fundamental forces at play remain familiar. In the following chapters we will build on those insights to find out what we may reasonably expect from the future, and how grasping this may help alter the outcome.

6 THREE PLAUSIBLE FUTURES

Time to look into the future. Our ultimate goal is to determine how the fate of humanity may be nudged in the best possible direction. In preparation, we first need to know what the realistic options are for humanity over the coming century. You may think that the number of possibilities is infinite, but reality could be simpler (Figure 6.1). Of course infinite variations are possible, but arguably those fall into three distinct categories, which simplifies the way we think about it a great deal. The reasons why this simplification makes sense are the feedbacks depicted in the map of trends (Figure 5.12). They tend to draw society in two opposite directions. Both Concerted Action and Social Disintegration are self-stimulating through the feedbacks with Deteriorating Earth and Concentrating Power. If such feedbacks are strong enough they can make our current moderate status quo unstable (Figure 6.1). It is impossible to quantify the entire dynamical system with sufficient accuracy to substantiate this picture, but qualitatively it makes sense, and I will use it as a framework to structure the discussion about potential futures. Before diving into the details, here are the three scenarios in a nutshell.

First, there is a failed-world dystopia in which the self-propelled power concentration and the crises triggered by a changing Earth stoke enough anger and fear to allow far-right populism to break up societies. States pull out of the global cooperation needed to stop and reverse the deterioration of the Earth. This is a global social trap where the loss of nature and climate change go unchecked, driving conflicts and migration waves, causing more fear and anger, and fueling more far-right

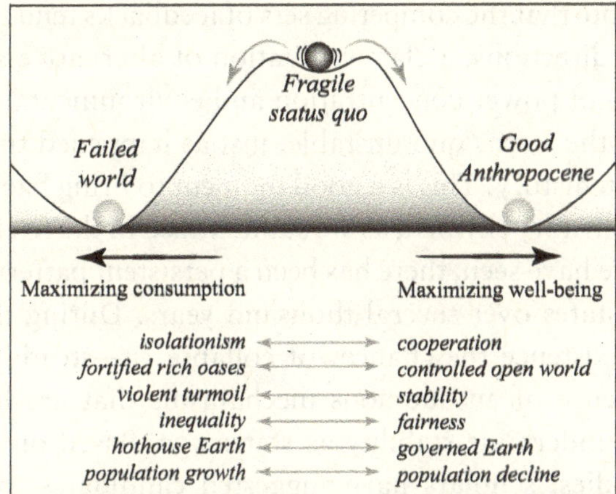

Figure 6.1 A schematic view of two contrasting future scenarios.

populism and autocracy. One might think that autocratic governments could perhaps be better placed to tackle the social ill of wealth concentration and its perverse effects forcefully, but this seems unlikely. As we saw, billionaires have been more successful in getting into political power in autocracies than in democracies. Thus, we have a twin self-reinforcing feedback linking societal disintegration with further deterioration of the Earth, on the one hand, and further concentration of wealth and power, on the other. This double feedback could let humanity fall into chaos as billions are driven out of their homelands by heatwaves, floods, droughts, famines, and conflicts spiraling out of control. A plausible scenario for a "failed world."

In the contrasting scenario, democracies manage to revise their institutions to meet the new demands and cooperate globally to control the deterioration of the Earth and state capture by populists or billionaires. Success in restoring equity and transparency boosts trust in institutions, making them more effective in turn. Also, positive results raise hope, encouraging more people to support the necessary change actively. Lifestyle movements and other prosocial and pro-sustainability initiatives nudge public attitudes to support policies that reduce ecological footprints and regulate corporations to become a force for good. This may seem a less likely scenario, but all the elements are in place already. What would be needed to reach such a "good Anthropocene" is a social shift in norms and values. More about that later.

For now, note that the competing sets of feedbacks tend to drive society in opposite directions, a classic situation of alternative attractors. The slow creep of power concentration and environmental deterioration have made the status quo unstable, just as happened time and time again in human history. This is a good moment to bring back some insights about how history rhymed, as we summarized in the ten laws of social tipping. As we have seen, there has been a persistent pattern in the wax and wane of states over several thousand years. During the first centuries of their existence the chances of collapse rise steadily. This points to the existence of autonomous mechanisms that are hard to avoid and tend to undermine stability as states age. Based on a wide variety of case studies, scholars have suggested candidates for such erosive mechanisms: autonomously rising inequity, environmental degradation, shortages, and rising insecurity. Various combinations of those tendencies have likely driven the senescence of states in the past, and it is hard to miss the parallels to the present. There is another hint from the past. Many premodern states collapsed after about two centuries. We are now roughly two centuries into industrial capitalism. Could modern versions of the social ills that slowly destabilized premodern states also undermine the globally dominant system we now live in? And if so, what could happen? The failed-world scenario is a real possibility. Discontent eventually destabilized many premodern states. Now discontent, anger, and fear are filling the sails of far-right populists. But history also tells us that collapse is not the only outcome. Some states persisted for over a millennium and, as we saw, part of their secret may well have been their capacity to change. To nurture inclusive institutions that could be reformed when needed. Such long-term thriving may happen in modern societies too. Indeed, trust and well-functioning institutions in the Nordic countries have long remained stable.[1] Those places have high social support, per capita income, life satisfaction, and low corruption.[2] They have relatively low inequality and high social cohesion, maintained by good governance. The Nobel laureate Joseph Stiglitz, who studied the problem of state capture for much of his life, summarizes it aptly in his latest book:[3]

> We can create public institutions with checks and balances that prevent the abuses the Right so fears. Some countries have done a remarkably good job of this. And there is a virtuous circle. Countries that have done a better job at creating trustworthy

governments have more trust in government and attract better people to public service. Indeed, so successful have some countries been that individuals willingly pay taxes knowing that "taxes are what we pay for civilized society," as Supreme Court Justice Oliver Wendell Holmes famously said. In Finland, for instance, a survey commissioned by the tax administration reported that "95% of Finns consider paying taxes an important civic duty … In addition, 79% of respondents were happy to pay taxes and felt that they get good value for the taxes they pay."

This raises the question of whether it could be possible for some countries to remain in good shape, even if many others spiral down into autocratic isolationism. Perhaps, but the problem is that we share the same planet. If global warming runs out of control with billions of people in search of better places,[4] stress will inevitably rise everywhere. Also, it is hard to see how a single country could be isolated from the implications of extreme global wealth concentration.[5]

This brings us to a third possible future: "buying time." It is quite likely that social change toward a good Anthropocene would unfold slowly. It would be a complex change requiring worldwide shifts in attitudes and institutions, likely resisted by powerful elites that benefit from maintaining the status quo. This is not unlike the change involved in abandoning the slave trade or the deep societal changes involved in improving fairness and redistributing wealth after the Industrial Revolution. Those changes had a timescale of about a century from start to finish. That may not be rapid enough to prevent the Earth from heating to a dangerous level where irreversible changes such as ice-cap melting and species extinctions happen.[6] In such an overshoot situation, much of the Global South would become uninhabitable. As we saw, our analysis of the future of the human climate niche suggests that about one-third of the global population may need to relocate. The good news is that there would still be space for everyone. That is because large pieces of land that were unlivable before would become well suited for humans and for agricultural production. The Earth will not become uninhabitable,[7] but people will 'just' need to move.[8] Clearly the emotional costs and social challenges of relocating billions of people would be enormous. However, as we will see later, migration, if managed well, may very well be a win-win for both the

Global North and the Global South. Also, over a few centuries, techniques for drawing carbon out of the atmosphere will slowly but steadily bring the climate back into shape, allowing the recovered Global South to be repopulated. Of course, such a relatively benign scenario of adaptive migration would become impossible if states in the Global North reject global cooperation and try to keep their borders shut in an 'eco-fascist' style, protecting their own turf. That would lead to a tense and violent failed world in which not just the Global South but eventually all humanity suffers.

One way to think of the costs and benefits of the three scenarios is to envision how human well-being would unfold over time (Figure 6.2). What works out best in the short term leads to the worst outcome in the long run. A swift social transformation toward a good Anthropocene asks for immediate investments but then allows humanity to live on in its current setting without the need for massive migrations. The eco-fascist scenario of strengthening borders while doing nothing about the deterioration of the globe allows the current pattern of overconsumption and fossil-fuel use to continue, resulting perhaps in a brief further increase in well-being. However, this approach steers the world toward collapse into a state of chaos and suffering from which it may be difficult to recover. The intermediate scenario in terms of global well-being is the challenging but feasible "buying time." In the following sections we will unpack those three scenarios in some more detail, laying groundwork for the final two chapters where we will ask if, and how, humanity may nudge its own fate in the best possible direction.

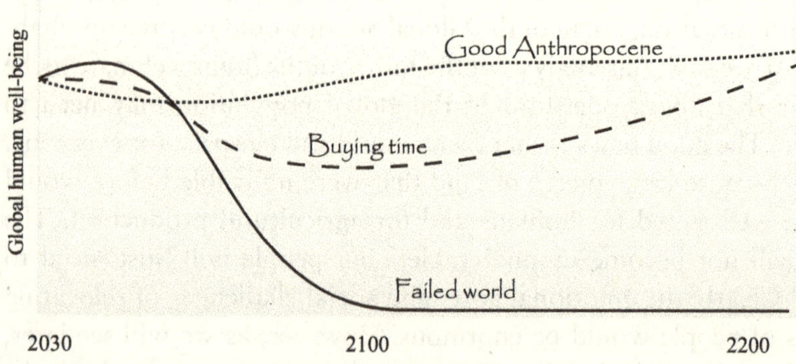

Figure 6.2 Long-term development of global human well-being in three scenarios.

A Failed World

Let's first deal with the easiest one, the road to collapse. Many things can go terribly wrong if discontent gets out of hand on a heating Earth. Self-reinforcing feedbacks could well make a failed world a nearly irreversible trap, a global version of the destructive systemic collapses that so many past societies have seen. Collapses that often came with suffering of biblical dimensions (in fact, the dramatic cascading collapse of societies during the Late Bronze Age inspired the Bible and other scriptures). I will briefly guide you through some end-of-times scenarios, but before that let's look in more detail at two dangerous tangles of already recognizable trends which could push us toward a world in which nationalistic countries led by autocrats find little incentive for global cooperation aimed at a just and sustainable world. First we will examine a possible spiraling down of trust, then we will consider how rising mental stress may degrade societies. Those different angles will allow us to get a deeper understanding of some of the most important self-reinforcing feedbacks emerging from the overall map of trends (Figure 5.12). In a nutshell, the storylines are simple: (1) dwindling trust leads to societal malfunctioning which further undermines trust; (2) stress leads to bad decisions and xenophobia, both of which push up stress even further. Those mechanisms may be drivers of runaway change toward a failed world, so let's have a closer look at the way they work.

Meltdown of Trust

I share a fascination for the fragility of trust with the economist Stephen Polasky and the mathematician Marty Anderies. We have discussed many aspects of this problem over the years, but eventually zoomed in on the question of what might be going wrong in the USA and other places today.[9] We found it easy to find support for the idea that trust is needed for a working democracy – indeed, for a functioning society.[10] Trust in politicians, scientists, medicine, and other institutions. Trust in others. These may seem very different topics, yet trust is related across domains.[11] Trust makes things work. To quote George Schultz, former US Secretary of State and Secretary of the Treasury:[12] "Trust is the coin of the realm. When trust was in the room, whatever room that was – the family room, the schoolroom, the locker room, the office room, the government room or the military room – good things happened. When trust was not in the room, good things did not happen. Everything else is details." Indeed, trust often seems to make the difference, from business deals to peace negotiations and pandemic control. For instance, negotiation studies stress trust management as part of strategies to get the best agreement,[13] and during the Covid-19 pandemic interpersonal trust was the single best predictor of a country's success at bringing down infection peaks.[14]

Although the importance of trust is widely accepted, it remains a somewhat vague notion. What exactly is trust, and how do you measure it? In the Covid-19 study it was defined as the percentage of respondents who agreed with the statement "Most people can be trusted." Comparable questions can be used to probe the trust in scientists, doctors, teachers, priests, bankers, journalists, government, police, and other groups or institutions. One can scroll endlessly through results on sites such as ourworldindata.org, revealing fascinating differences between countries and religious groups, as well as some puzzling trends. In 1958 more than 70 percent of people in the USA trusted the government, comparable to Scandinavian countries now. A long, wobbly downward trend brought American trust in government to around 20 percent (Figure 6.3). Trust in other people declined as well. Meanwhile, trust has remained much higher and relatively stable in Scandinavian countries.[15] Why such huge differences?

Perceived unfairness is probably part of it. For instance, there is an inverse correlation between inequality and trust (Figure 6.4), and it makes sense that there is causality involved. When people see economic inequality, they may feel that the system isn't on their side. This creates a breeding ground for conspiracy theories, pointing fingers at supposedly rigged institutions. As we saw, the downturn in the economic status of many working-class people over the past decade has likely fueled the rise of populism. Inequality also takes a toll on civic participation and social connections. All of this points to one thing: Wealth accumulation may erode trust due to rising inequality. However, as discussed in Chapter 1, there is also another way in which the concentration of wealth and power can be problematic for trust. People in influential positions, such as business leaders and politicians, may intentionally try to erode trust for their own gain.[16] A classic case is how tobacco companies have cast doubt on science linking cancer and smoking. The story has been repeated for climate change. Energy companies

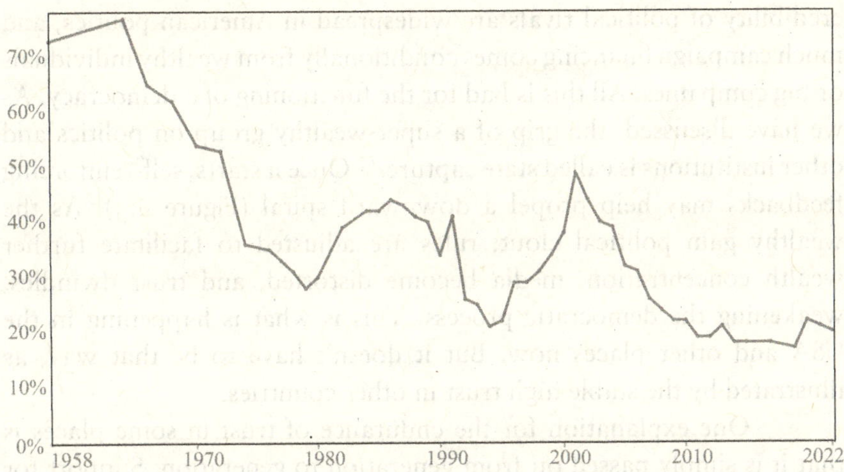

Figure 6.3 The percentage of people in the United States who say they trust the government to do what is right "just about always" or "most of the time." (Redrawn from ourworldindata.org/trust, based on data from the Pew Research Center, 2023.)

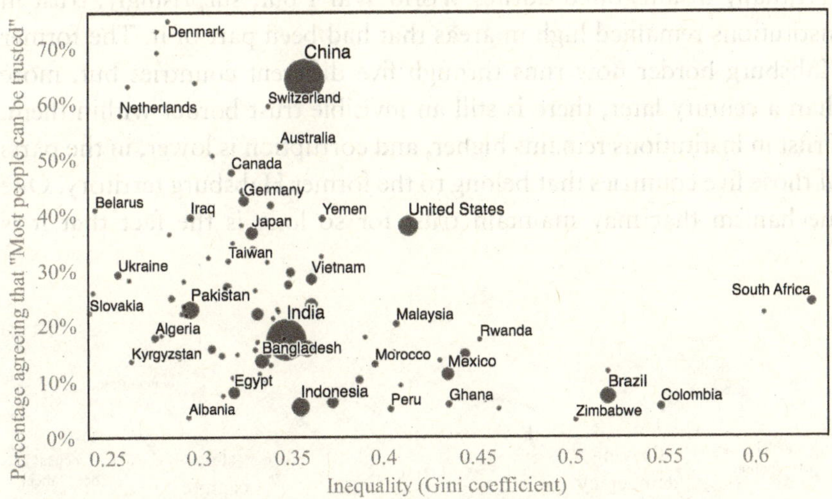

Figure 6.4 Inequality may undermine trust. In countries with high inequality, fewer people agree with the statement "Most people can be trusted." (Redrawn from ourworldindata.org/trust.)

have worked for decades at discrediting climate science to protect their profits. In such situations where undermining trust is cheap and brings large benefits, economists will tell you that it's not surprising to see efforts to destroy trust. Negative "attack ads" aiming to undermine the credibility of political rivals are widespread in American politics, and much campaign financing comes conditionally from wealthy individuals or big companies. All this is bad for the functioning of a democracy. As we have discussed, the grip of a super-wealthy group on politics and other institutions is called state capture.[17] Once it starts, self-reinforcing feedbacks may help propel a downward spiral (Figure 6.5). As the wealthy gain political clout, rules are adjusted to facilitate further wealth concentration, media become distorted, and trust dwindles, weakening the democratic process. This is what is happening in the USA and other places now. But it doesn't have to be that way, as illustrated by the stable high trust in other countries.

One explanation for the endurance of trust in some places is that it is simply passed on from generation to generation. Support for this was revealed by a fascinating study of trust after the fall of the Habsburg Empire.[18] The Habsburg dynasty managed to keep a relatively well-functioning – and therefore respected – bureaucracy for centuries. This likely helped maintain a stable society for centuries. The empire eventually disintegrated during World War I but, surprisingly, trust in institutions remained high in areas that had been part of it. The former Habsburg border now runs through five different countries but, more than a century later, there is still an invisible trust border within them. Trust in institutions remains higher, and corruption is lower, in the parts of those five countries that belong to the former Habsburg territory. One mechanism that may maintain trust for so long is the fact that it is

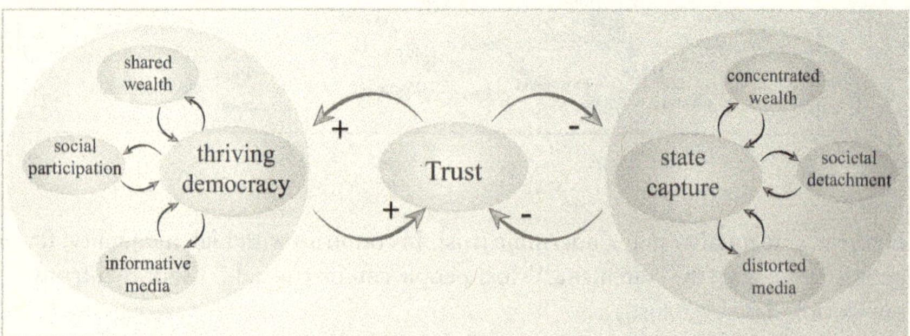

Figure 6.5 Trust and democracy have a mutually reinforcing relationship, while trust may dwindle in situations where state capture by vested interests undermines media, equality, and social participation.

anchored early in life, making it a slow cultural characteristic passed on from generation to generation.[19] This makes it even more striking that it has eroded so dramatically in the USA.

If self-reinforcing mechanisms such as the feedbacks in Figure 6.5 are strong enough, they may theoretically be expected to cause two basins of attraction, one with high trust and another one with low trust (Figure 6.6). Indeed, there is some evidence that there is a critical trust level (an unstable 'saddle point') above which trust tends to increase, while below it trust tends to decrease (Figure 6.7). The word 'tends' is important here, as the huge scatter of points around the curve tells you that factors other than trust must be important for the direction of change too. Those high versus low trust scenarios correspond to the opposing ways in which societies may respond to the deteriorating Earth and concentrating power

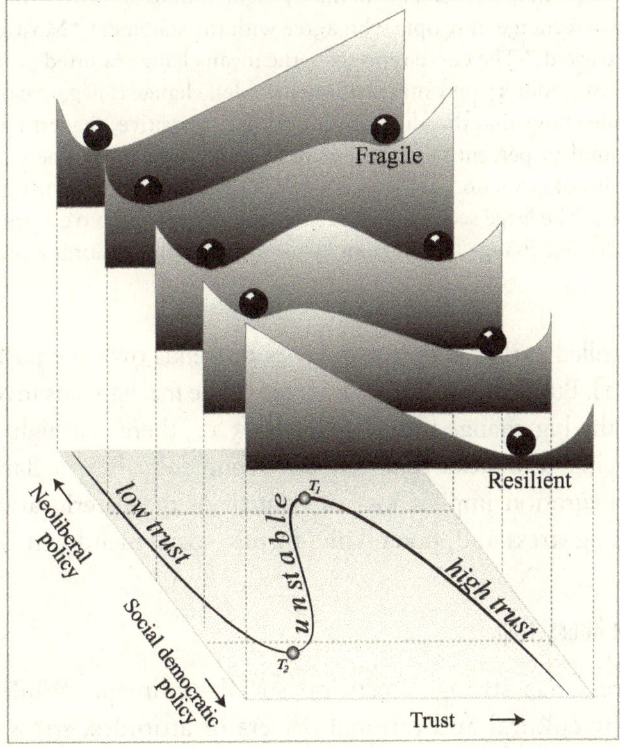

Figure 6.6 A schematic model of the effect of neoliberal policies on trust. When strong enough, the feedbacks depicted in Figure 6.5 may cause alternative attractors.

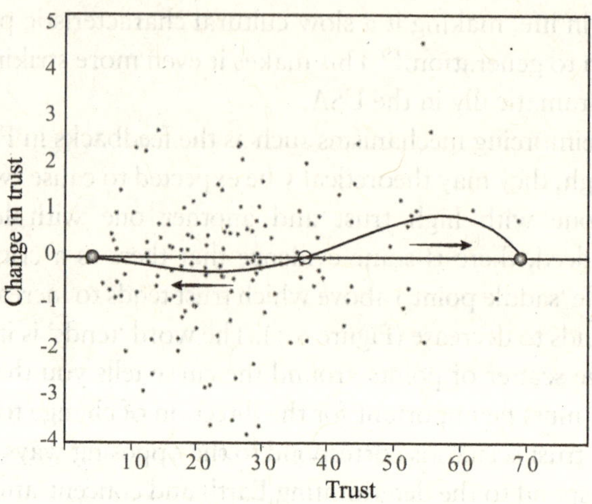

Figure 6.7 The relationship between trust and change in trust between subsequent measurements in ninety-eight countries. Trust is measured as the percentage of people who agree with the statement "Most people can be trusted." The curve represents the mean change (a fitted polynomial). Below about 37 percent trust (open circle), change is negative on average, while above that threshold, mean change is positive, suggesting that at around 37 percent trust there may be an unstable border between the basins of attraction of the alternative high-trust and low-trust states (solid dots). The large scatter implies that factors other than trust are dominant in driving change. (Data from https://ourworldindata.org/trust.)

that we distilled earlier from the analysis of trends over the past decades (Figure 5.12). But the trust trap is only one of the mechanisms involved. As you see in the big change model of Figure 5.12, there is a higher level of self-reinforcing feedbacks that can draw humanity into a dark future: social disintegration implies loss of control of the deterioration of the Earth, causing stress and, potentially, further social meltdown.

The Stress Trap

Stress has strong effects on social sentiment. While trust is anchored by cultural and rational drivers of attitudes, stress is something visceral. A focus on stress thus provides a complementary angle to look at feedbacks that could drag societies into trouble (Figure 6.8). We saw the main elements in the previous chapter, but here is a recap of how they hang together. Stress profoundly affects how the brain works. For

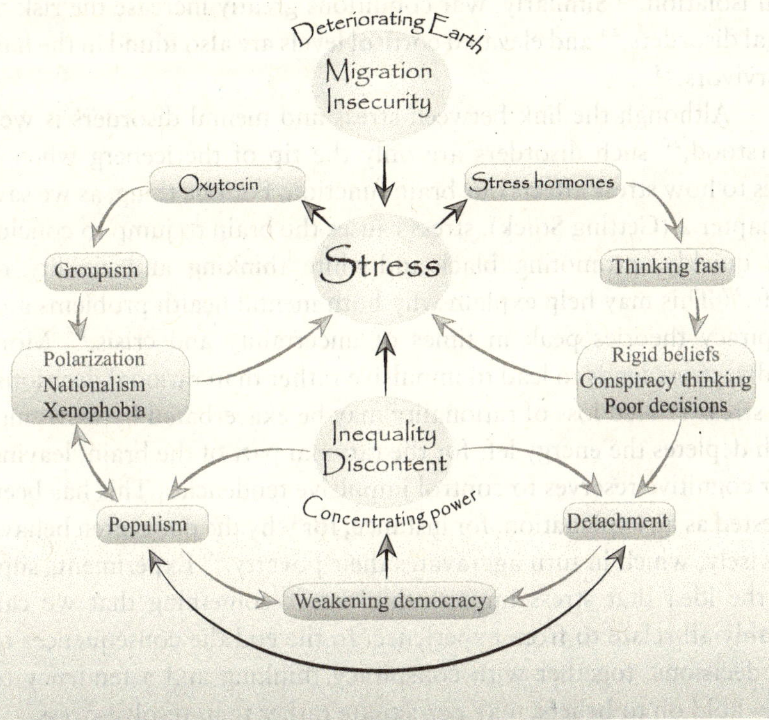

Figure 6.8 As with a loss of trust, rising stress may be involved in the self-reinforcing destabilization of societies.

instance, as we saw in the section on xenophobia, the hormone oxytocin makes us want to protect our group from strangers when social situations feel uncertain.[20] But stress also causes hormones such as adrenaline and cortisol to flip our thinking into a fast mode.[21] Evolutionarily speaking, such reactions have been a matter of survival, so they have become hardwired. Indeed, there is ample evidence that in modern societies those basic biological mechanisms still profoundly affect mindsets. For instance, population-wide surges in stress during pandemics or wars leave clear traces on minds, including elevated mental disorders. Over the first year of the Covid-19 pandemic, global prevalence of anxiety and depression increased spectacularly,[22] and traces of stress hormones in hair and nails point to stress as a likely driver. One study found the concentration of cortisol (in hair) to be associated with job loss, remote working, exposure to news, and social isolation. Meanwhile, child-hair cortisol was correlated with family job loss and social isolation.[23] Similarly, war conditions greatly increase the risk of mental disorders,[24] and elevated cortisol levels are also found in the hair of survivors.[25]

Although the link between stress and mental disorders is well understood,[26] such disorders are only the tip of the iceberg when it comes to how stress affects our brain function. For one thing, as we saw in Chapter 4 (Getting Stuck), stress causes the brain to jump to conclusions quickly, promoting black-and-white thinking and rigidity of beliefs.[27] This may help explain why both mental health problems and conspiracy theories peak in times of uncertainty and crisis.[28] More broadly, stress tends to lead to impulsive rather than rational decisions. Such stress-related loss of rationality may be exacerbated by worrying, which depletes the energy left for the rational part of the brain, leaving lower cognitive reserves to control impulsive tendencies. This has been suggested as an explanation, for instance, for why the poor often behave less wisely, which in turn aggravates their poverty.[29] Experiments support the idea that stress impairs thinking,[30] something that we can probably all relate to from experience. In the end the consequences of poor decisions, together with conspiracy thinking and a tendency to rigidly hold on to beliefs, may perpetuate rather than resolve stress.

The link between stress, anxiety, and cognition raises the question of whether such mechanisms might contribute to the puzzling decline of intelligence over past decades. As we saw in the section on distorted thought in Chapter 5, there has been an increase in language markers of cognitive distortions since the 1970s. Meanwhile, scores on intelligence tests have steadily declined in many countries. As the Norwegian study of military service IQ tests discussed in Chapter 5 showed, the decline in intelligence scores could not be explained by genetic factors. Instead, environmental conditions must drive the pattern. This leaves many possibilities open. For instance, changes in education or media exposure could play a role. Meanwhile, as we saw, inequality has increased, not only in the USA but also in many other places, including the relatively egalitarian Scandinavian countries. Stress-related inequality could thus contribute to dwindling thinking and reasoning capacities. Such an effect would be consistent with the pattern that a host of social problems increase with inequality (independent of the total wealth of a country)[31] and with the experimental finding that giving people an unconditional basic income reduces the incidence of mental disorders.[32] Also, the rise of loneliness in an automatized society with increasingly rare human contact may contribute to stress and has been suggested as affecting mental health.[33]

In addition to clouding our thinking, as discussed in the section on xenophobia, stressful situations cause oxytocin to show its nasty side.[34] When the social environment feels safe, oxytocin promotes all kinds of prosocial behavior. It is important in bonding mothers with their newborns and fostering in-group trust. But when the social environment is interpreted as unsafe, oxytocin also drives defensive antisocial behavior and emotions. It may promote discrimination against members of other groups and defensive aggression against those that are perceived as threatening. Again, this is not surprising when we see it from an evolutionary perspective. Being part of a group has always been critical for survival, and it makes sense that we evolved neural hardwiring that makes us contribute to the group by extending favors, cooperating, trusting, and complying with rules – but also, if needed, by aggressively protecting the group against threatening outsiders. This entire 'groupism' package is modulated by oxytocin. The 'cuddling chemical' transforms a person's mindset from that of a lone wolf to a valued group member. Experimental results are quite striking. Just a bit of added oxytocin drives participants to in-group favoritism, efforts to increase in-group well-being, and conformity to in-group preferences, and also increases lying for the group and aggressive protection against threatening outsiders.[35]

It is easy to see how in modern societies this package may promote xenophobia, polarization, and nationalism (Figure 5.12). All this is wind in the sails of far-right populists, which drives another self-reinforcing feedback. During calm times, cultural norms help to suppress overt xenophobia. But once populists are elected, the xenophobic narrative becomes more mainstream. Seeing someone who openly promotes xenophobic ideas succeed removes the stigma.[36] Even if formulations remain careful, disclaiming any prejudices ("some of my best friends are black, but … "), they can serve as dog whistles to mobilize the crowds. Populism is always about turning against the elite and, together with the tendency of disillusioned citizens to opt out, this often weakens democratic institutions. Also, there is much empirical evidence that when people see the world as dangerous they are more likely to choose authoritarian leaders.[37] The resulting downsliding of democracy weakens control over wealth concentration and its negative spillover effects, leading to rising inequality and discontent. This feeds back on rising stress levels and further promotes populism and social isolation.

Meanwhile, we should not forget the effect of climate news on stress levels. In a 2021 survey of 10,000 young people in ten countries across the Global South and North, 59 percent reported feeling sad, anxious, angry, powerless, helpless, and guilty about climate change. Moreover, about half of the respondents said that climate-related feelings negatively affected their daily life and functioning.[38] In short, on a deteriorating Earth, mass migration, insecurity, and inequality all fuel stress, and there is a real risk that this affects the minds of people in ways that drive societal dynamics to boost stress further.

Systemic Failure

To conclude this failed-world section let's look at how things may get totally out of hand. It's not a nice topic to think about. Also, it carries the risk of undermining the hope we need to fight the problems actively. Nonetheless, it is good to consider worst-case situations. Scientists tend to stay away from those scenarios, leaving them to the realm of fiction. That is not a good idea.[39] Understanding how things can go terribly wrong helps one see how rewarding efforts to prevent disaster can be – especially if those grim prospects turn out to be feasible. The hesitation among scientists to investigate worst-case scenarios comes in large part from a fear of being accused of alarmism. This has led to a tendency to "err on the side of least drama."[40] It is a bias we should get rid of just as much as we need to produce realistic positive scenarios. Both are necessary.

So here we go. Why could things turn out much worse than expected? The first problem is climate tipping. You may turn to any recent review for the details,[41] but here are the basics. The higher the Earth's mean temperature rises, the larger the chances of an element of the climate system flipping into runaway change. This may happen, for instance, as the Arctic permafrost starts thawing to the point at which the frozen ground releases massive amounts of greenhouse gases. Or, poorly understood cloud-formation mechanisms might produce changes that could cause the planet to run into an irreversible 'hothouse Earth' state.[42] Another worry is the irreversible collapse of the Amazon rainforests due to intense droughts and fires. Such tipping elements of the Earth system could give global warming an enormous boost, potentially causing other elements of the climate system to tip also, leading to a global domino effect. A well-known candidate for tipping is thermohaline circulation, sets of connected ocean currents that transport heat across the globe. The Atlantic Meridional Overturning Circulation (AMOC) has received much attention, as it transports heat from the tropics to places such as Europe and North America. If this circulation ground to a halt, those regions would quickly become very cold, disrupting agriculture, heating, and other essential pillars of society.[43] But the effects would be felt worldwide too. We know from the geological record that similar tipping events have happened in the past. Whether they are to be expected in the near future remains uncertain. Climate models have a hard time approximating the mechanisms that can lead to such tipping. In the early years this led the Intergovernmental Panel on Climate Change (IPCC) to leave them out of its reports, but that has changed. Climate tipping is now considered a low-probability yet high-impact event that should be seriously considered.

As we saw earlier, even without such climate-tipping events, warming may force 3 billion people in the Global South to migrate as their homelands become uninhabitable.[44] Other parts of the planet should become better places to live but, if poorly managed, the social challenge of moving a third of humanity could end in disaster. Climate change might also cause other problems, such as economic downfall, conflict, and failed harvests, to occur together in ways that may trigger larger crises that cascade across the globe.[45] It is conceivable that a rapid shift in climate could result in system failures that are serious enough to unravel societies around the world. In this context it is sobering to know that less extreme episodes of climate change than we are currently facing have repeatedly driven mass extinctions and the downfall of civilizations. The Late Bronze Age collapse was an early example of how such implosions can cascade through groups of connected societies.[46] The intense networks of trade and diplomatic relations around the Mediterranean allowed societies to thrive. But that very connectivity may also explain the cascading nature of this first global collapse – global in the sense that it pulled the entire group of states that formed the Bronze Age world into a spiral of chaos and destruction.[47]

We do live in a very different world now, but connectivity and climate change are elements we share with the Bronze Age, though on a much larger scale. Never has the world been so globally connected.

Cities depend on the countryside for food and energy, and countries depend on each other. This connectivity has provided an enormous boost to efficiency and productivity. It also allows for resilience, as challenges to parts of the network can be buffered by the whole. But connectivity is a two-edged sword. The benefits come at the risk of systemic failure. As mentioned in the Chapter 4, this dual effect of connectivity in networks is known as the robust yet fragile paradox. Like the idea of a tipping point, the robust yet fragile trade-off is universal. For instance, in building design the idea for many years was to connect the elements of a large building tightly so that they support each other in case of an earthquake. Now it is thought that it is better to include some weak connections, allowing a portion to collapse without taking the rest down.[48] Although the global web of interdependence as we know it is relatively new, the Late Bronze Age collapse remains a relevant example of how failure can cascade through a network of societies if they are connected too strongly. More recently, the start of World War I is an example of how perturbation can cause a domino effect in a closely linked set of alliances, and the 2008 global financial crisis and the Covid-19 pandemic illustrate that such collapses are not limited to wars. It is not just the web of countries and companies that has become more interdependent; the elements of our production systems are increasingly linked. For instance, a 2011 spike in global food prices – driven by failed harvests and increased demand due to the use of corn for biofuel production – contributed to the cascading of tensions in the Middle East unloading via the Arab Spring revolts.[49] In short, while we owe much of our current prosperity to unprecedented global connectivity, we have also become critically dependent on the stability of the whole.

So, what could disastrous 'endgame' scenarios with widespread harm and mortality look like in our connected world? The tangle of problems may include many elements, but the 'four horsemen' of global-warming disaster are likely to be famine, extreme weather events, vector-borne diseases, and conflicts.[50] They are not independent, of course. For instance, famines may cause conflicts and vice versa. Autocratic poor governance may make everything worse. For instance, the Great Famine in China that killed about 30 million people in 1959–1961 is thought to have been driven by droughts and floods combined with top-down policy changes that turned out to be disastrous.[51] While famines, wildfires, inundations, and pandemics are bad enough, conflicts boosted by stress-induced groupism exacerbated by populist narratives can be devastating. Recent wars provide examples, but we can easily forget that over half a million people were slaughtered within three months in the 1994 Rwanda genocide,[52] and over a million died violently in the Chinese Cultural Revolution started by Mao Zedong in 1966.[53] All this killing happened without sophisticated weapons. Meanwhile, there is a risk of global war. More countries than ever have nuclear arms. The idea is that they will never be used because no country would want to run the risk of escalating retaliation with mutual destruction as the end result. So far this has held true. But mistakes can be made, and the risk of mistakes might increase as rationality deteriorates further in a stressed world plagued by insecurities and migration waves.[54] International tensions involving nuclear powers are on the rise. Mortality in an all-out war would be huge, and a subsequent nuclear winter might lead to years of disastrous crop failures, famines, and chaos.[55] Another worry is the ease with which the information revolution has democratized access to instructions for making biological or chemical weapons of mass destruction.[56] In an increasingly unfair and unequal world, a growing group of potential terrorists may be motivated to use this information, with massive consequences for societal stability. So far, end-of-civilization scenarios have been explored mostly in fiction. Yet it is fair to say that the combination of the Earth's deterioration and societal trends that we have explored could plausibly end very badly indeed. We know from history that widespread discontent may destabilize societies to the point of collapse. The global interdependence of the food and production systems makes a modern version of the Bronze Age cascading collapse a real possibility. Such domino effects are always triggered by unpredictable events, as illustrated by the murder of Archduke Franz Ferdinand that led to World War I, or the street merchant setting himself on fire that triggered the Arab Spring. But whether such events result in a cascading conflict is less unpredictable. Put simply, it depends on the level of tension in the system at large – tension that might be managed; but that is for the next chapter.

You may wonder whether it might be possible to keep some places free from disaster in a collapsing global setting. You would not be alone. Researchers have tried to determine the places that have the best chances when things fall apart globally.[57] Studies of the collapse of states and civilizations reveal that falling apart may imply a loss of complexity. That happens when institutions fall apart, law and order are lost, and systems for the production and transportation of energy, food, and other essential things fail. The chances of a community surviving in such a world would then depend on whether it has a place where enough food and other essential goods and services for its people can be produced, while at the same time being inaccessible from mega-cities and other big population centers from which masses may be fleeing. This search boils down to a shortlist of island states, with New Zealand as the highest-scoring location. It would be very hard to keep your country or community safe in most of the world, and even if you could, it wouldn't be a pleasant world to live in. Even if you are a selfish person living in great wealth in a good place, the best option for you and your children is to do all you can now to cooperate with the rest of the world to prevent global collapse.

A Good Anthropocene

Time for happier thoughts. What could a good future look like? Not a utopia, but a realistic possibility? Just as the worst failed-world scenarios are understudied, integrative visions of attractive futures have barely been explored by scientists. In part this is because we tend to "err on the side of least drama," in part because the scientific approach tends to focus on well-defined subproblems rather than the whole. That should change,[58] but meanwhile let's have a go at it, starting with elements for which there is already strong evidence. To be realistic, scenarios for a good Anthropocene must meet two criteria. They need to spare the planet, otherwise humanity goes down the drain. However, they should also be compatible with human nature; otherwise they will never happen. This may seem an impossible combination; but, as you will see, it is not. We first ponder what a truly sustainable society could look like and then ask if such a situation is compatible with the behavioral tendencies that are hardwired in human brains through millions of years of evolution. Pathways to a good Anthropocene and how to get there will be the topic of the final chapters of the book. For now, we just explore the options for credible alternative futures.

Fitting Comfortably on the Planet

If we are to create an Anthropocene that we can be proud of, it should be one in which humans fit comfortably on the planet, coexisting with other species in ecosystems that provide so many indispensable 'services' to humanity. As mentioned in Chapter 1, it would help to have fewer people, but reducing the footprint of those living in the Global North would be far more effective. We know perfectly well what is needed to achieve that. We have to stop polluting the atmosphere and destroying nature. That can be achieved if we stop mass-mining fossil fuels and shift to a largely plant-based diet. More precisely, in a good Anthropocene, societies should be carbon neutral and have a modest ecological footprint. How would such a society look in practice? There is an enormous literature about that.[59] Here is an outline in broad strokes.

Carbon neutrality is probably the best-studied element of a good Anthropocene. Although progress so far has been too slow, it is clear by now that it is feasible. For instance, the small country of Bhutan captures four times more carbon than it emits.[60] Much of that comes from exporting hydropower generated in its mountainous territory to neighboring countries, so this model cannot be simply upscaled. However, the European Union has a concrete plan of how it can be carbon neutral by 2050, even if the details are not yet worked out.[61] Making the entire world economy carbon neutral by 2050 is estimated to cost the equivalent of around 7 percent of household incomes annually, and lead to a gain of 200 million jobs while losing 185 million.[62] Nothing outrageous. All remaining emissions should be compensated for by processes that remove carbon from the atmosphere, such as uptake in the oceans and forests, or engineered ways to capture and store carbon. Current plans for neutrality lean too heavily on optimistic estimations of potential carbon storage,[63] but that can be corrected. All the elements have basically been thought through, and even without assuming future novel techniques (which will emerge), carbon neutrality is possible. The same elements may allow for carbon negativity, a necessary phase during which we clean up the mess, sucking more carbon from the atmosphere than is emitted. There is extensive literature about all this, but to give you an impression, here is a rough sketch of what a carbon-neutral society could look like.

Solar, wind, geothermal, nuclear, and hydropower will be the primary electricity sources, with upgraded electricity grids to handle the fluctuating nature of renewable-energy sources. These grids integrate storage solutions and allow for better distribution of clean energy. Buildings will be designed and retrofitted for maximum energy efficiency using better insulation, heat pumps, LED lights, energy-friendly appliances, and smart controls. Cities will be more compact, walkable, and bicycle friendly. Almost all vehicles will be electric, and the extensive public transportation will be efficient and widely used. Biofuels made from sustainable sources will be used in the transitional phase for planes and long-distance transportation, where electrification is still challenging. Materials should be suitable for recycling and reuse to minimize waste and the need for damaging and energy-intensive extraction of virgin resources. Clean production processes will minimize emissions and waste. While some industries such as steel and cement production may still burn fossil or renewable fuels, carbon capture and storage (CCS) technologies can prevent the resulting CO_2 from leaking into the atmosphere, instead storing it in geological formations. Existing forests will be strictly protected. At the same time, large-scale reforestation will restore extensive and diverse forests to act as natural carbon sinks. Such restored natural areas can also help with regenerating soils, regulating moisture cycling, protecting bio-diversity, and offering wilderness for recreation and spiritual replenishment.

Many of the elements of a carbon-neutral society also help reduce the destruction of nature, but it is important to realize that nature suffers most from agriculture:[64] from pollution by pesticides, fertilizers, and soil erosion, but most of all from land transformation; from turning forests, wetlands, and other natural areas into intensively farmed cropland. There is enormous scope for improvements.[65] Farming practices on current land can be made less destructive by using less fertilizer and pesticides, promoting native plants that host pollinators and natural enemies of pests, improving manure management, growing crops with less soil disturbance, and producing rice in ways that emit less methane. But in addition to more nature-friendly agricultural practices, a sustainable Anthropocene will use less land for agriculture in total, allowing more space for nature.[66] This can be achieved in two complementary ways: improved efficiencies and reduced demand. Efficiency can be higher thanks to precision farming – giving crops and livestock the right treatment at the right place, time, and intensity – and vertical farming – growing crops in vertically stacked layers, optimizing growth with LED lights, and replacing soils with hydroponic or aeroponic techniques. Reduced demand is achieved in part by minimizing food waste along the supply chain from production to consumption. Most importantly, diets will be largely plant based, dramatically reducing the need for agricultural land. The animals we eat are fed largely on crops such as soy and cereals. A universal plant-based diet would reduce global land use for agriculture by 75 percent.[67] But a sustainable good Anthropocene with space for extensive natural areas is possible already with a diet that simply reduces meat consumption (Figure 6.9). This diet is a win-win for the health of people and the planet, as outlined by an interdisciplinary team put together by the prestigious medical journal *The Lancet*.[68]

As we will discuss in the final chapter, moving to such a society, which allows climate and nature to recover, would require a dramatic transition involving individual behavior, governance, and businesses. But before getting to the details of how that may be done, let's first ask whether a shift to such a low-footprint society is possible at all. Are humans simply hardwired for the destructive rat race of relentless competition, overwork, and overconsumption?

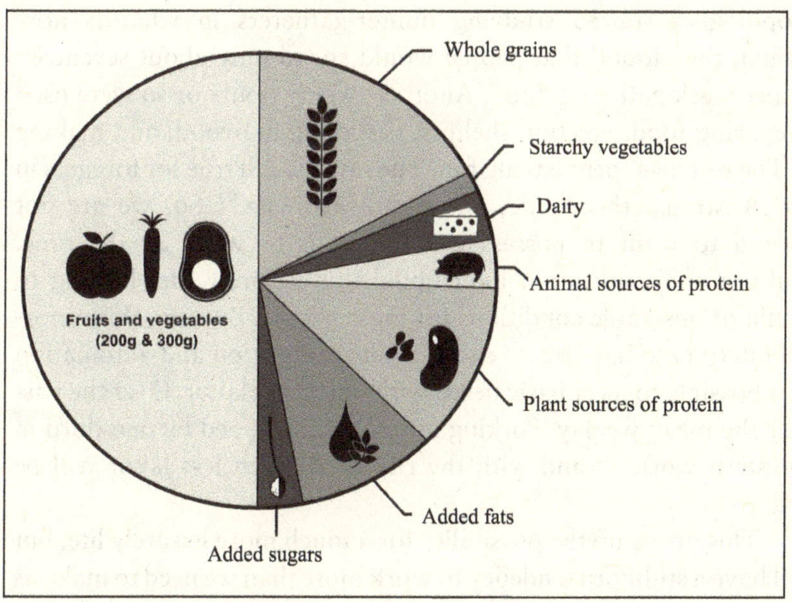

Figure 6.9 A diet that is healthy for people as well as the planet is largely plant based but leaves space for some meat and dairy too. (Redrawn from Haines and Frumkin, *Planetary Health*.[69])

Leisure as the Goal

The pursuit of ever more wealth and consumption has driven many of our problems. Fortunately, this is by no means hardwired in human nature. *Homo sapiens* walked the Earth in small groups, hunting and gathering, for hundreds of thousands of years, and earlier hominids did the same for millions of years. As mentioned earlier, the way we lived for more than 99 percent of our existence shaped our genetic setup. True, the rise of agriculture and civilization changed our way of living, but that started only 10,000 years ago. That is too recent to allow our hardware to change much. Our bodies and minds still work basically the same as they have done for millions of years. Among other things, this makes us want desperately to be part of a group and to strive for status. The latter is now often linked to displays of material wealth, but that is not hardwired at all. For nomadic hunter-gatherers, possessions were a burden and, as we saw, the few groups that have stuck to that lifestyle still don't see the point of having things. Neither do they spend much time getting food or running a household.[70] Enough is enough, which leaves plenty of time for leisure. For instance, in the 1960s, when anthropologists started studying hunter-gatherers in what is now Botswana, they found that people would spend only about seventeen hours per week gathering food. Another twenty hours or so were used for preparing food, erecting shelters, gathering firewood, and making tools. The rest was spent having fun. The same is still true for foragers in Africa, Australia, the Arctic, and Southeast Asia.[71] So, we are not hardwired to want to possess ever more or to work all the time. Agriculture and civilization interrupted this leisurely life, leading to millennia of miserable conditions for most people. By now, this unfortunate intermezzo has largely ended. Industrialization and automation made it possible to meet basic needs with much less labor. Over the past century the mean weekly working hours have dropped by one-third in the Western world,[72] and with the rise of AI even less labor will be needed.[73]

This opens up the possibility for a much more leisurely life, but we still have a stubborn tendency to work more than we need to make us happy.[74] More than is needed to meet what the legendary economist and philosopher John Maynard Keynes called "absolute needs":[75] universal requirements such as food, water, warmth, comfort, safety, and companionship. In the 1930s Keynes predicted that economic growth would allow those needs to be met in industrialized countries by around 2030. It turns out that progress went much faster than he anticipated, and by 1980 most people in the Global North were already on the safe side in terms of absolute needs. However, Keynes was spot on about another type of needs: the insatiable class of 'relative needs' that motivates us to work harder still, even if our absolute needs are met. Things like a second car, a bigger house, fancier food, greater wealth. Unlike absolute needs, relative needs are infinite. But runaway materialistic pursuit is only unleashed when the link between status and possession is activated. An illuminating illustration of how this happened in the USA was the reaction to a reduction of working hours in the Kellogg's cornflakes factory.[76] In 1935 W. K. Kellogg proudly stated that improvements in the production process allowed it to pay people the same for working six hours as they formerly did for eight. For two decades a thirty-hour work week remained the standard at their factories. Then, to the surprise of the managers, people wanted to go to a forty-hour week again. Why? According to another famous economist, Ken Galbraith, what happened in the 1950s in the USA was the activation of the latent force of Keynes's relative needs.[77] An artificial creation of perceived needs through mass advertisement. In the year when I was born Galbraith argued that in post-war America, just as goods were manufactured by factories, so were the material desires of people manufactured by advertising companies to keep the wheels of production and consumption spinning. They have kept spinning ever since, devastating the planet while not making us any happier.

Doesn't that hint at a recipe for a feasible good Anthropocene in which happiness is greater and the human footprint is smaller? What if we worked less and took the time to enjoy what really matters? Spend more time with friends and family. Engage in meaningful activities that make you feel part of something bigger than life. Enjoy your home surroundings. Sounds good, but can we really escape the grind? Aren't we hardwired to run the hamster wheel? No, we are not. We are hardwired to strive for status, but that does not need to be coupled to material goods. Advertising has cemented that artificial coupling, but it does not need to be that way. Status can be linked to different things. The focus of social valuation has changed over time. For instance, during the Industrial Revolution a curious type of person brightened up the streets of Paris: the *flâneur* (Figure 6.10) – literally, the stroller, displaying a slow way of enjoying life. In the most extreme caricatures,

Figure 6.10 A social obsession with wealth and consumption driving an unstoppable rat race arose only after World War II with the rise of mass advertising. It wasn't always like that, as illustrated by the image of the *flâneur*, reflecting a fascination with a strolling, idling lifestyle. (*Le flâneur*, drawing by Paul Gavarni, 1842.)

walking a turtle on a leash emphasized the luxury of slowness. A lifestyle to be envied. No rush. Just enjoyment.[78]

It may not entirely be a coincidence that this image emerged in Paris. There is a cultural component to what is socially valued. For instance, while wealth became the overwhelming focus of desire and social comparison in the USA, materialism remained somewhat shameful in France.[79] Yet, despite the cultural anchors, values may change. Just as the materialistic craze is a relatively young phenomenon, it could conceivably ebb away. That may seem hard to believe, but there are already unmistakable trends in that direction.[80] This has to do with concern for the planet while at the same time offering fresh ways to show high status. As luxury has become increasingly available to the masses, new symbols are needed to signal that you belong to a different league. For example, using sustainable alternatives to luxury goods, second-hand vintage items, and homemade clothes. The same holds for diet. High-end haute cuisine is moving toward local food and plant-based proteins. Consider the famous example of Eleven Madison Park, mentioned in Chapter 5. This three-Michelin-star restaurant in New York was considered one of the best in the world when the pandemic gave them time to rethink the concept. They decided to make their menu entirely plant based. A risky decision. Would they lose their star status? It worked out well, to say the least.[81] The menu remained equally expensive and the restaurant maintained its top rating with Michelin, its peers, and the public. So much for the inevitability of meat as the ultimate food to strive for.

Not only is conspicuous materialistic wealth falling out of favor with the elite, but being conspicuously busy is going out of fashion. For decades you could impress colleagues and friends by being so, so busy all the time, which showcased your work ethic and the importance of your career. Now, this busy-busy aura is becoming a loser attitude. Instead, like in the days when the *flâneurs* in Paris were envied, displaying your capacity to enjoy leisure time is again in vogue. Walking a turtle has been replaced by activities such as outdoor sports, the gym, knitting your own clothes, and slow cooking, proudly shared on social media. The signal is clear. It is not cool to be a workaholic. At least, that's the attitude of Generation Z.[82]

You may think that those are just fringe movements. Surely working less and consuming less will remain limited to small elite groups and have little global impact in the end? Not necessarily. There are two reasons why such changes could end up making a big difference. First, the current elites include the people with the highest ecological footprint in the world. So changes in their preferences have a disproportional impact. Second, and more importantly, there is a historical pattern that has repeated over and over again: Elite behavior is eventually copied by the masses in an attempt to signal belonging to the same elite.[83] That is how a massive decline in human impact on the planet could conceivably happen. An uncoupling of status from overconsumption. Status is hardwired as a driving force for behavior. High status comes with esteem, respect, and admiration, generating a plethora of benefits such as better access to scarce resources, better mating choices, better health, better treatment in social interactions, and more influence on joint decisions. We will always seek ways to improve our social status. But ruining the planet through overconsumption does not have to be one of them. Some may disagree,[84] but

I would say that it is perfectly compatible with human nature to form a society where status is not related to overconsumption. Where we work less and still obtain what gives us pleasure and satisfaction. A society of leisure.

Morality as an Invisible Hand

But surely we rely on the desire for money to incentivize people to do what it takes to make society function? Yes and no. Money is indispensable to make the division of labor possible on large scales. It allows me to buy a loaf of bread with the money I earn through teaching. I don't have to grow the grain, thresh, and grind it, and cut wood to heat the oven. In small-scale societies my bread could probably still be acquired without money if I taught the children of the farmer and the baker at the local village school. But obtaining my smartphone without monetary interactions becomes a different story. Money is indispensable to facilitate a global market for exchanging goods and services, and without such a functioning market we cannot keep global society running. Yet money does not have to be a whip to make people fall in line with society's needs. Adam Smith got it right when he coined the term "the invisible hand" to describe how markets miraculously organize what people do. As if directed by an invisible hand, people behave in ways that make sure that the necessary goods and services are available at good prices. But, as we have seen, this invisible hand needs help, or else things go wrong in many ways. Wealth becomes concentrated in the hands of a few, who subsequently corrupt society. Strong institutions are needed to prevent that. A centrally led system without markets is not the answer, as illustrated by the dramatic famines and other problems caused by misguided centralization in the former Soviet Union and China. We need the invisible hand of markets but cannot allow it to lead to rampant materialism or corrupt the way societies are governed, as that is precisely what pushed us into the hole we are in. Fortunately, there are other primordial forces that may drive human behavior. Forces that are more powerful in guiding human behavior and have fewer negative side effects: morality, altruism, and the deeply felt desire to be part of something bigger than oneself.

Humans are hardwired to be moral. For one thing, we reject unfairness. We have all seen how children go out of their minds when something is perceived as unfair. Anger over unfairness is deeply rooted in evolutionary history. A famous proof of that has been given by primatologist Frans de Waal.[85] During his professional life he has successfully challenged the view that we are fundamentally different from monkeys.[86] Obviously things such as language, culture, and science do set humans apart. But, as de Waal has shown, we are very much the same when it comes to social behavior or moral sentiments. For good reasons, his book *Chimpanzee Politics*, describing the social interactions and intrigues he observed in a group of chimps, was put on the recommended reading list for new members of Congress in the USA. The famous fairness experiment came later. I guarantee a good laugh if you watch it online.[87] The scientists have two monkeys in a cage, separated by bars but in plain view of each other. Their task is easy. If the monkey returns a pebble received from the scientist, it receives a piece of cucumber as a reward. This all goes well until the researcher starts giving one of the monkeys grapes instead of cucumber. Of course, a sweet grape is much more desirable than a boring piece of cucumber. The difference is immediately noticed by the disadvantaged monkey. Next time it is paid a piece of cucumber in exchange for the pebble, it immediately throws the cucumber back at the experimenter and angrily slaps the table to call for attention. The next time, uncertain what caused the situation, it examines the stone, as if something might be wrong with it, before turning it in. Then, when paid cucumber again, the anger explodes, and the outraged monkey shakes the cage in despair.

The strong aversion to unfairness is matched by an equally deeply rooted tendency to behave altruistically.[88] Experiments with monkeys, rats, and other animals show how widespread, and thus ancient, the capacity for empathy is. People are no exception. There is a widespread misunderstanding that humans are basically selfish. Nothing could be further from the truth, as argued beautifully in the book *Humankind* by Rutger Bregman.[89] Using a wide range of scientific studies and illuminating historical events, Bregman shows how important altruism is in shaping modern human behavior. Of course we know this. Strangers invariably try to help you if you lose your way. In the countryside you may well be invited in for coffee or more as a bonus. Ask a stranger for help, and they are usually happy to come to your aid. Happy indeed because it gives them pleasure. Doesn't it give you a good feeling when you get the ketchup bottle that was on a too-high supermarket shelf and hand it to that small lady who couldn't reach it? Or when you can comfort a person in distress? Or share your homemade lunch at work with a colleague who forgot to bring theirs? Helping, sharing, consoling – it all is very rewarding. This has an ancient neuronal basis that we share with monkeys, birds, and rats among other creatures.[90] For instance, elephants help each other out of the mud. Crows comfort distressed peers. Rats even prefer rescuing a drowning companion over getting a chocolate. And prosocial behavior is not limited to the same species. Your dog will comfort you when she feels you need it, and vice versa. Just like other social animals, we want to do good.

So where does our misguided selfish self-image come from? Economists could be partly to blame. An overly simplistic view of Darwin's principle of survival of the fittest, combined with the false belief that human behavior is driven by rational choices, was merged into the influential concept of *Homo economicus*. The idea is that humans behave by and large as wealth-maximizing machines. That is a convenient assumption for elegant mathematical models. But the concept is entirely flawed. It is a dangerous false belief. Dangerous because, despite good intentions, it has guided the design of counterproductive incentive systems. It may seem obvious that money is a good way to stimulate people to behave in ways that are best for society at large. In some situations that works. For instance, subsidizing solar panels and paying for excess generated power delivered back to the grid has boosted the spread of photovoltaic systems in many places. But there are also many examples of how monetary incentives can destroy prosocial behavior. A famous study illustrates how this may cause monetary incentives to have the opposite effect of their intention.[91] Parents often arrive late to collect their kids from daycare centers, forcing teachers to stay after closing time. To do something about that, a group of centers in Haifa, Israel, introduced a fine for late-arriving parents. Surprisingly, the fine caused the number of late-coming parents to increase further. Apparently, social pressure against coming late was more effective than the monetary incentive, which may instead have signaled that it was okay to collect your kids late as long as you paid for it. Strangely, it was also an irreversible effect. The behavior stayed the same after the fine was removed again. This is just the tip of the iceberg when it comes to the potentially antisocial effects of money, as shown by a host of studies in which people are subconsciously 'primed' to have money on their minds. This can be done, for instance, by giving half the participants mouse mats with dollar signs while the other half has nonmonetary images. Or by asking half of them to unscramble a text in which money plays a role and the others a control text without money cues. It turns out that priming minds with money causes people to behave more self-interestedly. They become less compassionate, empathetic, and helpful. At the same time, they become less likely to ask for help.[92] Thus, while money is needed for large-scale societies to function, it can also stand in the way of prosocial behavior. If it becomes too dominant, the new invisible hand of money-mediated interactions tends to undo the good work of the original invisible hand of moral behavior.

It is a tantalizing tension. For almost our entire evolutionary history, morality has guided behavior, making groups work. Money enabled civilization, the enormous upscaling of societies that came with the rise of agriculture and sedentary life. It has always been an indispensable part of the package deal, together with script, hierarchy, division of labor, and more.[93] The use of money is not in our genes, but we cannot do without it unless we return to the Stone Age. Fortunately, its overwhelming dominance is not set in stone. The degree to which people turn to money to get things done varies widely between cultures. Research shows that the motivating power of money is stronger in the United States and England than in China, India, Mexico, and South Africa. In the latter countries other motives, such as helping others, turned out to be more important. More generally, in collectivist cultures people live by informal reciprocity and see formal contracts as nuisances and threats to social harmony.[94] The other good news is that individualism is not hardwired either. Remember the change in the I:we ratio in books.[95] Extreme individualism in English-speaking countries and the rest of the Global North is a recent thing. It bloomed in parallel to the rise of neoliberal thought, which permeated societies and even changed the way people see themselves.[96]

In conclusion, the relentless pursuit of material wealth is not in our genes. It is a recent cultural phenomenon. That implies that we can get rid of it too. There is lots of good thinking about what an economy aimed at well-being rather than the consumptive rat race could look like,[97] but much less about the harder question of how a shift to such a new setting might realistically happen.[98] In the final chapter we will get back to the question of how some of the obstacles to our natural prosocial tendencies may be removed. But before I get to that, we have to face the elephant in the room. What if the change goes too slowly? Will humanity be inevitably drawn into a spiral of death? As I will argue next, the answer is: not necessarily.

Buying Time

Clearly, it is possible for humanity to fit comfortably on the planet. We can spare the climate, preserve nature, and, as a bonus, become happier and less stressed out. But there are formidable hurdles on the way there. Bad habits, stubborn false beliefs, outdated institutions, and also the vested interests of powerful players that try to prolong the planet-consuming rat race. None of this will prevent change in the end. But delay is a problem because it drives species to extinction and allows climate change to climb to ever more damaging levels. As we saw in the failed-world section, this could well destabilize civilization entirely. The obvious question, therefore, is whether failure to act quickly makes such doomsday scenarios inevitable. As briefly outlined at the beginning of this chapter, there are options to buy time. They will not lead to as much human well-being as acting fast would, but they could still prevent the worst depending on how long it takes for humanity to turn the ship. I will first address the question of how much time society might need to change and then look at two ways to buy time: (1) cooling the Earth while greenhouse gases are still high; and (2) helping people move from the Global South to cooler places.

How Long Will we Need?

As we saw in Chapter 3, revolutions can change societies rapidly, and some technological advances or shifts in specific social norms may also unfold within a few decades. Yet the sustainability transition we require does not fall into any of those simple categories. It needs to be more integrative, with change happening across institutions, norms, and behavioral attitudes. How long might such a profound transition realistically take? It is hard to think of any valid historical analogs for the current global sustainability challenge. The world has changed in so many ways. On the other hand, human nature has remained the same over the millennia. The longing to be valued and to belong to a group remains a primordial driver of behavior. Meanwhile, in-group empathy and favoritism are constants, and out-group hate may flare up in times of uncertainty. Also, the basic principles of capitalism and governance have not changed fundamentally over the past century or so.[99] In light of that, the Dutch economic historian Jan Luiten van Zanden suggested to me that an analog to a sustainability transition might be found in the wave of social improvements that swept across the world starting around the 1870s and culminated in the Western European post-World War II welfare states. Like the abolition of slavery – another profound socio-economic transition – the process of social improvements took almost a century to complete, with accelerations during the Progressive Era, the Great Depression in the USA, and the postwar rebuilding period in Europe. Could a sustainability transition follow a comparable path in terms of timescales? If we take the 1970s as the starting point of major worries about the environment, could a gradual push–pull process accelerated by one or more major crises be largely complete a century later, around 2070?

As we saw in Chapter 3, the century of social improvements came as a reaction to the massive social ills produced by the Industrial Revolution. While problems were addressed through revolutions in Russia, China, and other places, the response in Western Europe and the USA was more gradual. The improvements came about through a variety of changes. Reduced child mortality and increased vaccination rates were driven in part by technological advances. Other changes, such as the rise in literacy and the representation of women in government, reflect social emancipation. Importantly, taxation and other institutions for wealth redistribution drastically reduced inequality within countries from 1900 to 1980. In line with other emancipatory trends that allowed disadvantaged groups to rise to a more equal position in society, the incomes of rich and poor within countries became closer. For instance, the average income of someone among the poorest 50 percent nearly doubled relative to that of someone among the top 10 percent over those eight decades.[100]

Thus, in reaction to the problems caused by the Industrial Revolution, societies in most countries have become much fairer through a series of institutional revisions that unfolded over roughly a century. As we saw in Chapter 5, many positive societal trends began to backtrack around 1980. But while those reversals are worrying, humanity had by then realized massive social improvement within a century, through a combination of technological advances, shifting social norms, and a series of institutional revisions. This is precisely the mix needed for a massive sustainability transition. Would a century therefore be a realistic timescale for such change? And if worries about environmental degradation started around 1970 – accelerating around 2000 – could a parallel trajectory toward a full transition in the 2070s be possible?

This is, of course, impossible to say. One reason for this unpredictability is that big transformations are often triggered by unforeseeable crises. For instance, the Great Depression and World War II have played a role as catalysts in the century of social improvements. As argued, the reforms were accidents in waiting. Ideas about these new directions had been shaped over the preceding decades, but societies remained stuck in the status quo until a major perturbation allowed them to break loose. That raises the question of what crisis could possibly trigger a fundamental revision in the way economies are organized. Droughts, heatwaves, and wildfires in the Global North? Climate-triggered conflicts and mass migration from the Global South? Widespread psychosocial damage from social media?

Perhaps, but while such crises are largely unpredictable, the potential direction of the change they may unleash is not. What happens during such crises will depend largely on how we start to make sense of the sustainability issue now. That will be the topic of the next two chapters. The better we collectively understand the problems, the swifter society can tip out of trouble. That is hugely important because the longer it takes to curb the loss of ecosystems and climate change, the larger the overshoot and the more dangerous the effects.[101] By the time societies complete the sustainability transition, the climate may already have changed a lot. Such climate change can eventually be reversed by taking greenhouse gases out of the atmosphere. Much of nature may recover once we reduce our footprint. Yet other changes, such as the melting of ice caps, loss of soils, and extinction of species, are harder to reverse. Most importantly, recovering from such an overshoot scenario will also take time. Perhaps another century or more. Thus, humanity may face a few centuries during which much of the Global South is unsuitable for human habitation while vast areas in the Global North become better for agricultural production and human life. Making the best of such a scenario will require international cooperation to reverse planetary demise and facilitate the redistribution of people over the globe. More about that later. First, we should consider a more tempting way to buy time: cooling the Earth through geo-engineering.

Dimming the Sun

Cooling the Earth may be done in ways that are relatively easy and cheap, but also very risky.[102] Although the effects on global weather patterns are uncertain, the basic principles of how the planet could be cooled are easy to understand. The temperature of the planet is the result of a dynamic equilibrium between incoming radiation from the Sun and outgoing radiation from the Earth back into space. The two have different colors – or, more correctly, wavelength spectra. Incoming radiation is mainly visible light. Outgoing radiation is more infrared, especially when it comes from dark surfaces. The wavelength of such heat radiation is longer than that of red light, making it impossible to see without the use of infrared cameras. Infrared radiation does not penetrate glass. That is why greenhouses and cars get so warm in the sun. Infrared light also struggles to pass easily through air if CO_2 and methane concentrations are high. Hence, the greenhouse effect that is warming the globe. Understanding how all this works in more detail points to ways in which the balance may be changed (Figure 6.11). To give you an idea: Snow and ice or other light-colored surfaces reflect

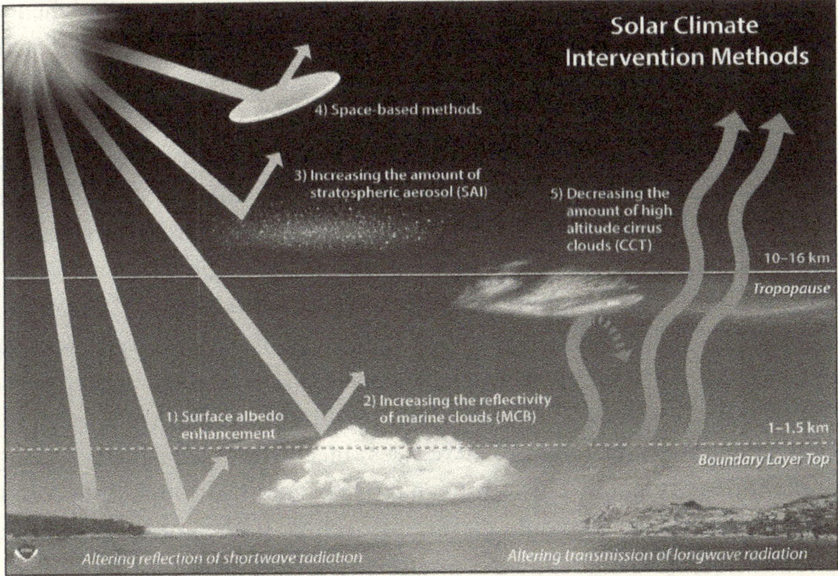

Figure 6.11 The radiation balance that controls the planet's temperature may be influenced through geo-engineering. (Figure by Chelsea Thompson, NOAA/CIRES, public domain.)

light before it can be turned into heat radiation. That is mostly bad news, of course, as the melting of ice and snow makes warming worse. A bit may be done about that by creating snow and painting roofs and roads, but the effects would be small. Low clouds also reflect incoming radiation, and those may be enhanced, for instance, by using ships to spray seawater into the air. By contrast, high clouds add to the greenhouse effect, so thinning those by injecting different substances could help cooling. More popular and better researched is the idea of using airplanes to inject tiny particles known as aerosols high into the atmosphere. Something similar also happens naturally when large volcanoes erupt. For instance, when Mount Pinatubo in the Philippines erupted in 1991, global temperatures dropped temporarily by 0.5 °C, and a cooling effect remained measurable for nearly two years. Engineering such effects is relatively cheap. An estimated annual amount of about $18 billion would be needed for each degree of avoided warming,[103] a tiny fraction (c. 1/10000) of the $80 trillion global economy. In fact, Elon Musk alone could foot the bill for the coming decade using his current worth of hundreds of billions of dollars.

What are we waiting for, you may say. But not so fast. It is indeed cheap. But it also has an element of playing Russian roulette with humanity and the planet. Effects are hard to predict, especially when it comes to the global distribution of precipitation. For instance, it is uncertain whether the Asian and African summer monsoons could be harmed,[104] implying potential food insecurity for billions of people. Theoretically, there are many ways to fine-tune the process. But the problem is that it will be hard to agree on what must be done. This is because there will always be winners and losers, and there will always be disagreement on whether changes are due to the engineering activities. As is the case with assigning current extreme events to global warming, uncertainty will remain large. If potential interventions went wrong, and indeed drove mass mortality and political instability, it might also ignite global conflict.[105] Another issue is the risk of becoming complacent. If it works well enough, there is less incentive to curb further rising greenhouse gas levels. This means that ocean acidification, killing corals and other organisms, would go on, unchecked. It also means that if the permanent replenishment of the stratosphere with particles is interrupted – due, for instance, to sabotage or wars – we would all be cooked, quite literally. Temperatures would rise very rapidly, creating havoc in ways that are hard to fathom. Those risks have led to a widespread opinion that we should not go down the path of solar radiation engineering, not even do research in that direction. As we have seen, it would not be the first time in history that technological advances created unintended collateral damage. Nonetheless, the effects of continuing along the current path of climate change would be disastrous too, so it is a tantalizing choice. To settle this dilemma, the US National Academy of Sciences has looked into the issue carefully, eventually recommending research into the effects and risks that would be intensified rather than halted.[106]

Moving the People

Another way to buy time as greenhouse gas concentrations keep rising is equally challenging. As large parts of the Global South and other regions become nearly uninhabitable, vast areas in the Global North would become available (Figure 6.12). It thus makes sense that in a warmer world people would move. The geographical distribution of many animals and plants is already shifting in response to climate change.[107] In my country, winters have become milder, summers hotter, and spring arrives about a month earlier than it used to. Like my great-grandfather I have kept a nature diary for half a century, and the change

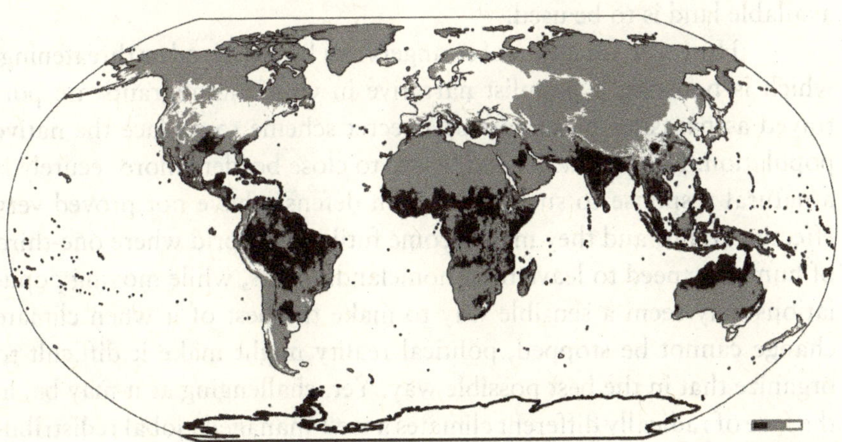

Figure 6.12 Global patterns of anticipated change in climate suitability for humans at the 2.7 °C of global warming expected under current policies. Black areas will deteriorate, grey regions remain roughly equal in suitability, while the white land regions will improve in terms of the human climate niche. (Figure by Xu Chi based on Lenton *et al.*, "Quantifying the human cost of global warming."[108])

is striking. Many species that I used to know from Mediterranean areas have now come to Holland. This is how nature has responded to climate change many times before. With the come and go of glaciation periods, species have always shifted their living areas. This allowed most of them to survive in the long run. Humans have been no exception. But this way of adjusting to changing conditions has become more complicated with the rise of nations and borders. Two centuries ago the world consisted of unclaimed land, empires, and city-states that could be crossed without passports. Not anymore, and that makes it more difficult to move to better places if necessary.

Climate change affects nations very differently. There will be winners and losers in terms of livability. The winners are mostly in the Global North and the losers in the Global South, boosting the already existing inequalities. This may seem a recipe for a disaster in which the Global North keeps its borders shut, leaving the Global South in ever more misery. But that is much too a simple view. The vast areas in the north that become better for human occupation and agriculture can lead to great prosperity, but only if people relocate to make that happen. As it stands, many nations in the Global North are facing declining populations increasingly dominated by elderly people. Countries such as Germany and Canada are already adopting policies to attract immigrants. With climate change, that demand will increase if the newly available land is to be used.

However, an influx of strangers can be perceived as threatening, which is boosting a populist narrative in which immigrants are portrayed as parasites or as part of a secret scheme to replace the native population. Building walls and fences to close borders more securely is a natural response to such fears. Such defenses have not proved very effective so far, and they may become futile in a world where one-third of humanity need to leave their homelands. Thus, while moving populations may seem a sensible way to make the best of it when climate change cannot be stopped, political reality might make it difficult to organize that in the best possible way. Yet, challenging as it may be, in the face of radically different climates a well-managed global redistribution of people would be best for the Global South and the developed world alike.[109]

To make that happen, global coordination would be essential. This is already being prepared. For example, there is an agreement on how to ensure "Safe, Orderly and Regular Migration" signed by 164 nations.[110] That is just a first step. When a groundswell of mass migration grows, it will be vital that such intentions are translated into concrete plans to match migrant flows with the demand for labor in ways that benefit both the Global South and North.[111] But agreement on where people should move is not enough. Making the most of it requires organizing infrastructure such as new roads, villages, and cities with all facilities, services, and jobs. Furthermore, when a few billion people go to live in different parts of the world, the food system needs to be redesigned.

Many of the world's farmlands will lose their productivity due to heat, drought, salinization, and soil erosion. Such losses will be strongest in the Global South, where much of the agricultural production is now used for local consumption.[112] As this traditional local system coupling agricultural production and employment vanishes, it needs to be replaced by something working equally well or better on the new lands in the north. A fresh start should not repeat the errors made by the devastating industrial agriculture mentioned earlier. Instead, this will be a good moment to move to more elegant food production. More efficient, less wasteful, and more sustainable.

But perhaps the greatest challenge will be to make sure that newcomers and the receiving population integrate smoothly. We know from experience that this works best if housing and job markets work to mix ethnic and religious groups,[113] but making that happen requires effort, as segregation is a natural human tendency. While negative forces may be dominant, there are also some examples where receiving climate migrants has been perceived positively as an act of collective solidarity.[114] A lot depends on cultural sense-making, norms, and values, which are, in turn, closely linked to institutions ranging from media, arts, and law to education. For instance, primary schools may run dedicated programs that increase genuine interest in different cultures and experiences.[115]

Clearly, moving the people will be an immense social challenge. But if it is done well, there is a bonus in the long run. It is likely that, with the current and future array of techniques, atmospheric carbon can be brought down sufficiently to restore the preindustrial climate within a few centuries. The tropics would become livable again, and meanwhile, nature in other parts of the world would have bounced back too,[116] ready to receive people eager not to repeat the mistakes of the past. Ice caps and oceans are notoriously slow components of the

Earth's system, so they would need a little more time. This also means that we will have to go below historical carbon levels to cool the Earth to preindustrial temperatures. This is because a world with smaller ice caps absorbs more heat, and the huge volume of ocean water takes time to cool down. Nonetheless, the potential long-term perspective of a well-managed phase of adaptive migrations looks good.

In summary, even if we cannot stabilize the climate rapidly, there is reason for hope. But hope is not optimism. If humanity does not get its act together the current trajectory is grim. And the longer we wait, the higher the price. In the next chapters we ask how the systemic shift of attitudes that will be needed to stabilize and redistribute the Earth might happen.

7 THE INVISIBLE STRANGLING HAND

In the end a massive transformation of our societies is inevitable, but it can be for better or for worse. We are now ready to address the big question of our time: How can we enhance the odds of a graceful transition to an Anthropocene that we can be proud of? In this chapter we will analyze what precisely keeps us trapped on the wrong track. Why is there so little progress, despite the fact that most people feel they are doing the right thing? In the next chapter we will then ask how that gridlock may be solved.

Cleaning Mood

The good news, as we have seen, is that humanity has an impressive track record of social tipping, in which self-propelling mechanisms led to swift change, even if hopes were close to being dashed by long periods of stagnation. Time after time, cascading change has whisked societies out of trouble. Perhaps the most inspiring examples of social tipping are those where changes in social norms and values brought progress. Enlightenment thinking brought rationality and ethics to the fore. Over the centuries this mindset contributed to scientific progress and social justice in countless ways, including the end of slavery and child labor, and other movements of emancipation. But not all social transformations have been happy ones. Technological advances brought progress, but unforeseen problems too, including the climate crisis that may now push humanity to the brink. Meanwhile, rising discontent has caused states to collapse.

This finished off many evil and incompetent rulers, but their replacements were not always better, and the human costs of the conflict and chaos during such transformations were often overwhelming. A warning indeed. Change is desperately needed, but a collapse of the way in which modern societies are organized could play out in disastrous ways. Fortunately, a fundamental revision of the rules of societies does not have to be so violent.

To get our spirits up, let's remind ourselves once more of the American Progressive Era. The progressive movement was an escape from state capture. In many countries the Industrial Revolution had led to a situation in which wealth had accumulated in the hands of a small group, which used the resulting power to corrupt politicians. This allowed pollution, poverty, and other social ills to grow uncurbed in order to facilitate further wealth concentration. What I find especially inspiring about the American period of societal improvements is that there was no central planning. There was no one in the cockpit. The change movement emerged spontaneously. Growing discontent across all layers of society led to a broad progressive movement, making sense of the web of forces that kept them stuck. That ultimately powered an unstoppable wave of reforms that got society out of trouble, solving several problems at the same time. That's precisely what we need today, as we are facing the climate crisis and crumbling ecosystems amidst an unjust world. This confluence of problems may seem overwhelming, but it might be just what is needed to trigger a true rethink of the way we run the world. Something that gets the world out of the boiled-frog situation where the slow pace of worsening inhibits action.

Especially when it comes to the loss of nature, there is this kind of shifting baseline syndrome. The demise of nature has been a creeping issue to which humans have grown accustomed over millennia. Plato wrote in 360 BCE in his *Critias*:[1]

> What is left then, comparing that era with the present, resembles the skeleton of a diseased body. ... The mountains contained lots of trees of which there is still evidence nowadays, for ... it was not long ago that roof timbers were cut from the trees there for use in huge buildings and the rafters still survive to this day. ... What's more the soil was made fruitful by the annual rains sent by Zeus which were not wasted as happens

> nowadays by flowing into the sea from land that has been made
> bare. Rather since the land had plenty of soil it could indeed
> receive the water and store it in impervious clay ground. The
> water stored there was sent forth from the heights through
> hollows, providing plenty of flowing water for springs and
> rivers. The shrines that still remain where the springs once
> stood are an indication that what we are now saying about
> this region is true.

That sounds familiar, and indeed, not much has happened since Plato to protect nature. The problem has become worse and worse, bit by bit.[2] It was only about a century ago that worries about the destruction of nature led to a rise in state and private initiatives to establish protected areas. In America this happened as part of the progressive movement.[3] Social ills had been the main driver of discontent, but environmental protection became firmly integrated into the package. Although the upswing made a difference, pollution and encroachment on natural areas have proved hard to stop. The scale of the problems grew exponentially during the great acceleration. Yet somehow the threat to nature is not widely felt as a crisis.

Not so with the climate. Climate change was discovered only in the 1970s, and was initially hidden from sight to protect economic interests.[4] After a few decades of delay the public eye was suddenly opened to the astonishing scale of this global problem. Not only is climate change more recent than the loss of nature, it is also more obvious. Destruction of nature took place out of direct sight for most city dwellers, and the negative consequences for society remained unclear. Climate change, by comparison, arrived as a big bang that could not be missed. Awareness rose from marginal to massive within a few decades, as virtually everybody started to feel that it would threaten their children's lives.

Perhaps that makes it easier to spring into action. The upswing proves that once society awakens, problems can be addressed as a package rather than competing for attention. Triggered by the social crisis, what emerged around 1900 was an integrative problem-solving period. We need something like that now, only bigger. A movement in which the urgency of the climate crisis inspires global systemic change that also addresses social unfairness and the demise of ecosystems. An upswing into a good Anthropocene.

Of course this sounds easier than it is, and there will be trade-offs that can make it hard to address different problems in one shot. For instance, some forms of climate action can hamper nature or social justice.[5] The production of biofuels or of biomass for underground storage of carbon requires arable land. This competes with land needed to produce food and protect nature. Clearly, integrative problem solving is challenging and we shouldn't be uncritical of the achievements of the Progressive Era in that sense. The Americans got a lot done, but the emancipation of black people was not part of the package at that time. Yet this historical period illustrates that out of a seemingly hopeless situation in the grip of a powerful corrupt elite, society can get in a 'cleaning mood,' addressing a range of problems at once. The question thus is how we can make that happen again.

Free Will

If you ask people how things should be changed, many point to their fellow citizens or to the government. They are right. Everyone's behavior matters, and good policies are needed to improve well-being, fairness, and sustainability. But behaviors and policies are emergent features of society. They arise from the complex whole. My behavior, choices, and attitudes are not as intrinsic to me as I like to think (more about that later). Thus, I cannot change them by myself. The same applies, on a different level, with governance. We cannot simply change policies. They emerge. That doesn't mean we cannot change at all. Rather, it means that if we want to change behavior, attitudes, choices, and policies, we should understand how they emerge and change their drivers. Rather than relying on those in the cockpit, it is wiser to assume that the cockpit is essentially empty. Societies with their laws, policies, and elites emerge from all participants' interactive attitudes and behaviors. In a way we are all just ants in a big ant colony. That may seem to suggest that no one can have any effect on humanity's direction. But that is too simple, just as it is too simple to point fingers at conspicuous players. Certainly, some have much more impact than others. Think of Vladimir Putin, Elon Musk, Karl Marx, Adolf Hitler, or Mahatma Gandhi. Of course such key persons do not come out of thin air to play their role. Elon Musk comes from a wealthy entrepreneurial background, and Gandhi saw how the suffragettes got female emancipation going in London.[6] Counterintuitively, rather than being independent original agents, such exceptional individuals and their opportunities for change-making are also part of the emergent dynamics of society. Yet there are huge differences in the capacity of individuals to nudge societies in particular directions. Such potential comes in different flavors. Marx and Gandhi had a very different kind of power than Putin and Musk. In politics the term 'soft power' is sometimes used to capture the capacity to shape the preferences of others through appeal and attraction rather than coercion.[7] But appeal and attraction to what?

As we have seen throughout the book, societies may be attracted to states of being that are bad for most of their citizens. Such traps may function via coercive power or appeal, drawing people to the wrong thing. That is precisely the problem we have now. Societies are complex adaptive systems[8] but, rather than smoothly adapting to new evolving situations, they tend to get stuck in traps that are not good for the vast majority. Fortunately, unlike ant colonies, coral reefs, and many other complex adaptive systems, we have the capacity to analyze, understand, and resolve our traps. Or do we? To what extent can a society change course when it becomes clear that it is in a trap? This is analogous to the question of whether individual humans have free will. Does everything flow from the past in a deterministic fashion? Or is there scope for deliberate action? Like the individual free will dilemma, neither complete determinism nor smooth maximization of well-being characterize reality well. Traps are real, but societies can tip out of trouble when collective sense-making destabilizes the status quo.

On a deep philosophical level you may wonder if there is any scope for us to carve out our own future. Doesn't everything flow from the past in a deterministic way? Is free will an illusion? A tantalizing question that has been discussed since Aristotle. In a recent book the neuroscientist Kevin Mitchell presents a sophisticated argument in favor of free will.[9] During our lives we develop actorship, the capacity to act according to our own insights. As those insights evolve we may gain a better grip on the world around us. For instance, a person who suffers from recurrent depression may seek help and be trained in a set of cognitive and behavioral skills that can subsequently fend it off for decades.[10] Thus, if you are able to recognize destructive dynamics it may be possible to change them.

I like to think about society's free will along the same lines. Societies in trouble may be able to reshape the rules that govern their own dynamics. To see how, let's start with the counterintuitive fact that the actions taken by individuals and that ultimately shape the world flow largely from 'the system' that surrounds them: the options, prices, choices, ideals, norms, and values. Our behavior is guided by an invisible hand, as framed so powerfully by Adam Smith. Smith was thinking of the effect of supply and demand on markets, but the concept of emergent – rather than centrally planned – drivers of behavior makes sense more broadly too. The invisible hand that emerged from the mechanisms of civilization, technological advances, markets, and so forth has done much good. But now it is strangling us, keeping us stuck in a social trap. If we want to shape the future we should find out how to channel the forces that guide behavior in ways that lead to a good Anthropocene rather than the spiral of death.

Revealing the Hand

A necessary first step to liberate us from the strangling grip of the invisible hand is revealing how it works (Figure 7.1). Whether we are preachers, scientists, or CEOs, we do what we are driven to do, consciously or subconsciously. Let's take shopping as an example. What we purchase depends on our intentions and desires, and on the choices at hand. All of this is influenced by the invisible hand. The decision to go to a supermarket rather than several small, specialized shops depends on convenience, preference, and expected prices. Once inside, the choice of meat versus a meat substitute or vegetables depends on the options you see: The prices, the displays, how you feel about the products, the things you think you know and desire. Much of this is shaped by what we could call vested interest parties (VIPs), big corporations that need to grow to satisfy their stakeholders. Advertising companies, marketing specialists, and influencers are paid to advance the agenda. This edifice shapes what appears in the media, whether advertisements, news, movies, or stories on social media. All this can be regulated by governments but, as we saw, VIPs also have a strong grip on policies. Voters get the politicians they voted for, but not necessarily the policies that resolve their real issues. Thus, powerful parties with a vested interest in the status quo shape the conditions that drive choices to sustain that status quo. This maintains market dominance by fossil fuels, animal-based products, and consumption-based status signaling. Meanwhile there are counterforces too. People in a diverse range of societal roles, including

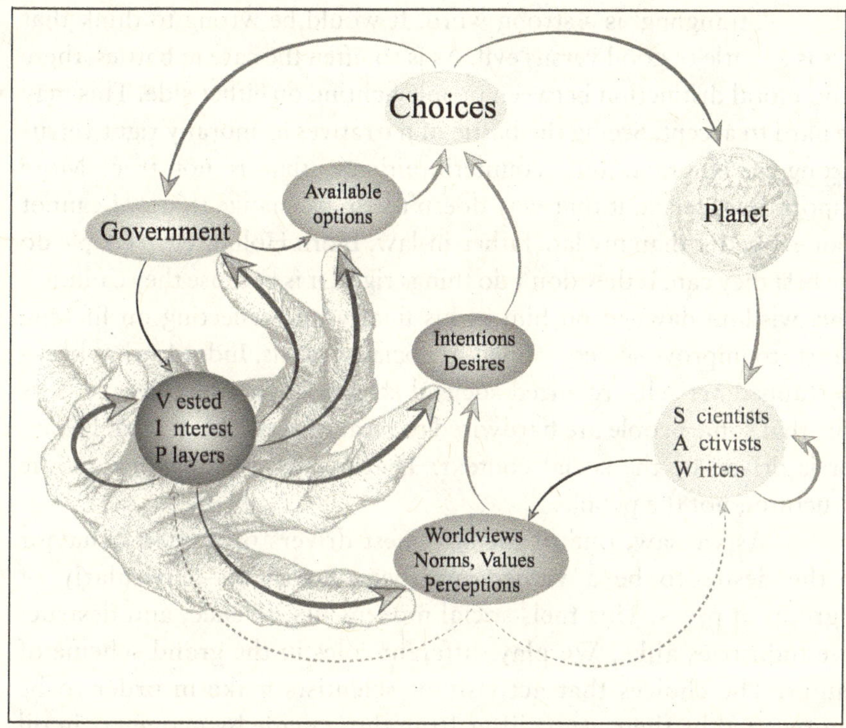

Figure 7.1 Revealing the invisible strangling hand. People's choices affect the planet and policies. Those choices depend only to a limited extent on our intentions. In practice, they are strongly shaped by the 'ecosystem' of what is on offer and the perceived costs and benefits. Marketing by corporations with vested interests in the status quo shapes that ecosystem. Through a range of media, the same vested interests have a disproportionately strong effect on the perceptions, norms, and values that shape the desires and intentions behind choices. Policies can control the power of vested interests but are themselves vulnerable to state capture by the rich and powerful. Counterforces come from citizens informed by changes in the planet and society revealed by scientists and journalists. However, for serious change to happen the grip of vested interests on perceptions, policies, and the ecosystem of choice must be broken through addressing state capture, market capture, and media capture. As discussed in Chapter 8, such change requires addressing the incentives that drive the behavior of individuals in professional groups ranging from policy makers and scientists to CEOs and educators.

scientists, activists, and writers (SAWs), see it as their task to point out things that are going wrong. Their contributions to sense making blend with the influence of VIPs and others in a battle of narratives shaping the social norms and values to which we are subject.

'Strangling' is a strong word. It would be wrong to think that this is a battle of good versus evil. As is so often the case in battles, there is no moral distinction between people fighting on either side. This may be hard to accept. Seeing the battle of narratives as morally right versus wrong is tempting. But, counterintuitively, that is not true. More importantly, seeing it that way doesn't help us change things. I cannot frame it better than my late father-in-law, Bjorn Holmgren: "People do the best they can. If they don't do things right, it is because they cannot." This wisdom dawned on him in his final years, reflecting on lifelong efforts to improve society guided by socialist ideals. Indeed, what keeps us trapped are self-organized societal structures, not bad people. It is true that some people are hardwired to be antisocial,[11] but most behavior is driven by the social context. That means we must change the structures, not the people.

As we saw, one of the strongest drivers of human behavior is the desire to be a valued member of society, particularly of a group of peers. This fuels social movements, science, and destructive industries alike. We play different roles in the grand scheme of things. The choices that activists or scientists make in order to be appreciated by their peers differ from those made by managers in oil companies or the meat industry. Each community has its own specific set of incentives to guide behavior. For instance, scientists gain respect from their peers if they publish in famous journals and are cited by many other scientists. Meanwhile, employees of corporations are valued if they make the company more profitable, help its market share grow, and make its shareholders wealthier. Following such incentives in the effort to become a valued member of one's peer group is part of why humanity's current trap is so resilient. Widely cited science does not necessarily produce the holistic insights needed to inspire attractive futures, and company profits may come at the cost of the planet and people.

At the same time, the desire to be a valued member of society may also be the key to escaping this trap. Despite differences in professional roles and peer groups, all of us are connected to an overarching set of perceptions, values, and norms. Conforming to this omnipresent cloud of norms is a prerequisite to being accepted as a valued member of society. So, how can people do so many bad things? That is largely because everyone tends to believe they are doing the right thing. We already saw how cognitive dissonance caused by inconsistencies in what people believe and observe can be resolved surprisingly well. Similar mechanisms achieve self-justification. In this case, the tension to be resolved is due to a moral dissonance resulting from inconsistency between unethical behavior and a moral self-image. Research shows that virtually all people want to be moral and honest.[12] But that does not mean that they behave accordingly. Instead, a range of coping mechanisms helps – often unconsciously – reduce the moral dissonance.[13] For one thing, the truth can always be stretched in many ways. But there are other mechanisms that help justify bad behavior. For instance, morally wrong behavior can be presented as altruism. An iconic example is Robin Hood, who robs the rich to help the poor. Power and status also justify immoral behavior. Surprisingly, experiments suggest that this is accepted not only by the powerful but also by their victims, who agree that power makes bad behavior more acceptable. Then there is the strategy of distancing, masking one's own moral failings while pointing to others' moral violations. Versions of this old trick have become increasingly popular in polarized debates where they are known under the apt name of 'whataboutism'. For instance, Putin, on being accused of atrocities in Ukraine, might well reply: "But what about Gaza? Isn't what has happened there much worse?" Moral licensing is another powerful mechanism, when people resolve moral dissonance resulting from bad behavior by doing something good too.

All these mechanisms have been demonstrated through elegant, controlled experiments,[14] and it is not hard to see them play out in real life. Billionaires' nagging guilty feelings about the questionable ways in which they acquired their wealth may ebb upon donating a few million to a good cause. People working for environmentally destructive companies may argue that their activities help mitigate poverty: regulation would hurt the poorest and, moreover, would only allow worse companies to take over. I am not saying that such reasoning does or does not make sense. Just that humans want to be moral, but also have effective coping mechanisms that make it easier to live with immoral behavior. Such coping mechanisms are the basis for narratives that make people feel good doing their jobs even if that involves promoting fossil-fuel use, destroying rainforests for meat production, making social media addictive, evading taxes, or undermining democracy. Also, narratives that appear plausible become shared beliefs through social reinforcement within groups. That is a powerful mechanism, as we saw in the section on beliefs. At the extreme end this is illustrated by the seemingly outra-geous beliefs held by some sects. Or on a smaller scale by shared delusions that may occur in isolated couples (*folie à deux*) or families.[15]

So, if everybody believes they are doing the right thing, how can we possibly tip society out of trouble? How can we get off the road to the collapse of climate, ecosystems, and human civilization? As I will argue, the answer is to make the dissonance more salient. People can be freed from society-wrecking bubble thinking. Consider the words of Andy Fastow, former chief financial officer of Enron who was responsible for one of the most prominent frauds in history: "I didn't set out to commit a crime. I certainly didn't set out to hurt anyone. When I was working at Enron, you know, I was kind of a hero, because I helped the company make its numbers every quarter. And I thought I was doing a good thing. I thought I was smart. But I wasn't."[16] We need such awareness of perverse incentives to become common. The way to make corporations behave better is to make the justification of unethical choices more difficult. At the same time, we must develop attractive prospects for a good Anthropocene. Make low-footprint choices easy and attractive. In other words, do all we can to reduce the resilience of the bad basin of attraction and to let the good basin of attraction grow. There is no silver bullet that will make everything change. Instead, there are many different things that can be done to increase the odds that humanity will shift into a better future. Some of those actions may seem futile, but in the grand scheme of things they are not. This is not so much because of their environmental impact but rather because they help nudge society toward a tipping point where change in the direction of a new and sustainable setting may become self-propelling. Throughout the book we have seen how such mechanisms work. Now, we will begin to specify what can be done.

Unmasking Bullshit

To help society release the grip of the invisible hand, it is vital to reveal explicitly how that grip is maintained. Stories are an import-ant part of that. Our brains did not evolve to look at numbers and graphs. We are guided much more by narratives. Narratives may inspire change, but can also prevent it. What, precisely, makes us falsely believe that change is impossible? What makes us believe that things should stay the way they are? Can we recognize the delusive narratives that delay progress? 'Delusive' sounds bad but, again, this is not about morality. Almost everyone believes they are doing the morally right things, even those who are opening new coal mines or destroying the rainforest. There is always a good story to justify one's actions, and that is a big problem. I say "almost everyone" because it would be naïve to neglect willful self-interested behavior that damages society. Some people are intrinsically antisocial,[17] and it is also true that the mere sensation of power can boost bad behavior.[18] Power matters, and we must be realistic. Massive resources are mobilized to maintain the status quo. Still, individuals playing their parts often do so with the best intentions, given the narratives, beliefs, and incentive structures that surround them. Of course they may feel some tension between broader societal norms, values, and perceptions, but their behavior can be driven by more direct incentives. Mechanisms of self-justification help overcome that moral dissonance, especially in the context of self-amplifying group dynamics. This is part of the invisible hand that keeps the ship on course for disaster. Therefore, the struggle to escape the grip of the strangling hand largely boils down to a battle of narratives. A continuous battle to debunk lines of seemingly convincing reasoning that discourage change.

Fortunately, the set of narratives that delays change is, in fact, limited. They come in endless variations, but seeing the archetypal storylines helps to recognize them. Making it easy to recognize the delusional narratives is important, as it allows us to address the bullshit head-on. In a way, that is how vaccination works. By presenting the body with fragments of specific pathogens. That teaches the immune system to be alert and recognize the real thing when it comes, allowing a quick, effective reaction to neutralize the pathogen before it has the chance to do too much damage and replicate. There is good evidence that this works for recognizing bullshit too. For instance, such an 'inoculation' strategy is effective in making people immune to fake news by showing them a range of examples that allow them to recognize the phenomenon in the future. In fact, this method works better than tagging messages on social media explicitly to warn people that it is fake news.[19] So here we go with some framings that are often used. After reviewing the archetypes, I will dig deeper into the intricate nature of bullshit and its antidotes.

Doubt Seeding

The book *Merchants of Doubt* is perhaps the best illustration of how effective delaying narratives can be, but also what unmasking them can do. The writers, Naomi Oreskes and Erik M. Conway, reveal striking parallels between the fabrication of controversy over climate change and earlier dynamics that delayed the regulation of smoking, DDT, acid rain, and the hole in the ozone layer. In each case the controversy was kept alive by spreading confusion and doubt, even though scientific consensus had already been reached. As historians of science, Oreskes and Conway meticulously reconstruct how such dynamics emerged. Key players in the book are physicists Fred Seitz and Fred Singer, scientists who challenged scientific consensus in fields ranging from the dangers of smoking and pesticides to the existence of anthropogenic climate change. Seitz and Singer were, along with a few other scientists, linked to conservative American institutions such as the Heritage Foundation that aim to prevent regulation in all kinds of ways and later helped prepare the agenda for the second term of Donald Trump. All of this is supported by private funders and large corporations with stakes in the game, such as Dow Chemical, ExxonMobil, and General Motors. Over time the tactics remained the same: discrediting the science, spreading false information, and creating confusion. That sounds morally wrong but, according to Oreskes and Conway, the dissenting scientists felt they were working for a good cause. They viewed any government regulation as a step toward socialism and communism, which they fiercely rejected. They thoroughly believed in free-market capitalism and wanted to prevent overreaction to problems, claiming that government intervention would be an intrusion into people's lives and freedom. *Merchants of Doubt* highlights one aspect of how sneakily the invisible hand works. While the effects are evil, the actors involved feel they are doing the right thing. Singer and Seitz were not entirely fringe scientists either. In fact, the work of Seitz on the behavior of atoms and electrons in the solid matter was respected, and in the 1960s he served some years as president of the American National Academy of Sciences, dedicated to making the world a better place.

The work of Oreskes and Conway reveals just how vulnerable scientific guidance is in society, even when virtually all science points in the same direction. The stories illustrate how easy it is to seed doubt. Even though scientific consensus on climate change was overwhelming, a tiny group kept a large audience believing that there was no consensus at all. The approach of the press didn't help. Giving equal space to skeptics and other scientists to highlight both sides of the argument may seem like good practice, but in the end it helped delay climate action for decades, with massive suffering projected over the coming century as a result. All with good intentions, of course.

Even when the doubt seeding was unmasked it proved exceedingly difficult to do something about it. Researchers became overly cautious. No one wanted to be seen as an irrational alarmist. The result was systematic "erring on the side of least drama." The scale of that problem dawned upon me in 2009 at a science-policy conference on global warming in Copenhagen. Upon listening to the scientists' explications, politicians asked us why we had not been clearer before. They had never imagined the problem was so serious. Science communication has improved since then. In a joint effort, the Intergovernmental Panel on Climate Change (IPCC), comprising hundreds of scientists globally, more clearly summarizes what is known and what is unknown. Yet, even if we know how it works, doubt seeding remains a hard nut to crack. Have you ever seen a kid meticulously building a tower of blocks and then knocking it over with the press of a finger? The effort necessary to destroy is much smaller than that needed to build. As we saw, that is very much true for trust. Trust in science. Trust in institutions.

Complicating

Although doubt seeding affected the notion that climate change was real, it only delayed action. A very costly delay, but still. Now almost everyone, everywhere, is convinced that humans are profoundly changing the climate. We can see it with our own eyes, just as we can see that nature is being destroyed. But that doesn't automatically translate into action. That is where other delaying narratives come into play. One archetype is 'complicating.'[20] It goes something like this: "You may think we can resolve the problem that way, but you are hopelessly naïve. You clearly do not understand how the world works. It really is not as simple as that." Of course, everything is always complicated. Also, much may be uncertain. But that does not mean that we do not know enough to act. For instance, the effects of plastic on biodiversity and ecosystem functioning are complex, uncertain, and perhaps minor. The first pictures of albatrosses dying from ingestion of plastic were published in 1969, but it took at least four decades for the topic to attract public attention. The eventual rise in interest was in part due to some iconic 2009 photographs that touched people's hearts:[21] remains of decomposed albatross chicks in the sand, their bones and feathers surrounding plastic cigarette lighters, bottle caps, and so forth. Scientists have studied the impacts of plastic in many ways but haven't quite agreed on the severity of the problem for natural populations. Indeed, that is a complicated topic, but isn't the mere image of plastic on the beach sufficient to spur action? A few dramatic pictures got the ball rolling, and now plastic has risen to the top of environmental concerns. Perhaps unjustly so, as other forms of pollution are much more dangerous for people and nature.[22] Yet plastic has become a poster child of environmental concern and has helped people see how pollution works and how it can be solved. It also allows everyone to engage and show they care about the environment. It shows that we don't need to know how everything works to get mobilized. Although the effects on nature and human health are not yet resolved, the UN is slowly working on a global ban on single-use plastics.

The plastic story is also a reminder that visual representation of a problem may sometimes do more than hundreds of scientific articles. Seeing is believing. Seeing complete forests die helped with solving the acid rain problem.[23] And even though it took decades, plastic pollution is an easier target than invisible pollution. By contrast, air pollution by fine particles and gases is still responsible for nearly 7 million deaths annually,[24] even without taking climate change effects into account. But invisibility is only one aspect. Regulation of pollution is hard in part because the problems are perceived as complicated. Industries may argue that the processes and products such as pesticides or per- and polyfluoroalkyl substances (PFAS) are indispensable and that closing down polluting factories would only allow worse ones to flourish in other places. Most governments don't even try. As *The Lancet Planetary Health* wrote in 2022:

> Despite strong and growing evidence for pollution's contribu-
> tion to . . . mortality . . . control programmes focus almost exclu-
> sively on behavioural and metabolic risk factors such as tobacco
> use, exercise, and obesity, while ignoring pollution . . . our
> review of pollution policies in countries around the world
> finds little substantive progress in the development of pollution-
> control policies, even in the most severely affected countries.[25]

Indeed, it is easier to tell people they should exercise and eat healthily than to change their environment. That environment is shaped largely by corporations with vested interests and sophisticated storytelling power to convince you that it is all more complicated than you think, and that change is virtually impossible.

Fear Seeding

Another aspect of delay arguments is focused on predicting that regulation would have disastrous effects for ordinary people. A typical narrative goes something like: "You cannot do that. The prices of food, transport, and heating would go up, hitting the poorest most of all." This may sound like a convincing argument, but it is not. The real problem here is inequality, not the cost of abolishing practices that will ruin the future of humanity. Taxation of fuel powered the Yellow Vest movement. But there would have been no problem without conspicuous wealth inequality or if the reduction of carbon output had been realized in ways that would not disproportionally hurt the poor. An elegant example of a solution to the latter was France's eventual decision to make small electric cars available at a low monthly cost to everyone. The cars soon ran out because of the overwhelming success.[26] But it proved my point: You can't expect broad support for climate issues if it injures the masses. I think Thomas Piketty is absolutely right.[27] To get majority support for tackling the climate issue, it needs to be shaped as a matter of social justice. Change won't happen if we frame the choice in such a way that environmental protection comes at the cost of the common people. However, that often happens despite massive inequality being in plain sight. Not only do the richest 1 percent own almost half the global wealth, they also emit more carbon than the poorest two-thirds of humanity.[28] Clearly, the cost of solutions does not have to amplify inequality. More about practical ways to do that later. Nevertheless, creating fears of an unbearable rise in the cost of living is a sure way to gain support for populist narratives against climate action or the protection of nature.

Seeding fear and doubt. Making things seem overly complicated. It all feeds into something we could call hope dashing. As we have seen, hope stimulates people to act. The idea that nothing can be done is one of the great threats to progress. Malicious regimes make their populations feel powerless, thereby increasing their grip. Similarly, narratives that make people believe that it is too complicated and risky to change are dangerous because they take the wind out of the sails of change.[29] A sustainable good Anthropocene is perfectly possible. Let nobody make you believe otherwise, or else it will become impossible to achieve.

Greenwashing

There is something else that can take the wind out of the sails of change. Something deceptively positive: offering fake 'green' products that promise to somehow mitigate their environmental impact. Greenwashing is an elephant in the room when it comes to bullshitting.[30] Taking advantage of the desire of people to do good, draining good intentions of their power. As soon as people feel that something is morally wrong, be it child labor, pesticides, or carbon emissions, they are motivated to do something about it. This massive energy can propel change. But it is also an opportunity for companies and entrepreneurs to gain a competitive edge by presenting their products as morally better in order to charge a higher price.[31] The invisible hand will, of course, push companies to do this at the lowest possible cost. For consumers it feels great. That way we can fly on planes and eat beef without feeling guilty. The catch, of course, is that greenwashing is often based on a thin veneer. The environmental impacts of green-washed products are not much less than those of the competition. It may seem that this is relatively harmless, but it isn't. That is because of the moral licensing effect. If we do something morally good, we are more likely to do something morally wrong later. Subconsciously we are keeping a moral balance over the course of the day. For instance, in one study researchers found that people behaved less altruistically and were more likely to steal and cheat after buying green products than after buying conventional ones.[32] Greenwashing is thus a huge problem. Regulation is starting to improve, but greenwashing is like a hydra, a multi-headed monster in Greek mythology on which two new heads appeared every time one head was cut off. That is the work of the invisible hand. There simply is a massive economic incentive for this way of cheating. And greenwashing is not alone. There are variations ranging from we-washing and she-washing to bee-washing, appealing to emotions about the lack of community, female participation, and honeybee protection, just to name a few. Beware. As my bee-studying long-time friend Katja Hogendoorn put it succinctly, "Washing stinks!"

The Myth of Free Choice

Another delaying strategy is the suggestion that change must come from the wishes and behavior of individual consumers. On the surface that seems to make sense and empower us all. Except that, as we saw, that our decisions are driven largely by our environment, on what is available, and how we feel about it. That, in turn, is largely shaped by companies. The same companies meanwhile promote the idea that consumers should be free to choose. A sneaky strategy, because shifting the responsibility to the consumers lets such companies off the hook. A good illustration of how this works is the concept of the carbon footprint. Online calculators allow everyone to compute their CO_2 output, giving insight into how we may shrink it. That is a good idea. But guess who popularized it? Big Oil behemoth BP, along with its advertising, marketing, and public relations agency Ogilvy & Mather. The explicit strategy of shifting responsibility to the consumer combined with other deceptive framings has been revealed nicely in a systematic analysis of four decades' worth of climate communications by ExxonMobil.[33] This is how the researchers present their findings for a general audience:

> A dominant public narrative about climate change is that "we are all to blame." Another is that society must inevitably rely on fossil fuels for the foreseeable future. How did these become conventional wisdom? We show that one source of these arguments is fossil fuel industry propaganda. ExxonMobil advertisements worked to shift responsibility for global warming away from the fossil fuel industry and onto consumers. They also said that climate change was a "risk," rather than a reality, that renewable energy is unreliable, and that the fossil fuel industry offered meaningful leadership on climate change.

Adjusting to the reality of public opinion, ExxonMobil shifted in the mid-2000s from seeding doubt about climate change to two other narratives: a socioeconomic threat narrative (seeding angst about a transition) and a fossil-fuel savior narrative stating that fossil-fuel companies are passive suppliers, and that customers are to blame for demanding their damaging products. They also stressed that continued fossil-fuel dominance is inevitable, given the insufficiency of low-carbon technologies (hope dashing), and that fossil-fuel use is reasonable and responsible because it has profound benefits and only ambiguous, uncertain climate effects.

The constructed myth of free choice has been particularly well studied for the fossil-fuel industry, where it helps to turn the focus away from their pervasive marketing, disinformation campaigns, and lobbying against climate and clean-energy policies. But, just like the other false narratives, promoting the myth of free choice is a common pattern across industries. Most companies now offer more sustainable options. Sometimes heavily greenwashed, sometimes real. Food companies offer vegan alternatives. Shell offers electric car-charging stations powered by renewable energy. All this is good, but we should keep our eyes on the ball. In the end, consumer demand is largely shaped by companies and policies.

Debunking Bullshit

The term 'bullshit' may seem a bit rude to use in a civilized book like this, but, with respect to the narratives we discussed, it gives us food for thought. Originally vulgar slang, the word bullshit captures something deep and important. No one has argued that more succinctly than the philosopher Harry G. Frankfurt in his famous short work *On Bullshit*,[34] which builds on an earlier piece, "The Prevalence of Humbug"[35] by Max Black. Both are hilarious reading, but they are also dead serious. Each author makes the point that bullshit and the related humbug are slippery phenomena. Different from lies and, because of their murky nature, more dangerous too. Frankfurt's opening sentences are fabulous: "One of the most salient features of our culture is that there is so much bullshit. Everyone knows this. Each of us contributes his share. But we tend to take the situation for granted."

Black opens: "Humbug has the peculiar property of being always committed by others, never by oneself. This is one reason why it is universally condemned," and provides the reader with a tentative definition as a "deceptive misrepresentation, short of lying, especially by pretentious word or deed, of somebody's own thoughts, feelings, or attitudes." To illustrate the dangerous nature and the subtle contrast to lying, he quotes the poet William Blake (in his famous poem "Auguries of Innocence"):

> A truth that's told with bad intent
> Beats all the lies you can invent.

Frankfurt unpacks the difference between bullshit and lying as follows:

> It is impossible for someone to lie unless he thinks he knows the truth. Producing bullshit requires no such conviction. A person who lies is thereby responding to the truth, and he is to that extent respectful of it. When an honest man speaks, he says only what he believes to be true; and for the liar, it is correspondingly indispensable that he considers his statements to be false. For the bullshitter, however, all these bets are off: he is neither on the side of the true nor on the side of the false. His eye is not on the facts at all, as the eyes of the honest man and of the liar are, except insofar as they may be pertinent to his interest in getting away with what he says. He does not care whether the things he says describe reality correctly. He just picks them out, or makes them up, to suit his purpose.

Do you recognize some political debating styles in this? Those philosophers were not referring specifically to the delusive narratives that tighten the grip of the invisible hand. But it is easy to see how their observations apply. None of the narratives are outright lies. They consist of elements that make sense, and the narrators may even believe the stories themselves ("second-degree humbug," according to Max Black). But, once you recognize bullshit, what can be done? For short-term remedies in a debate, Black recommends asking the humbugger questions such as "Do you *really* believe that?" or "Do you really *mean* that?" (If the answer is yes, he recommends saying, "How extraordinary!") But this strategy may backfire, as it cynically hints at immoral motives in the bullshitter. That is not helpful. Experiments show that moral questioning pushes subjects into a physiological threat state reflected in a distinct set of cardiovascular markers.[36] This threat response causes rigidity and anchoring in conflict situations, derailing all possibilities for a fruitful further exchange of thoughts.[37] As I argued earlier, it is much better to assume that everyone is trying to do their best. Acknowledge the good intentions, but then reveal how this line of reasoning, convincing as it seems, may frustrate our common challenge of stopping the invisible hand from pushing all of us to the abyss. Assume moral equity while at the same time offering corridors of clarity that prevent becoming bogged down by bullshit. Corridors of clarity that help see how, working together, we may bring positive futures within reach.

Unleashing Cascading Change

Revealing the invisible strangling hand and disarming bullshit serves a single goal: tipping the system. Or, more precisely, reaching a critical point where change becomes self-propelling. Snowballing into a set of widely shared social norms that make it very hard to escape the moral dissonance that comes with excessive fossil-fuel burning, meat eating, and wealth accumulation. Such a sea-change may seem impossible, but history tells us that it is not. Time and time again the tipping of social norms happened after long periods during which seemingly nothing changed. In those periods, tension between common practices and emerging new visions increased slowly but steadily. Eventually this allowed society to break loose from its trap. That is how the slave trade, foot binding, public smoking, and many other practices vanished. All such things were taken for granted and considered unchangeable until tipping suddenly happened. Perhaps most surprisingly, the new setting always seems so natural: "Really? Did people smoke in the office and in the car with their children?" Yes! And what is more, they had cars that burned huge amounts of fossil fuels. Fuels that had been stored underground from before the time of the dinosaurs. Stored for hundreds of millions of years and then burned in a century or so. How absurd! Norm tipping has happened many times before. Each time, ways of doing things that were considered totally acceptable seem unimaginable in hindsight. By extension, what we now consider set in stone does not need to be. We just find it hard to imagine that our current practices might be seen as unbelievable by our grandchildren.

So, how do we get to the new norms? Of course, by building more and more tension between those practices and emerging worldviews. Again, there is no silver bullet. Or rather, the tension itself is the silver bullet. That is where everything comes together. Countless small and big things contribute. From a teenager turning vegan to a lawsuit against the government for not doing enough to protect its citizens against climate change. From cooking lentils to developing a meat substitute. From teaching preschool kids to redirecting science. From nudging small talk to writing books. From in-depth reporting to making a blockbuster movie. It all reduces the resilience of the status quo. Lost attraction is what we are looking for. Once the ball is pushed over the rim, there is no way of stopping it. Alas, the same can be true for the descent into a failed world. Discontent with the status quo can propel societies in opposite directions. A battle of narratives determines the outcome.

In a good Anthropocene the invisible hand guides individual behavior in sustainable directions. This requires systemic change. As we saw, free will is limited when it comes to the formation of individual attitudes, not just when it comes to political opinions but also in shaping our implicit biases and prejudices. And, of course, in channeling the pursuit of status toward a relentless rat race for material gain. Intuitively this is hard to believe. We tend to overestimate the power of free will. That is what makes it so easy for corporations to evade regulation by saying that people are free to choose and for governments to ask people to change their behavior. It doesn't work like that. We need to change the choices we have and the way we think and feel about them. In short, we need a system shift to create an Anthropocene we can be proud of. More than a century ago, Max Weber captured the way our primordial behavioral tendencies can be guided in entirely different directions by shifting worldviews. He likens such changes to the role of switchmen, the people who operated railway switches to guide trains from one track to another.[38] As Weber writes: "Not ideas, but material and ideal interests, directly govern men's conduct. Yet very frequently the 'world images' that have been created by 'ideas' have, like switchmen, determined the tracks along which action has been pushed by the dynamic of interest."

Could humanity become its own switchman, exercising its free will to step over its own shadow and move the behavioral train to a different track? It may seem overly ambitious to talk about such a system shift. Why not be content with more feasible and concrete tipping points, such as a shift from fossil-fuel to electric cars and a ban on single-use plastics? Indeed, such shifts are important. But remember, global road transport accounts for only 12 percent of carbon emissions,[39] and compared to land conversion, plastic waste is probably a relatively minor threat to ecosystems.[40] Also, there is the risk that doing the easy things will have a moral-licensing effect. It makes us feel good, reducing the urge to truly address the hard problems.

Nonetheless, as argued, the small steps toward sustainability are very important for another reason. Participating in aspects of sustainable behavior signals to others that we care. We care about handing over the planet to our children in good shape. Policies to stimulate sustainable choices send a signal too. They suggest that thinking this way is credible. All of this is nudging shared worldviews, which is the key to the systemic shift we need.

One way to highlight the key role of worldviews is to see society as a web of institutions that are all interacting with the shared cloud of beliefs, perceptions, norms, and values. I know I have shown many maps of causal links by now. But we cannot pretend to capture how the world works in one graph. That is what true complexity is about. You can capture aspects in different theories, all valid, but they cannot be collapsed into one. We saw that for the complementary theories of social change. Is it tipping, a sand pile, a cycle, Panarchy, a braided river, or all of them? All, of course, but if we tried to combine all insights it would simply become too big to wrap our minds around. The only correct map of the world is the world itself. But that is not very practical, as captured so brilliantly in a famous dialogue by Lewis Carroll, the pseudonym of mathematician Charles Lutwidge Dodgson.[41]

> "What a useful thing a pocket-map is!" I remarked. "That's another thing we've learned from your Nation," said Mein Herr, "map-making. But we've carried it much further than you. What do you consider the largest map that would be really useful?" "About six inches to the mile." "Only six inches!" exclaimed Mein Herr. "We very soon got to six yards to the mile. Then we tried a hundred yards to the mile. And then came the grandest idea of all! We actually made a map of the country, on the scale of a mile to the mile!" "Have you used it much?" I enquired. "It has never been spread out, yet," said Mein Herr.

Later, the famous Argentinian writer Jorge Luis Borges and others elaborated on the theme of the entirely complete map,[42] which sounds a bit silly but captures something deep and important. To be useful, a theory must isolate a limited set of aspects that we can wrap our minds around. Maps that show only the parts that we want to emphasize.

So, let me present you with yet another way of depicting forces that govern societal inertia and change: the institution map (Figure 7.2). It shows one of the many ways in which societies are structured. This way of mapping societies is complementary to looking at social networks linking groups of people. That is because an institution has a life of its own. It is fundamentally different from a group of people. Language, laws, and religions emerge as self-sustained entities. Although institutions evolve, their relative stability makes them serve as anchors for our beliefs, perceptions, norms, and values (in other words, our worldviews).[43] Such institutions do reflect our worldviews. However, at the same time they also affect our worldviews. The resulting web of feedbacks tends to stabilize the status quo.

In view of all those conservative forces, it may seem unlikely that we can truly break away from the status quo. But as we saw, some of those stabilizing feedbacks are more flexible than others. For instance, scientists and journalists may suggest new ways of seeing

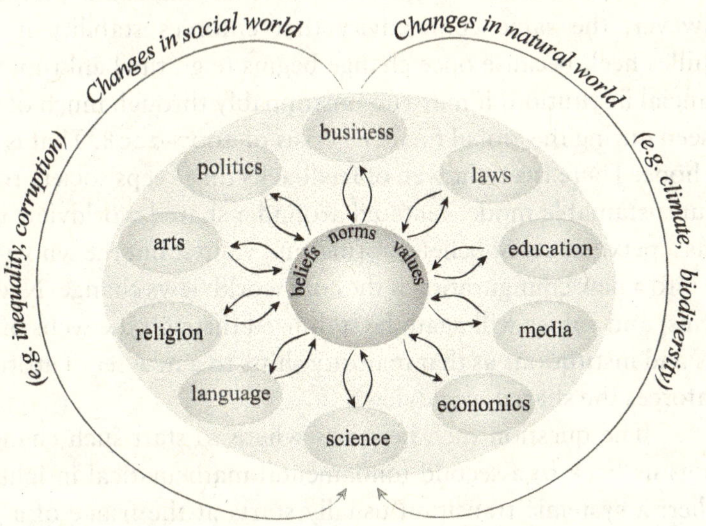

Figure 7.2 Worldviews encompassing beliefs, values, and social norms are anchored in institutions. Change in any of those institutions affects worldviews and may thus nudge the entire web that shapes society toward a tipping point for systemic change. (Adapted from Chapin *et al.*, "Earth stewardship[44].")

things, and changing education may help raise a generation that is more aware of the problems and solutions to the climate and biodiversity crises. Most importantly, the same web structure that stabilizes the status quo can allow cascading change to happen once a critical point is reached. Worldviews are a central hub in the web of connections and are decisive in eventually tipping the whole system. The central role of shared values, norms, and worldviews also holds for networks of individuals. Societies are often viewed as intricately organized networks of individuals. The big network contains layers of clusters with varying sets of attitudes. Such complexity is important, but it almost makes you forget that we are united in most of our worldview. Many beliefs, values, and norms are shared among society as a whole. For example, today nearly everyone disapproves of slavery, a stance that used to be a fringe attitude. Social tipping happens when fringe attitude becomes mainstream.

The fact that shared worldviews may be seen as the core of webs of individuals and institutions allows us to tap into fundamental insights into the nature of systemic transitions in networks[45] An obviously relevant insight is the robust yet fragile paradox that we saw earlier. It implies that systems with strong connections (e.g., the global web of financial institutions) are generally able to withstand perturbations. However, the same connectivity that enforces stability is also the Achilles heel, because once change begins (e.g., the bankruptcy of one financial institution) it may run unstoppably through much of the web, as seen during the global financial crisis of 2007–2008. That is a reason for hope. There is a tight web of feedbacks that keeps society trapped in an unsustainable mode, centered around a shared worldview that contains a perverse set of beliefs, norms, and values. But the whole web will flip into a new configuration if the core worldviews change. New beliefs, norms, and values will again be stabilized through the webs of individuals and institutions as that majority shifts to a new set of attitudes that reinforces the shared worldviews.

The question then becomes where to start such change. That brings us back to a second fundamental mathematical insight we saw earlier: a systemic transition usually starts at the fringe of a network rather than at the core.[46] This is because other nodes stabilize the core from all sides. There is pushback from all sides. Therefore, change is more likely to start at the edge, gradually winning more ground until the core is won and the whole network flips. As discussed in the section on

Breaking Loose in Chapter 4, this theoretical insight is supported by evidence that innovations often start in the peripheries of organizations or societies. All this implies that worldviews are an unlikely starting place themselves. Instead, a sea-change involving a shift of beliefs, norms, values, and worldviews is more likely to be set in motion from the corners of a web. Communities of young people becoming vegan. Groups of early adopters picking up solar panels and electric vehicles. Movements of change that revise institutions such as arts, business, politics, law, or science. In the next chapter we will make that concrete, and ask questions about each individual's role in the big scheme of things, and which policies we should prioritize.

8 WHAT CAN BE DONE

I hope you are convinced by now that a good Anthropocene is not impossible. We can all fit on the planet, and we know how that could be achieved in a sustainable and comfortable way. Carbon neutrality may theoretically be achieved by 2050 through a combination of existing techniques. It would require radical policy choices and massive investments. In principle, that could allow us to keep traveling and consuming, just as we do now. However, such an all-encompassing technological revision seems unlikely to happen any time soon. More realistically, feasible technological solutions would need to be accompanied by behavioral change to stop climate change, and certainly to stop the food-driven destruction of nature. Such behavioral change will not happen on a sufficient scale unless the regulations and prices are changed. And regulations will not be fundamentally revised unless social norms, values, perceptions, and worldviews have shifted sufficiently. As those are anchored in education, law, business, religion, art, science, and other institutions, change toward a tipping point may be nudged via many different societal roles. At the same time we must start thinking about fundamental changes in the way our societies are regulated, pragmatic approaches that may facilitate a sea-change when the time is ripe. Those are the two categories of change-making for which this final chapter offers suggestions: individual action to nudge worldviews, and sweeping policies once people's minds are ready.

What You Can Do

Let's start with what you can do as an individual to help nudge society toward a positive tipping point. In the first chapter, I asked, "Who are we?" That was an important reflection because I was going to use the word 'we' freely, even though there is no single *we*. Are *we* the people in the Global South, in the USA, in Russia, in Holland? The rich, the poor, the young, the old, the garbage collectors, the farmers, the lawyers, the scientists? Of course, there is a near-infinite number of identities and societal roles. We all have several. I am a parent, a son, a neighbor, a consumer, a scientist, and a violinist – to name just a few. A large part of our change-making power is relatively independent of our identities: the goods we buy, the number of children we have, the politicians we vote for, and the stories we tell. All that makes a difference, and I hope the book has inspired you to think about what anyone can do to help nudge the world toward a good tipping point. But identity does matter for what you can do. What Elon Musk or the Pope does matters more than what you and I do. Wealth and power matter. But for the rest of us it is useful to think of the specific role of institutions in which you may be involved. How can *you* have the largest impact possible?

Democracy

As you may guess, my top suggestion is to improve democracy. Here is why, and how. You may associate the term 'democracy' with voting and government. But movements, NGOs, investigative journalism, and law continuously correct and nudge the way things work. Regulations may, in theory, liberate us from the strangling hand. But as I have argued, you can't just prescribe policies and regulations. Instead, policies are emergent properties of society. They emerge from the many forces in society, including the same strangling hand that we would like them to disarm. That can be frustrating, and if progress happens at all it tends to be slow. Indeed, democracies are wired to accommodate incremental improvements. As we saw, adaptive capacity is a strength of democracies. But adaptation tends to be imperfect and chronically overdue. Thus, democracy is, in many ways, conservative. Democracies struggle to reduce the grip of wealthy elites and transnational corporations. Such power does not have to be overt. Instead, it is often exerted more subtly through soft but influential mechanisms such as media nudging, agenda setting, and narrative shaping. Resolving the resulting stagnation may seem to require a revolution. I think it does, but not a revolution to put a strong leader in place. Autocracy, in the end, has never worked. It has the advantage of allowing forceful, coordinated action. But, as we saw, there is a reason why famines killing millions of people have consistently happened in autocratic societies. The wisdom of the crowd outsmarts that of any single person, even if distorting mechanisms affect that wisdom. Also, as we saw, autocracy and wealth concentration often go together, strengthening the strangling hand. Indeed, the strangling hand of autocracies is increasing its meddling with democracies worldwide. Pulitzer Prize-winning historian Anne Applebaum gives a sharp analysis of the problem in her recent book *Autocracy, Inc.: The Dictators who Want to Run the World*.[1] Her introduction immediately sets the stage:

> All of us have in our minds a cartoon image of an autocratic state. There is a bad man at the top. He controls the army and the police. The army and the police threaten the people with violence. There are evil collaborators, and maybe some brave dissidents. But in the twenty-first century, that cartoon bears little resemblance to reality. Nowadays, autocracies are run not by one bad guy but by sophisticated networks relying on kleptocratic financial structures, a complex of security services – military, paramilitary, police – and technological experts who provide surveillance, propaganda, and disinformation. The members of these networks are connected not only to one another within a given autocracy but also to networks in other autocratic countries, and sometimes in democracies too.

Applebaum documents the many ways in which the emerging autocratic networks deliberately destabilize the institutions that are hindering their strangling kleptocratic hand globally. She calls for a war – not against autocratic states, but against autocratic behaviors. A global anti-kleptocracy network in which there are roles for governments and institutions, but especially for individuals. I couldn't agree more. Such an approach is very much in the spirit of this chapter. One of the main action points Applebaum proposes is to take on the information war. As she observes, the Western democratic world naively embraced Francis Fukuyama's "end-of-history" argument, which suggested that after the collapse of the Soviet Union all countries would automatically evolve toward Western liberal democracy as the endpoint of humankind's ideological evolution. This idea was based on the false assumption that good information would inevitably win the battle in the "marketplace of ideas." The problem is that there is no free market of ideas. Instead, a subset of ideas is being turbocharged by disinformation campaigns. The solution is for a coalition of actors to expose how that works, to aim for radical transparency, to revise the rules and regulations of the information system, but also to "break the autocrat's monopoly on the use of strong emotions."

Far-right populist leaders within democracies such as Donald Trump, Viktor Orbán, and Jair Bolsonaro openly admire autocratic leaders. They promise to break away from the perceived elite and advance a nationalistic agenda in which international cooperation is a low priority. Such nativist approaches make it hard to solve the big challenges of the coming decades. Addressing the climate crisis, loss of nature, mass migration, and runaway wealth concentration all require global cooperation. Thus, the best we can do is focus all our efforts on defending and improving democracy. An ideal situation can never be reached. Instead, we chase the moving target by continuously revising and improving. That may feel disappointing. Can't we do better? No, we cannot. Democracies are our best bet for guiding a graceful transition to a fundamentally revised world. We need cooperating democracies that are continuously corrected and updated.

I do realize that my point of view may be biased. I talked long about that with my Chinese friend Xu Chi (with whom I worked to show the existence of a human climate niche). He made me see that while the call for change based on democracy may be naturally accepted by most people in Western nations, the situation may be different in many Eastern societies. For example, China has an ancient hierarchical culture, which is trusted and relied upon by the majority of its people. This affects how people exert their influence on policies. For instance, people in China are most likely to take part in local protests if they have a greater trust in the central government than the local government. One interpretation is that, in a society without meaningful elections, participating in protests is a way of attracting the attention of the upper-level authorities to problems, in the hope of redress.[2] Whichever way things work, China is firmly planning for ecosystem restoration and the energy transition.[3] This is just to make the point that the ideas in this chapter are unavoidably limited by my Western democracy-oriented point of view. Consider that an invitation to expand the lines of reasoning for other societies. How might we best strive for a sustainable future within other forms of governance?

In the remainder of this chapter I ask how, within the limitations of democracy, we can break free from the grip of the strangling hand. That is not just the work of politicians. Again, there is no pilot in the cockpit. Policies emerge from society. Change is the responsibility of us all. What follows are some ideas for how you can help, depending on your societal role. These are hints, not recipes. I am not an expert on any of the institutions (except science). However, I highlight those complementary angles to show some of the many different roles that can be played to nudge society toward the desired tipping point out of trouble.

Government and Law

Most of you will not work in government, but those who do can have a disproportionate effect on moving society toward a good tipping point. When it comes to policies for a sustainable and just world there is no shortage of suggestions in the literature about a post-growth economy, focusing on well-being rather than economic output.[4] Great ideas, but getting it done is altogether a different challenge.[5] We will only get there if social norms and worldviews shift. How to make that happen? Coming from an action-oriented perspective, Cass Sunstein and Richard Thaler have explored possible practical ways for governments to change behavior and, ultimately, social norms.[6] That sounds like manipulation – and, indeed, it is. But then again, we are manipulated by commercials aimed at nudging our behavior all the time. Sunstein and Thaler find it naïve to leave all the nudging to the companies, and show that similar tactics may also be a useful tool to stimulate people to make choices that are better for their health and the environment. The idea is to change the so-called architecture of choice. Things like putting plant-based food at eye level in the supermarket. A nudge makes it more likely that you will behave in a particular way. It changes the environment in such a way that your automatic cognitive processes are triggered to favor a desired outcome. Could we nudge society over a tipping point for social norms? Sunstein argues for that in the book *How Change Happens*.[7] That sounds almost as presumptuous as *How Nature Works*. But Sunstein's arguments align well with what we have seen in past norm changes. He focuses on a situation in which many people privately disagree with an existing norm but fail to say so, precisely because it would be against the norm. This is the situation close to the tipping point in our graphical model (Figure 4.1). Smart nudges may invoke behavior that signals disagreement with the status quo, bringing forward preferences that have existed all along but remained hidden. This, in turn, may nudge more people to go against the status quo, causing a cascade if a tipping point is reached. In this view, the goal of a 'norm entrepreneur' may be to reveal silent majorities who are secretly already against the norm. Indeed, people often underestimate how many others agree. For instance, as we saw earlier, supporters of climate policies in the USA outnumbered opponents 2:1 in 2022, but they mistakenly thought that the opposite was true.[8] Revealing such hidden majorities may help escape social traps.

Meanwhile, there are two obvious key issues to keep an eye on if you are in the policy-making game: populism and the invisible hand. As we saw, the global trend toward far-right populism is a problem because the associated isolationism makes it hard to coordinate global action on climate, migration, and other critical issues. However, rather than brush populism aside as a nasty aberration, it is important to understand and address its causes. As argued in the sections on weakening democracy and the populist Zeitgeist, there is much confusion about potential drivers.[9] Counterintuitively, poverty is not what drives people toward populists. There is simply no correlation between the economic condition of people and their support for populists. However, perceived unfairness, envy, or a drop in social status do drive people toward populist narratives. Another misconception is the idea that attraction to populism results from a cultural backlash against things such as gay rights or ethnically different immigrants. Instead, the backlash is largely driven by populist narratives themselves. Thus, the drivers of populist appeal are issues of perception that require good facts and framing to address. At the same time, there are legitimate underlying drivers of discontent, such as austerity measures and neoliberal policies that disproportionately hit the least well-off, and sustainability measures that affect the poor most sharply, such as the tax raise on fuels that triggered the Yellow Vest movement. Seeing the wealth of the richest rise with each crisis does not help. Such drivers of discontent must be addressed so that they don't fuel attraction to far-right populist leaders who promise to solve unfairness while letting the world slide toward a potentially calamitous future. The costs of sustainability policies should not affect the well-being of ordinary people. There is no need for that, given that the richest 1 percent own more wealth than 95 percent of humanity.[10] As the philosopher Bruno Latour so sharply observed, the only way to gain a majority for sustainability policies and to avoid populism from taking over is to get the rich to pay for it.[11]

Of course, this can only be done if you address the other priority: ensuring regulation to weaken the grip of the invisible strangling hand. The grip of vested interest parties on markets and media, but also on government itself. So, do not just ask, "How can we tax the rich better?" or "How can we stop subsidizing fossil-fuel use?" But also, "Why has that not happened earlier?" and "What can be changed to remove those barriers?" In the next part of this chapter, there are some suggestions that may get you going with some more out-of-the-box thinking about governance.

It can also be helpful to use the existing structure of checks and balances in more forceful ways. Democratic governments have a separation of powers between the institutions making the laws, executing them, and adjudicating them: the legislature, executive, and judiciary. There are many variations, but for centuries it has been agreed by thinkers that such a separation is better than having the power combined in a single institution such as a king or dictator. Somewhat unexpectedly, judges are now rapidly becoming more important in reminding executive governments of their responsibility to act according to legally binding agreements, such as the task to protect their citizens from harm. Lawsuits organized by NGOs or autonomous groups of citizens are increasingly reminding governments of their task when it comes to implementing climate policies promised in international agreements. Although there are of course backlashes against this approach, such lawsuits are starting to make a real difference and greatly help governments to resist the strangling hand of vested interests.[12] Also, greenwashing is now considered unlawful in some parts of the world.[13] Lawsuits are waking up companies, making them correct misleading communication strategies, and the European Union has started regulating green claims more firmly.[14] The power of using the law in such novel ways is also inspiring a tendency to start defining rivers and other natural elements as entities that have rights just as humans do, an entirely new tool for the protection of nature.[15] You may think that those are all just incremental twists, but remember the main goal: tipping social norms. Like all institutions, laws interact with social norms. They reflect norms, but they also affect them. For instance, when a country legalizes same-sex marriage, attitudes to sexual minorities improve.[16] Thus, whether you are working on legislation or thinking of the possibility of starting a lawsuit to correct a government or companies, all that can have positive spillover effects on social norms and values that go beyond the direct goal you may have in mind.

Protest Movements

An enormously important correction of government comes from protest movements. This was recognized by early thinkers about the modern state, such as Thomas Jefferson, who – reflecting on the pros and cons of democracy versus feudalism in a letter to James Madison – noted that the turbulence that can arise when people don't agree "prevents the degeneracy of government, and nourishes a general attention to the public affairs. I hold it that a little rebellion now and then is a good thing."[17] It is important that people get together outside the traditional democratic institutions to rethink the policies and even the fundamentals of government. One way to do that is by bringing a 'mini-public' together that represents a demographic and attitudinal cross-section of society. Such deliberative citizen forums are increasingly embraced as a tool to help shape ideas outside the political arena where hidden agendas and legacies can blur discussions and cause stagnation.[18] While such venues for deliberation help weigh a diverse set of arguments, protest movements are complementary, helping to emphasize positions. This is the useful turbulence that Jefferson was thinking about. Such movements nurture so-called enclave deliberation among like-minded people.[19] This helps articulate minority views that are easily drowned out in mainstream debates. Organized protests and civil disobedience also help raise the perceived tension between the status quo and important values or goals. A classic example is Gandhi's Salt March, when he led a swelling crowd of people on a 387-kilometer march to the sea where they could harvest their own salt illegally, avoiding the high British taxation on such a basic need. The protest did not immediately end British colonial rule, but it was a watershed moment, something seemingly small but unforgettably symbolic.[20] After that event, feelings about colonial rule started sliding in another direction, among both Indians themselves and the global community. It also inspired later change-makers, including Martin Luther King, and it is no coincidence that Greta Thunberg has been called the "new Gandhi."[21] In December 2019 *TIME* named her person of the year, the youngest person ever to receive the honor, just sixteen months after she started her solo "school strike" in front of the Swedish parliament building. The intensity of her impact has puzzled analysts ever since, but one important element was certainly her fierceness and emotion, exemplified perhaps most powerfully in her "How dare you" speech to world leaders at a UN summit.[22] Democratic deliberation remains mostly focused on rational arguments. Meanwhile, our attitudes and choices are guided by intuition and emotions. Just like King's "I have a dream," Thunberg's "How dare you" has played an enormously important role in crystalizing how people feel about important problems. The avalanche of movement that such emotional framing triggers is not just a release of existing tension. It also helps build further tension, which can move problems up policy agendas. Perhaps most importantly, movements help erode the worldviews and norms that stand in the way of progress, making it increasingly hard to ignore the moral dissonance between common practices and common goals. This holds not just for organized social movements but also for lifestyle movements such as veganism.[23] Such emergent movements have neither explicit leaders nor organized mass actions. Yet adherence to a lifestyle also nudges social norms and values, simply through the small, everyday implicit statements that the visible choice embodies. While some conspiracy-theory-based movements may disrupt much-needed social coordination – as happened during the Covid-19 pandemic – movements in general are an important correcting force in democracy.

Participation in movements does not fit every personality. Nor does it have to. It is only one of many ways in which you can make a difference. For instance, supporting an NGO. Non-governmental organizations are complementary to social movements in the way they are organized. They are like corporations operating in a market of public attention.[24] They become bigger if they can attract more support from donors. Thus, the evolving landscape of NGOs is coordinated by an invisible hand, much like classical markets. This allows successful NGOs to grow and to hire professional staff to coordinate, investigate, and guide communication strategies. Their actions help set agendas, nudge norms, and reveal the strangling hand of vested interests. Meanwhile, their structure and professionalism make NGOs good partners in round-table initiatives, deliberations, and negotiations with governments and transnational corporations.[25] Working for an NGO or supporting one financially is thus one of the many effective ways to help nudge society in the right direction.

Religion

Religions have historically been major players shaping the dynamics of stasis and change in societies. There are many examples of wise advice in religious texts and scriptures. Much of it points to ways of maintaining peaceful, egalitarian societies. However, despite all this good advice, inequality has persisted. Also, the destruction of our natural resource base has proceeded unhalted, even though from Christian stewardship to the Andean Pachamama views, spiritual guidance has included the need to protect natural resources for future generations. Clearly, religions have turned out to be relatively weak when it comes to discouraging wealth concentration and emphasizing the protection of the environment. A more cynical view is that religion has often been a repressive tool for elites, promoting acceptance and discouraging radical change. As Karl Marx put it: "Religion is the opium of the people." A "just-world view," accepting the world as it is, ameliorates discontent,[26] reducing the social tension that can fuel transformations. Seen in this light, religion can be seen as undermining change. Yet, at the same time, religious institutions could be uniquely placed to help society focus on important goals and values, free of the turf war of politics that is clouded by power structures protecting vested interests. This could theoretically help in places such as the USA, with its highly polarized politics. In such a setting, positions on climate, food, or environmental protection have become part of the political package deals that split the country, along with the choice of car, music, sports, and so on.[27] Alas, religion turns out to be strongly implicated in American polarization.[28]

Still, spiritual leaders have the potential to step outside such schisms and formulate overarching visions of sustainability and justice. They are also trusted more than politicians (albeit less than scientists). Indeed, there is a lot of interest in the potential for religions to reshape values in ways that help the world shift to a more sustainable path.[29] At the same time, not much of that seems to be happening on the ground. Here are a few characteristic quotes on the topic from interviews with religiously active Buddhists, Muslims, and Christians (in that order):[30]

> "It is not the task of Buddhist communities to educate people about environmental protection. . . . The task of Buddhism is the training of the spirit. I mean a sports or football club does not have the task to enlighten about environmental protection either."

> "Environmental protection is an issue for the wealthy. If you do not have any financial difficulties, if you know, yes tomorrow I have enough to eat, tomorrow I can pay the electricity in the mosque, tomorrow I can also pay the Imam, that will not be a problem, then you can say: Okay, now we can also dedicate ourselves to this topic. But if you're always in a state of financial emergency, as is the case with 99 percent of the mosques . . . you just don't have time to deal with this topic properly now."

> "Although they [the Catholic Church] have actually received the boost with Laudato Si', very little has actually happened so far."

Such inertia raises the question of how the potential for religious leadership in reshaping values may be unleashed. If you are part of a religious community, you could work actively to help see the big picture, escape unproductive polarization, and make sure the visions vocalized by the Dalai Lama, the Pope, or other leaders are translated into action on the ground.

Business

Perhaps business has more potential than religion for change-making? There are countless small companies and start-ups experimenting with sustainable ways forward. Those lead by example, spreading awareness and serving as a source of inspiration and hope. At the same time, most of humanity's impact on the planet runs through a handful of transnational corporations. Globalization has elevated the economic winner-takes-all effect to an unprecedented level. We are used to seeing the latest reports, again and again, revealing the growing wealth of individuals such as Elon Musk, Jeff Bezos, and Bill Gates. The same concentration of power happens at the level of companies.[31] Some 10 percent of the world's corporations generate 80 percent of all profits globally. A few tech companies control over 90 percent of the global market share of search engines, operating systems, and social media, and three investor firms manage over 90 percent of all assets in passive equity funds. Meanwhile, 80 percent of global emissions from 2016 through 2022 can be traced to just fifty-seven corporate and state production entities.[32] It is tempting to think of the role of business as morally dubious, but, as argued before, this is the wrong way to look at it. As we saw, virtually all people like to think of themselves as moral and have a strong drive to do the right thing. Things go wrong not because of the people, but because of the beliefs, framings, and incentives that surround them. So, that is what must change. The sheer weight of giant corporations makes them influential in many ways, including in nudging the rules of the game by influencing governments to shape the system in which they operate. Dominance by the few is a double-edged sword. The power of such corporations allows malicious state capture. On the other hand, if the key players are on board to work toward sustainability, social justice, and other laudable goals, progress can be achieved much more efficiently and rapidly. Of course, that is tricky. If you suggest transnational corporations as partners in making the world sustainable, aren't you dealing with the devil? This is a deeply contentious issue. So contentious, in fact, that when we wrote an opinion paper on the topic after discussing it for days with a broad group of influential scientists,[33] several of the discussants refused to sign as authors.

Indeed, big companies have played dubious roles in many ways. As we know, they nudge worldviews through media and try to influence government rules to benefit themselves, even if it means weakening environmental and social standards. But, as we stress in our review,[34] the influence goes further. For instance, big companies often control who can enter a particular industry, slowing down progress toward sustainable practices and new technologies. They also tend to pay their suppliers very little, which limits the suppliers' ability to adopt sustainable approaches, forcing them to go with what they know will work. For good reason, many people doubt that businesses are really committed to being environmentally friendly. On the other hand, if these large companies start demanding eco-friendly practices from everyone in their supply chain, it stimulates smaller businesses to follow suit. How can you help to make that happen if you are an employee or shareholder of a company? Basically, by making everyone in the company more aware and pushing it higher up the agenda. Most big companies are already quite aware of the need for change, and many participate in initiatives such as the UN Global Compact, where companies work with NGOs and other participants to find ways of aligning their strategies with societal goals such as human rights and sustainability.[35] But progress is much too slow. A core impediment is the almost intrinsic tension between the drive to do the right thing morally and the need to remain competitive. An obvious way out is to construct regulations that result in a level playing field.[36] But that is not the only way. Consumers are interested in buying morally right things. As we saw, this stimulates greenwashing. But space for such suspect practices is shrinking under rising pressure from investigative journalism, NGOs, and governmental agencies. One of the ways to enhance the sustainability of your business is thus to cooperate with such partners to scrutinize not only you but also your competitors and to make sure that your company is ahead of the competition when greenness comes under closer investigation. Of course, your impact depends on where in the corporation you work. Progressive CEOs such as Paul Polman of Unilever can be role models for a culture shift. Reflecting on his career, he challenges other business leaders to reflect on questions such as "How can a company profit from solving the world's problems, not from creating them? Is the world better off because your business is in it, or not? How far are you willing to push your companies to help solve them?" Meanwhile, he proposes practical ways to change the culture in a corporation, such as defining the company's long-term purpose, spelling out the economic case for sustainability, and designing practices and incentives that stimulate working towards sustainability. In other words, he is creating an invisible hand within the corporation that guides a pursuit of sustainability at all levels of the corporation.[37] While few people get to be CEOs, this conversation can be triggered from anywhere in the corporation, or among the shareholders. A conversation about the question of how the culture and incentive structure may be changed so that people make better choices.

Education

Schools and universities are important parts of early life in which worldviews are shaped. Educators teach the way the world works, but this is almost inherently anchored in the status quo. What if we want the world to work differently? And what if the playing field is already shifting rapidly? Knowledge and skills that were once essential to understanding the world and meeting the challenges of life can become irrelevant. But how can we replace them with new knowledge that may come from outside the traditional disciplines? What would you like to teach your students? Of course, I hope that you are inspired by the content of this book. Lift them out of hopelessness. Show how change can happen and how the invisible hand can trap us, even if everyone is trying to do the best they can. How to detect fake news and artificial realities. Encourage them to appreciate many cultures and religions in order to prepare for productive and inspiring integration when a redistribution of people on the globe becomes a reality.

But just as in business and any other institution, there is systemic inertia in educational institutes that holds us back. Teachers have some freedom to innovate in the classroom, but they are limited by curricula that are notoriously hard to update. One analysis identified nine categories of constraints to change, including: fuzziness of new ideas, vested interests, teacher education, lack of consequence when everything is kept the same, and lack of space and motivation for initiative.[38] On a small scale, the question of how to change education resembles the challenge of tipping society out of trouble. First, reveal the strangling hand that prevents change. Then stimulate people to do something about it. It's the same recipe. Reveal the tension between current practices and a vision of what would be needed to prepare students to become effective actors in a new world. Raising the perceived tension will nudge your school closer to tipping points for institutional rejuvenation. But don't wait for institutional change to happen. It may take too long. You can still stretch your freedom and change your teaching within the existing constraints.

Science and Arts

Science has shown us the trouble we are in. Frustratingly, those insights have not led to much action. In part, this may be because the urgency of the problems is not yet sufficiently salient. As we have seen, a crisis is often needed to trigger change. Yet the foundations for the new directions are typically built by earlier thinkers. The potentially massive power of ideas was also recognized during the era of great social improvements. Remember Max Weber's statement that "ideas have, like switchmen, determined the tracks." Later the influential economist John Maynard Keynes echoed that thought in his book *The General Theory of Employment, Interest, and Money*[39] when he wrote: "Madmen in authority, who hear voices in the air, are distilling their frenzy from some academic scribbler of a few years back. I am sure that the power of vested interests is vastly exaggerated compared with the gradual encroachment of ideas." One way to think about this is that, as scientists, we have already done enough to explain the problems and potential solutions. From that perspective, at this point we cannot do anything more, but must wait for a crisis that finally wakes up the decision makers. But I would say this is not true.

Scientists certainly have a role to play in clarifying the costs and benefits of major societal choices. But scientific insights are only part of what people use to make sense of the world (Figure 8.1). Thought leaders ranging from politicians and influencers to priests and activists play a big role too. Should we abandon slavery, foot binding, and fossil fuels? Whose lead will we follow? Stakes are high for everyone, not least

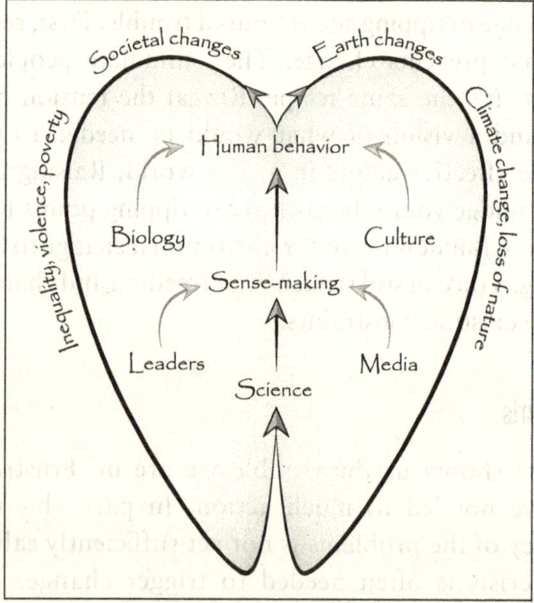

Figure 8.1 The heart model of social change. Human behavior drives some detrimental trends in the Earth system and society. Science can help make sense of those to guide changes in behavior. However, other opinion leaders and media have a strong impact on sense-making too, and behavior is largely determined by nonrational forces rooted in biology and culture. (Adapted from Scheffer *et al.*, "A heart model of Earth stewardship."[40])

for the rich and powerful, who often have vested interests in keeping the world the way it is. They have a disproportionate capacity to influence information and worldviews. Indeed, the strangling hand plays a big role in public sense-making, and the VIPs (Figure 7.1) often use much better communicators than the scientific community. Such competing communicators also understand that rationality is just a small part of what drives the choices people make. As argued, revealing how this invisible hand works is one priority for science, with journalists and NGOs as obvious partners in explaining such insights. But there is more.

If our aim is to catalyze change, we may not be producing the most useful science. As we saw, many feel hopeless about the possibility of shaping a positive future for humanity, and lots of research has shown that this undermines the motivation to act. Thus, to motivate action, science must show how positive futures can realistically be reached. Presenting such insights in an appealing way is not something science can do by itself. Arts have often pushed for societal change at pivotal moments. Think of Thomas More's book *Utopia*, which inspired thinking about better ways of organizing society half a millennium ago; of Bob Dylan's lyrics on social struggles, political protest, love, and religion that helped an entire generation decide what matters in life; or, more recently, Kim Stanley Robinson's science fiction book *The Ministry for the Future*,[41] which describes vividly what can be done to save our planet. Despite the huge need and potential for change-making, most of the science and art produced today remains irrelevant to that challenge. Prompted by that mismatch, we gathered a group of thinkers from the arts, humanities, and sciences to ask how our fields could be made more useful.[42] Lots of fascinating stuff is produced in each of our fields of expertise, but most of it is irrelevant to the big challenge of our times. In a world heading for the abyss, surely we should be able to do better. But how? The diagnosis from this introspection was that our professional worlds suffered from similar issues to the world at large, locked into place by their own invisible hands. Some individuals will always escape that pressure. They don't care about the written and unwritten rules, and just do what they feel is needed. But in order to direct more brilliant thinkers over to change-making work, we need a shift of incentives in our disciplines.

In the world of science, decisions about who gets tenure or funding are often made by small committees that rely on a handful of peer reviews and publication metrics. This drives scientists to focus more on boosting their superficial performance indicators than on doing truly important work. They also spend way too much time chasing grants and judging proposals by others. For instance, in Australia researchers collectively spend about three centuries of working time each year in writing and reviewing project proposals.[43] Worst of all, the whole thing makes no sense. It turns out that there is no correlation between how proposals are rated and how impactful the resulting research is.[44] My computer-science friend Johan Bollen designed a brilliant alternative to this pointless, time-consuming machinery.[45] The idea boils down to using the wisdom of the crowd. In a nutshell: give every qualified scientist the same amount of funding with the understanding that they must anonymously give a fixed percentage away to others based on whatever they think is important. The system allows the current inequality in fund allocation to be tuned to a desired level and removes gender and other biases. Many similar ideas are floating around, all triggered by the same observation: the current system does not work. It's time for a shake-up, a real change in how we do things. We need to shift away from this obsession with metrics and start focusing on what really matters: pushing the boundaries of knowledge and making a difference. Experiments in that direction are already happening, but progress must come faster.

Chasing status also hampers progress in more subtle ways. Cultures of hidden rules in each field dictate what topics to study and how to study them.[46] One example is the prestige of mathematical proofs. While math has helped us understand a lot, its allure sometimes makes scientists focus only on problems solvable mathematically, ignoring real-world relevance. This leads talented researchers in fields such as economics and ecology to waste their time on irrelevant problems just to impress others and secure their positions. Similarly, there is a big push for 'hard evidence' from controlled experiments. While this is natural in some areas, it just does not make sense when studying how complex systems such as ecosystems or societies work. In ecology, for example, proving mechanisms using replicated experiments in jars or aquaria is cool, but such knowledge simply doesn't add up to understanding the response of entire forests, lakes, or oceans to climate change or pollution.[47] The same goes for climate research – we can never fully verify our models, but that doesn't mean they're useless.[48] Insisting on strict methods discourages approaches that could give us insights into the most important issues facing humanity today.

Meanwhile, disciplines such as social science and humanities are struggling with their own rigid culture.[49] Traditionally the idea of trying to change human attitudes and behavior has been discouraged. But things are changing. Humanities scholars are teaming up with other disciplines to break free from this mindset and start making a difference. Economists, too, are shifting toward a more effective approach, moving away from the old idea that people always act rationally. They're finding new ways to motivate behavioral change beyond monetary incentives. In ecology the focus used to be on what was going wrong in the natural world. Now there's a movement toward looking at how we can make things better. Instead of just lamenting losses, scientists are exploring ways to restore ecosystems and create a more sustainable future. Meanwhile, the arts are changing too. Working for the masses or aiming to change public attitudes used to be undervalued by experts deciding on grants. But the world is moving on. As commentator John Holden expresses it: "Under the old model funded, or high culture, could be marginalised as the elite preoccupation of a small minority, commercial culture could be dismissed as mere entertainment, and home-made culture could be patronised as being merely amateur. But put them all together and they become … 'the second ecosystem of humankind'."[50] This is becoming an influential ecosystem today indeed. Amanda Gorman created a shockwave as the youngest inaugural poet, performing "The Hill we Climb" at President Biden's 2021 inauguration, and Kim Stanley Robinson's *The Ministry for the Future* became a favorite book of Bill Gates and Barack Obama.

In conclusion, what you can do as a scientist or artist to nudge the world toward positive tipping is similar to what people in government, religion, business, or education can do: help change the system of incentives within your institution, but don't wait for change to happen fully. Reveal how the invisible hand keeps your discipline trapped, but don't wait for that to change. Go ahead and investigate the nature of the invisible strangling hand at large, design credible routes to attractive futures, facilitate cooperation between artists and scientists to leverage the profound emotional force needed for moving worldviews. In short, create powerful visions of realistic and appealing ways forward.

Tip by a Thousand Cuts

Each of these contributions from different societal perspectives helps nudge the cloud of worldviews, norms, and values to which we are all connected. Nudging this cloud is how we build the tension between practices and ideals needed to make big change happen. The specific societal-role actions aimed at nudging institutions add to the many other things anyone can do. Things that be no surprise: eat less meat, drive an electric car, recycle your waste, participate in political protests, support candidates who protect democracy, etc. None of that is revolutionary in the slightest. But the question lurking in the backs of your minds may always have been "Do these things *really* make a difference?" I hope that after reading this book your answer is a resounding YES. This is the point: Do the things you've already been doing, and push them as far as you can, because they absolutely contribute to tipping us out of trouble. More specifically, all those efforts help to grow support for a fundamental revision of our society, a revision of the rules of the game.

The Invisible Hand Revisited

Big change, in the end, can only come through a change of the rules. A change of the structure of incentives that drives our behavior, consciously or subconsciously. That is how tipping out of trouble must happen. As we have seen, ideals and good intentions have only limited effects on the choice of food, travel, and other things that affect our footprint. Much more influential are the options we have and the prices that are asked. And – not to forget – our manufactured desires. As Galbraith observed so sharply, the insatiable hunger for luxury consumption was created artificially through mass advertising after World War II. It shaped the great acceleration that fundamentally changed the planet and the climate in a matter of decades. Climate change and the destruction of ecosystems can be curbed. We know that, and we know how. It will not come from spontaneous changes in individual habits. It can only come from a change of rules. A change of policies beyond incremental tweaking. But that, in turn, is only possible if perceptions, norms, values, and worldviews change. All the "What *you* can do" suggestions in the previous section are geared toward nudging such a shift. Once institutions such as laws, education, businesses, and science start changing, this will feed back on worldviews. That is how the self-reinforcing runaway change we need can happen. The tipping out of trouble.

At the deepest level, many perverse incentives could evaporate if society starts to value prosocial contributions instead of money or consumption. This makes all the sense in the world, and change in that direction is already starting to unfold. However, as argued by the economist Branko Milanović in his book *Capitalism, Alone*,[51] it will be impossible to abandon capitalism altogether. Instead, the invisible hand must be repurposed. Turned from a strangling hand into a helping hand that frees humanity from our trap. So, what might a revisited hand look like? There are, of course, endless possibilities, but to get you thinking, here is a sketch of three scenarios. In the 'loosening hand' scenario, the grip of each of the five fingers of the strangling hand is loosened through dedicated policies. The 'second hand' scenario involves an independently elected climate-governance system that redistributes resources globally. Finally, the 'visible hand' instead accepts the runaway concentration of wealth but makes the associated power transparent in order to press for morality.

The Loosening Hand

Helping to loosen the grip of each of the fingers of the invisible strangling hand is essentially what *you* can do depending on the societal role you play, as I argued in the previous section. Here is a recap showing how it corresponds to each of the strangling fingers (Figure 8.2).

The *thumb* represents incentives that drive the choices of the people working for vested interest parties, such as the super-wealthy and transnational corporations. As we saw, the innate desire to be a valued member of a group plays out in this setting as a drive to help meet the goals of the company. Naturally, these goals include increasing profits and market share, boosting the value of the company for shareholders. But there is room to extend this narrow focus. Much depends on leadership, as illustrated by the success that CEO Paul Polman had in embedding incentives for sustainability at all levels in the multinational Unilever corporation. Such attitude changes are, of course, inspired by the cloud of shifting perceptions, worldviews, norms, and values. But there is also contagion between corporations. Polman is actively inspiring other companies to do the same, and many engage in roundtable

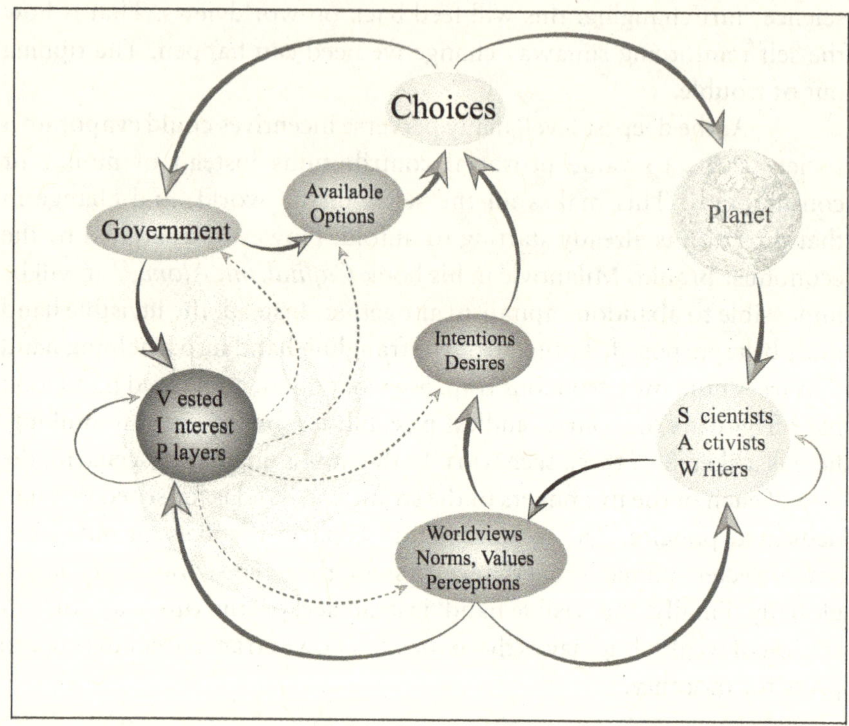

Figure 8.2 Loosening the grip of the strangling hand allows well-informed worldviews to play a larger role in shaping the choices of governance and lifestyle.

initiatives and other forms of cooperation aimed at boosting sustainability while remaining competitive. Sometimes scientists can serve as catalysts for such dynamics. A good example is a global fisheries cooperation influenced by Henrik Österblom of Stockholm University.[52] This Seafood Business for Ocean Stewardship (SeaBOS) initiative is a collaboration between some of the largest seafood corporations in the world, aiming to develop an improved stewardship of the ocean. Henrik and his colleagues realized that if big corporations cooperated to address overfishing, by themselves and illegal fisheries, they would all benefit. Convincing the companies to cooperate wasn't easy, as some of them deeply mistrusted both science and the other companies. In the end the repelling forces were overcome, and a sustainable win-win pact was formed. I like this example, as it shows how a marriage between profit-seeking incentives and sustainable goals may sometimes be arranged via entrepreneurial scientists like Österblom. Of course, the scope for such self-regulation of the thumb of the strangling hand remains limited. But it addresses the core of the problem, making it an important mechanism. In the end, the stronger the moral dissonance between shifting societal norms and corporate practices, the more prominent such self-regulation may become.

The *little finger* represents the grip of corporations and concentrated wealth on policies. Loosening of this finger of the strangling hand is an ongoing effort with varying degrees of success. The grip works through a range of mechanisms, including the soft forces of lobbying, framing debates, and setting agendas. But political finance is perhaps the largest direct force. To cite a handbook on the funding of political parties and election campaigns:[53]

> The role of money in politics is arguably the biggest threat to democracy today. This global threat knows no boundaries and is evident across all continents from huge corporate campaign donations in the United States and drug money seeping into politics in Latin America, to corruption scandals throughout Asia and Europe. Attempts to tackle these challenges through political finance laws and regulations are often undermined by a lack of political will or capacity, as well as poorly designed and enforced measures.

Resolving that is a tantalizing challenge, as the invisible strangling hand resists regulation, both of and through this little finger. The whole problem has been thoroughly analyzed and is well understood, but this doesn't mean that solving it is easy. Yet elements for improvement are clear. The dependency of politicians and parties on donations can be reduced by having a good public-funding system, including free or subsidized media access, to reduce finance-induced biases. Countries can also limit the amount of money that candidates or parties are allowed to spend during election campaigns. Corporate funding can be banned altogether. While many regulations exist, monitoring and enforcing is often weak. This should be done by an independent agency that has the power to track money flows and make all information available to the public. Investigative journalists add an extra layer of monitoring, and – if sufficiently independent – media can make in-depth journalism exposing the influence of powerful players on politics an editorial priority, for example, mapping the main donors and explaining the damaging effects.

The *ring finger* shapes the collection of choices of goods and services and their pricing. For instance, the availability of public transport and the pricing of train versus plane tickets. Or the availability and prices of plant-based food versus meat and dairy. Policy makers can shape much of this landscape of choice through taxes and subsidies, but again, the invisible hand is holding back change. As we saw, the data speak for themselves. For instance, public funding for animal products remains much larger than for plant-based alternatives,[54] and subsidies for fossil-fuel use amount to $6 trillion annually, despite broad agreement over the need to cut down on their use.[55] Agreement, but no action. The situation is similar if we zoom in on the massive subsidies for unsustainable forms of industrial agriculture and fisheries.[56] Thus, while policies ranging from regulation to subsidies and taxation are obvious, the little finger tends to allow the ring finger to sustain its power.

The *middle finger* shapes our perception of the attractiveness of different options. While forms of advertisement have existed since ancient times, manufacturing desires on massive scales became a game-changer after World War II. As we saw, this is what powered the consumptive drive of the great acceleration as well as our insatiable drive to accumulate and display wealth. It is not much of an exaggeration to say that without advertising in all its wide-ranging forms, we would not be in such trouble. It doesn't take rocket science to come up with the solution: ban advertising. Not surprisingly, any such suggestion can count on fierce reactions from the advertising industry. The right to advertise is often defended as freedom of speech, but as the effects of our overconsumption become increasingly damaging and novel techniques keep boosting the power to steer minds, this defense is hard to sustain.[57] I know it sounds ridiculous, but just pause a minute to think about it. A ban on all advertising would solve a lot of problems and give us enormous peace of mind too. Even if a complete ban may be impossible, the perverse influence of advertising can be reduced. Movements such as badverts.org aim to stimulate pushback against 'badvertising' – adverts that fuel the climate emergency. Small successes include France's somewhat futile move to oblige car advertisers to add a clause to their advertisements encouraging people to use more eco-friendly means of transport. More meaningfully, some governments and NGOs are starting to crack down on companies for blatantly misleading greenwashing advertisements. Yet, to really harness the drivers of the great acceleration, much more forceful regulation is needed. Advertising of alcohol and tobacco has already become increasingly restricted, and in 2025 The Hague became the first city to ban fossil-fuel advertising.[58] It may seem a bold idea, but to curb planet-ruining consumption patterns, it would be best to ban all advertising. Advertisements for things like SUVs, air travel, fast fashion, or beef are only the tip of the iceberg. Loosening this finger of the strangling hand is a tough task, but in my view it must be done to get rid of the planet-consuming rat race. The good news is that legally, a ban on advertisements could be more feasible than you might think.[59] In the mid-twentieth century courts ruled that persuasive advertising by big corporations is, in fact, anti-competitive and harmful to consumers. That did not lead to a ban, as in those days there was still the argument that advertising provided consumers with valuable information. By now, however, that function of advertising is arguably obsolete as consumers can find any information they need on the Internet.

Lastly, the *index finger* of the invisible hand nudges media content beyond advertising. It has a profound but diffuse effect on our perceptions, worldviews, aspirations, and attitudes. In democracies globally, television channels, radio, newspapers, and social media are largely owned by a small group of billionaires. While not comparable to state control of media under totalitarian regimes, the influence of private owners cannot be ignored. Media derive much of their credibility from their perceived independence, but shielding them from the influence of the state or private owners is hard. Also, the ways we receive the information that shapes our views and aspirations are bewilderingly diverse, ranging from sponsored influencers or their AI versions and internet bots to traditional newspapers and public radio. In the end there is no such thing as total independence, since media will always be affected by a multitude of constraints and external influences.[60] It is up to the public which media they trust. The good news is that awareness of the quality of information sources is rapidly co-evolving to combat the emergence of new strategies of manipulation.

The Second Hand

As global warming continues, the tension between worldviews and practices will become increasingly salient, and each of the fingers of the strangling hand may relax bit by bit. Due to feedback effects, such change is self-reinforcing, and the resulting accelerating change in worldviews can prepare minds for more profound revisions of the system. One radical idea is pioneered by Kim Stanley Robinson in his novel *The Ministry for the Future*.[61] In the face of accelerating climate disaster, an international body is created to advocate for the world's future generations. This ministry helps catalyze the – chaotic, violent, and slow – transition to a world in which, eventually, climate is successfully controlled through a broad mix of approaches. Robinson's fictional ministry made me think of a very real semi-autonomous institution we have in the Netherlands to manage our major environmental threat: water. The country lies low and flat in the delta of the Rhine and Meuse rivers, and one-third of our land is below sea level. Since medieval times people have cooperated on an increasingly large scale to construct dikes and to pump water using windmills. The resulting institutions are interesting because they have a high degree of autonomy. For instance, the twenty-one water boards that control regional water levels and water quality hold elections, collect taxes, and function independently of other government bodies.[62] We thus have an old, resilient, and effective parallel democratic structure that controls the largest environmental issue we face. There is also a national institute in charge of the larger defenses. In 1953, when a major storm surge overwhelmed the dikes and killed 1,836 people in one night, the national defense was scaled up to create the Delta Works, a huge set of structures to protect the country against the sea. Since then, 'keeping dry feet' has remained a priority, with a massive separate budget that is never threatened. Despite the usual political push and pull over budgets for education, roads, healthcare, etc., the massive water-management budget is never touched. Never even discussed. Isn't that interesting? We have the normal government guiding everything, but we keep water management separate because it is too important for political compromise. Nobody disagrees with the need for this autonomous 'second hand' of governance.

As the global sense of urgency accelerates, might this principle provide a model for global climate government? A body that holds elections, levies taxes, and functions independently from governments to manage the crisis of climate or even overall planetary health? Could it be an independent democratic structure? Perhaps sanctioned by the UN? For instance, consisting of locally elected climate boards that in turn elect representatives for regional or national boards, which then elect representatives to join the global climate board. Given massive funds (more about that later), what might such a board do? Subsidize the development of new technologies to help reduce greenhouse gases? Fund adaptation measures? Create a network of local boards creating housing and other facilities in places where climate migrants and locals may merge to form thriving, productive communities? Install a global universal basic income?

Let's pause to consider that last option. The idea of unconditional payments to all citizens is an old one. Early examples date back to antiquity, and proposals and experiments have come and gone over the centuries. But recent interest has grown so much that there is an academic journal titled *Basic Income Studies*, an authoritative handbook of basic income,[63] and – if you are looking for a simpler narrative – Rutger Bregman's bestseller *Utopia for Realists*.[64] Universal basic income is feasible, and has remarkable positive effects on society. Intuitively it might seem like a bad idea, as it would reduce the incentive for people to work. But experiments show that that is not what happens. Salaries can be lower, which interests many on the right. Meanwhile, appealing to the political left, it reduces the stress that comes with poverty and income insecurity. That has been shown to reduce the incidence of psychiatric illnesses, and it may have even more profound social effects. As we saw, rising stress is at the core of a set of mechanisms that could allow humanity to spiral into the chaos of a failed world. It reduces the capacity to reason thoughtfully, instead driving people to unwise decisions that may aggravate poverty,[65] to conspiracy theories that may destabilize society,[66] and to populists and authoritarian leaders.[67] Moreover, uncertainty tends to boost aggressive defense of the in-group against outsiders.[68] Thus, in addition to eliminating poverty, a global universal basic income would greatly reduce the risk of slipping into the tracks of a self-propelling failed-world scenario.

These possibilities for a second hand all sound great, but where would the money come from? Taxing countries based on their GDP is one option, but there are other interesting possibilities. One idea, designed by a small group of economists and cited in *The Ministry for the Future*, is to create a parallel world currency for climate-change mitigation. This complementary currency for climate change would be a multi-trillion-dollar crypto fund backed by central banks and provided to persons, organizations, or states that store carbon. This would incentivize funding of costly transition plans and stimulate fossil-fuel-producing countries to stop oil drilling without crashing their economies.[69] Another radical possibility is to take the money from the billionaires and multimillionaires. As we saw, climate measures funded by the poorest will never have sufficient public support. The alternative will become more and more obvious. Inequality has increased with nearly every crisis since medieval times,[70] and that pattern continues. For instance, most of humanity has grown poorer during the pandemic and cost-of-living crisis (2020–2023), while billionaires became 34 percent richer.[71] One proposition to halt this tendency is to put a cap on how wealthy an individual is allowed to be. Again, such limitarianism is an old idea. Indeed, Plato argued that no cohesive society could be created if the richest earned more than four times the wages of the poorest. But while it is ridiculed by some economists, there is much to be said for the idea that no one should have more than, say, €10 million.[72] Taxation of extreme wealth makes all the sense in the world. Moreover, this is agreed upon by the hundreds of billionaires and millionaires who signed an open letter [73] stating:

> Our request is simple: we ask you to tax us, the very richest in society. This will not fundamentally alter our standard of living, nor deprive our children, nor harm our nations' economic growth. But it will turn extreme and unproductive private wealth into an investment for our common democratic future. The solution to this cannot be found in one-off donations or in philanthropy; individual action cannot redress the current colossal imbalance. We need our governments and our leaders to lead. And so we come to you again with the urgent request that you act – unilaterally at the national level, and together on the international stage. Every moment of delay entrenches the dangerous economic status quo, threatens our democratic norms, and passes the buck to our children and grandchildren. Not only do we want to be taxed more but we believe we must be taxed more. We would be proud to live in countries where this is expected, and proud of elected leaders who build better futures.

The Visible Hand

It is encouraging that so many millionaires and billionaires signed a letter asking for taxation. Yet they may not be representative of the extremely wealthy in general. It turns out that ideology matters when it comes to willingness to pay taxes. On the left of the political spectrum, willingness to be taxed rises with income; but on the right, that pattern is reversed.[74] Many billionaires give away a substantial part of their wealth to charity, but like to do so on their own terms rather than leaving such decisions to the state. So, rather than taking their money and redistributing it, why not leave it up to the billionaires themselves?

Many would object. Indeed, giving away money for society's benefit may seem laudable, but it arguably has its darker sides. It is a way to buy public influence and it is largely unaccountable. It raises the fundamental question of whom we trust to have the power. In feudal times, birth into the upper class gave a person power, but that was no guarantee of intelligence and integrity. The same holds for being born a billionaire, or even for becoming one. Just as the counts and lords often felt capable of and responsible for making societies run well (*noblesse oblige*), so do many modern billionaires (the messiah attitude). There are more similarities: just like traditional royalty, billionaires aim to maintain their position, and this may often come at the cost of the common people. So, after getting rid of feudalism, why would we now allow billionaires to run the world? One reason is pragmatic. As we have seen, after societal transformations the same powerful families often remain in charge.[75] This pattern may be explained in part by a tendency for the powerful to prevent a transition unless it keeps their power intact. As we saw, the abolition of slavery in the Netherlands had to be enacted by parliament, which was dominated by wealthy individuals directly or indirectly dependent on slavery. Payment of a lavish compensation per released slave (to the owner, not to the slaves), allowed the same economic elite to stay on top, changing their investments to railways and other new profitable developments. Thus, transformations needed to tip out of trouble could well be more likely if they leave the wealthy in charge. A more positive way to look at it is that, done well, mass giving is simply a good way to decentralize power for the benefit of public goods, such as the climate, nature, arts, education, and science.[76]

If we accept continuity in the way wealth and its associated power is distributed, how might that situation be harnessed in ways that benefit the transition to a good Anthropocene? One thing that would help is finding ways to ensure transparency. Radical transparency about the way wealth is used, and not just the charitable donations. Making all fingers of the invisible hand explicit. A *visible hand* would help make the power of wealth accountable. Not in a formal way, but in a potentially more effective way. Many social experiments confirm that when people feel they are being watched, they behave better.[77] It is a powerful force. All people like to think of themselves as moral, and strive for social valuation. So, if escalating climate problems shift the cloud of worldviews, perceptions, and social norms, could radical transparency make the 'united billionaires' as benign as the United Nations, only more effective? Could monitoring be crowd based, using techniques such as AI-aided open-source intelligence, or should it be institutionalized, supervised by the UN or by the climate boards? Many questions remain, but this is just meant to get you thinking.

Turning the Ship

The loosening hand, the second hand, and the visible hand are not mutually exclusive. Nor are they instruction manuals that must be followed to the letter. Such changes may, in fact, seem far off from the current perspective. Yet most of the elements of those scenarios are plausible. Once the pressure rises and perceptions change, combinations of those elements may self-organize, boosting the big structural transition needed to capitalize on the collective "what *you* can do" efforts. This view of how many different nudges – bottom-up and top-down – may eventually interact to cause a sweeping systemic transition is starting to emerge as a consensus from different angles of research.[78] For instance, a diverse group of researchers led by social scientist Ilona Otto searched for social tipping interventions that might help to "activate contagious processes of rapidly spreading technologies, behaviors, social norms, and structural reorganization."[79] Based on a literature review and input from a broad group of 133 experts, they produced six action items: (1) removing fossil-fuel subsidies and incentivizing decentralized energy generation, (2) building carbon-neutral cities, (3) divesting from assets linked to fossil fuels, (4) revealing the moral implications of fossil fuels, (5) strengthening climate education and engagement, and (6) disclosing information on greenhouse gas emissions. Although these mostly sound like policies, the study identified a broad group of actors that could contribute, including international agencies, national and local governments, business, the financial sector, the agriculture industry, the car industry, the food industry, and the media. As we have seen, these institutions are closely intertwined with the invisible strangling hand, but the experts also stressed the importance of active roles for citizen organizations, NGOs, intellectual leaders, spiritual leaders, journalists, writers, wealthy fashionable people, scientists, teachers, political elites, and the public. Thus, while the emphasis and details differ, it is fair to say that experts who have been thinking deeply about these problems converge on the view that humanity may be nudged toward a sustainability tipping point through the actions of people from a wide range of societal roles.

In the end, laws and policies are important, but it all starts with changing attitudes. That allows for changes in laws and policies which in turn signal broad consensus, further promoting attitude shifts. Most empirical studies have focused on specific examples of attitudes such as veganism, recycling, or renewable-energy use. However, arguably such elements are all linked to the larger web of norms, values, worldviews, and perceptions. As research across countries in the Global South and North showed, a vast majority of people already want to protect the planet for future generations. This is considered the most important benefit from acting on climate change. As we saw, "protecting the planet for the future generations" has twelve times more support than "increasing jobs, opportunities and economic growth" or "reducing social inequality and supporting those impacted by climate change."[80] There is massive potential energy for change, and it is directed toward the holistic goal of passing on the planet in good shape. To reach that goal we must disarm the invisible strangling hand and increase the salience of the dissonance between current practices and the widely shared wish to pass the planet on to future generations in good shape. That is how we can start an avalanche of change toward a good Anthropocene. The alternative is spiraling toward a dystopian future, as captured so powerfully by William Butler Yeats amidst the Spanish flu pandemic that followed World War I:

> Turning and turning in the widening gyre
> The falcon cannot hear the falconer;
> Things fall apart; the centre cannot hold;
> Mere anarchy is loosed upon the world,
> The blood-dimmed tide is loosed, and everywhere
> The ceremony of innocence is drowned;
> The best lack all conviction, while the worst
> Are full of passionate intensity.

History shows that humanity can tumble the wrong way, but also has the power to change course and steer toward a desired future. If I were to choose two examples from the past, one scary and the other encouraging, it would be the Late Bronze Age collapse and the American Progressive Era. Both were the result of rising trouble. As we saw, the Late Bronze Age collapse was a chain reaction of conflict, taking down one state after another in a devastating crumbling of what had once been a thriving network of trading partners, quite literally a tragedy of biblical dimensions. By contrast, the Progressive Era was an 'upswing' of prosocial values and policy measures. It allowed the society to tip out of a situation of trouble which has many similarities with what we face today. Environmental degradation, inequity, and politics corrupted by the power of hyperconcentrated wealth. But change became inevitable and the growing support for action was channeled into a broad spectrum of institutional improvements. Environmental protection, anti-corruption laws, better access to education, and more. The Americans were not alone. A worldwide wave of much-needed social improvements repaired the damage of the Industrial Revolution. History rhymes. But with which past episode will the coming decades rhyme? The outcome is in our hands. Society's free will is an emergent property of common-sense-making, ultimately allowing us to reshape the invisible hand that guides our choices.

EPILOGUE

Never before has humanity been able to see its past so clearly. And never before could we foresee the long-term consequences of consumption and pollution so well. Science has been a game-changer in many ways. It has given us the atomic bomb, new medicines, the Internet, the smartphone, and social media. Humanity's history of invention and transformation has brought us a lot. Arguably we live in the best of times. Over the past two centuries, people have been living ever longer, and the percentage of the global population living in extreme poverty has shrunk. Progress has been highly unequal, but things have become better overall. This is also true for the way we treat each other. The abolition of slavery, the Universal Declaration of Human Rights, the emancipation of women, and the legalization of gay marriage are just some examples. Of course not everything is ideal, and there are occasional setbacks, but historical progress is undeniable. Remembering this is important because it is a source of hope. Hope is different from optimism, the belief that things will turn out well. Like pessimism, optimism invokes a passive attitude. By contrast, hope is the belief that things may turn out well if we do the right things. Hope implies that we see the future as open rather than predetermined. Hope invites agency. History provides good reasons for hope. We have achieved great things that we now take for granted, forgetting that they were the fruits of Enlightenment, science, and technology. And we forget that major social breakthroughs were invariably brought about by decades of activism.

Many of us who seek to inspire positive change are now realizing that it is important to remember the good things humans achieved. One of the most powerful voices in this field is the writer Rebecca Solnit. In preparation for a workshop that we both attended I read her book *Hope in the Dark*. If you are looking for compelling arguments for hope, read her work. Somewhere in the middle of her book she casually drops in the notion that depressed patients have a memory problem. They cannot recall instances of agency when their actions worked out. The other day I brought this up to Claudi Bockting, a psychologist with whom our team works on tipping points for depression. She told me that indeed, one of the ways to help people climb out of a depression is to ask them to bring back memories. Memories of when good things happened to them, or when they did something that worked out well. Surprisingly, even bringing back memories of things that went wrong may help. What matters may be memories of agency, irrespective of results.[1] In fact, psychiatric problems such as depression and anxiety disorder can be rooted in "learned helplessness," a feeling of having no agency at all.[2] People who have long been subject to abuse or other overwhelming challenges can come to believe that they have no control over their situation. Anxious or depressed, they may give up trying and accept their fate.

Could such psychiatric disorders and their drivers have a social parallel? Could entire groups in society become anxious, depressed, hopeless, and passive? If so, could it help to bring back memories of our agency? That is certainly what Rebecca Solnit proposes, and I think she is right. She goes even further and suggests that promoting the feeling that nothing can be done is a deliberate strategy of powerful players that benefit from prolonging the status quo. Whatever the causes, climate anxiety is real. According to an international study, in 2021 a majority of young people felt very worried, sad, anxious, and angry about global warming.[3] They also felt helpless and betrayed because of inadequate government response. Could societal versions of depression or anxiety make us passive? Let's not allow that to happen. As I have argued, society does have its own version of free will, and that free will does not want us to spiral into a failed world. Vision is shaped by all of us. Once the way to go is clear, there will be no way to stop the transformation. As has happened so many times before in the history of civilization.

Perhaps it seems unlikely that concerted global action will tip us out of trouble given the worrying trends in societies. But the response to the Covid-19 pandemic has been an eye-opener. First and foremost, it revealed that when the shit hits the fan, people and governments can move quickly and cooperate effectively worldwide to control the problems. Of course it wasn't easy at all, but people quickly adapted to new life patterns, such as working from home and spending holidays locally. As Bruno Latour said:[4]

> The pandemic has reopened the debate about what is necessary and what is possible. It has put us in a position where we can decide what is useful and what is not. That choice disappeared before. Everything seemed relentless like a tsunami. Now we realise it was not. We can see things are reversible. What we need is not only to modify the system of production but to get out of it altogether. We should remember that this idea of framing everything in terms of the economy is a new thing in human history. The pandemic has shown us the economy is a very narrow and limited way of organising life and deciding who is important and who is not important.

Of course, with hindsight we did not take the opportunity to "get out of the system of production altogether." Depressingly, once again the rich got richer and the poor poorer. We may be better prepared for the next pandemic, but altogether nothing really changed. A lost opportunity perhaps, but the pandemic revealed an immense capacity for concerted action once the need is urgent enough. That mechanism was suggested by experiments on cooperation years earlier.[5] Economists had long considered humans as selfish, rational actors. Reality couldn't be more different. That is why, after years of fundamentally misunderstanding humanity, Nobel Prizes in economics were given to Daniel Kahneman, who showed that we are only marginally rational, and to Elinor ("Lin") Ostrom, for showing the conditions under which humans cooperate to reach a common goal. In this spirit, economists Astrid Dannenberg and Scott Barrett asked what it would take to make humanity cooperate to avoid climate catastrophe.[6] The answer, based on an experiment with 500 students, was that cooperation only arises if uncertainty about the potential catastrophe is small. They found a critical threshold of understanding beyond which, suddenly, cooperation emerged. Before that threshold the students were trapped in the classical situation where they would not commit to cooperation because others were free-riding on their efforts, contributing nothing. Clearly, the pandemic pushed humanity to the cooperative side of such a threshold. Apparently, climate change and the demise of nature have not quite reached a similar salience. Yet the pandemic response shows that a massive leap into action is possible after all.

During the pandemic we were lucky with the state of science. An effective vaccine could be rapidly mass produced and rolled out. Not that there was any strategy behind getting science ready to come to the rescue. Quite the opposite. Researcher Katalin Karikó eventually received a shared Nobel Prize for getting the revolutionary new mRNA technique to work. But in fact, she had faced decades of scepticism.[7] It was her persistence that, in the end, saved millions of lives. This is a character trait shared by many successful scientists.[8] Karikó grew up in Hungary, living with her family in a single room without running water or a refrigerator. In 1985 she sold the family car and, hiding the money in her daughter's teddy bear, moved with her family to Philadelphia, where she was offered a post-doc. The years that followed weren't easy. At one point she was even demoted for failing to generate enough funding for her research. When the pandemic broke out it became clear that she had been right all along. A great moment after decades of swimming against the stream. As she told *The Guardian*:[9] "I always wished that I would live long enough to see something that I've worked on be approved." There could hardly be a better illustration of how visionaries in the periphery of the networks of power, money, and prestige eventually lead the way. A reason for hope and an encouragement to anyone contributing in their own way to making a difference, even if it seems pointless at times.

In the end, we cannot predict the future, but one thing is clear. A big change will come. That may feel unlikely. It always does. But time capsules are a powerful reminder that this feeling of inertia is a delusion. When Ova, my great-grandfather, started keeping his diary in 1904, the world looked very different. Over his half-century of writing, much changed. But the great acceleration really happened only after he finished in 1950. How would he look at the world today? As a doctor, he might be surprised at the advances in life expectancy; as a pianist, he would be stunned by the technical mastery of the latest generation of musicians; as a gourmand, he would marvel at the range of worldwide

Figure 9.1 Me looking at my great-grandfather, with the two intermediate generations sharing the moment.

products available and the sophistication of chefs. As a naturalist, he would probably be shocked to see the Dutch landscape transformed and many of his favorite species vanished. On the other hand, he might smile on learning that many new species have colonized our country. He might well like how his great-grandchildren enjoy life.

Thinking of my great-grandfather (Figure 9.1), I can't help wondering how my great-grandchildren will look back on our times. That is impossible to foresee. However, one insight emerges firmly from the reasoning in this book. Scenarios over the coming century may differ hugely, depending on social choices in the coming decades. Those social choices emerge from individual choices. What you and I do to help disarm the invisible strangling hand matters. Our great-grandchildren will be proud if we help turn the ship. History shows that it can be done. That is no reason for optimism, but it is reason for hope.

ACKNOWLEDGMENTS

The insights reflected in this book have emerged to a great extent from cooperations with colleagues who over the years became dear friends. Cooperations that involved countless discussions, often starting over long walks or at campfires in the breaks of workshops. Some of the emerging thoughts ended up in papers we co-wrote, but those are just the tip of the iceberg. For the content of this book the 'trust group' has been very important. Steve Polasky, Marty Anderies, and I started working on stability of trust in societies; our weekly online chats pulled us through the pandemic and helped shape my thoughts on society's free will more broadly. Then there is the 'surprise group,' named after a surprise that brought us together. The 2010 Eyjafjallajökull eruption disrupted air traffic just when we were heading home after a workshop in Sweden. Frances Westley, Steve Carpenter, Carl Folke, and I were happily biding our time, uncertain whether this would last for days, weeks, or months. It led to the ideas reflected in our paper "Dancing on the volcano: social exploration in times of discontent." Many more fruitful retreats followed. Both the trust group and the surprise group exist thanks to the vision of Buzz C. S. Holling, who brought ecologists and social scientists together on islands to get a new kind of interdisciplinary science going to unravel how people and nature interact. Over the years I have come to work more and more with artists too. Extensive talks in the forests of Norway, the pampas of Uruguay, and the high Andes with Tone Bjordam, Francisco Gazitua, Angela Leible, and others helped me get a more sophisticated view of what moves people.

Versions of the manuscript have been read by Koen de Gans, Bas van Bavel, Duur Aanen, Bert de Vries, Roger Cremades Rodeja, Stephen R. Carpenter, Alison A. Kalett, and Rinse Boersma, and by master storytellers Len Fisher and Rob Dunn, who all gave enriching and complementary suggestions. William Boggess edited the final text, smoothing my non-native English and suggesting some good improvements of the logical flow. I am also happy that I met Tim Lenton. Such a kind and brilliant mind. We discussed tipping points in the climate and societies for many years. We have very similar interests and our complementarity greatly helped deepen my thoughts. While I wrote this book he was writing his on positive social tipping. Two different symphonies on an overlapping collection of themes. When Xu Chi came visiting me from China for a sabbatical it marked the start of another long-lasting friendship that proved scientifically very fruitful. Xu, Tim, and I formed a 'power trio' that became the core of a range of cooperative projects with archaeologist Tim Kohler, Luke Kemp, and others. We came up with the idea of the human climate niche and found evidence for the loss of resilience in aging societies. Meanwhile, with economic historian Bas van Bavel we explored how inequalities in nature and society relate, and Bas taught me that since medieval times crises have generally widened rather than narrowed the power gap in societies. Historian Jan Luiten van Zanden suggested using the period of great social reforms after the Industrial Revolution as a model for the kind of complex social change we need now. Naomi Ellemers helped me think about social attitude change in more profound ways, and in discussions with Appy Sluijs we developed the idea that even seemingly futile steps toward sustainability matter because of their positive signaling effect. My fascination for language change was fueled by the enthusiasm and expertise of Johan Bollen. Whenever we talked, new plans and ideas came up. None of those cooperations can beat the duration of my companionship with Egbert van Nes. As I write this, we have been working together on the principles of tipping points for thirty-three years. Joined over the last decade by Ingrid van de Leemput, we now have our little 'troika.' I couldn't dream of more kind and smart friends with whom to explore the miraculous world of complex dynamical systems. Lastly, Milena, Pablo, and Camila are my source of happiness and inspiration in life. They also made me keep my feet on the ground, while their deep insights helped me understand humans and nature more profoundly.

FIGURES

NOTES

Prologue: Change is in the Air

1. Pinker, S. *Enlightenment now: the case for reason, science, humanism, and progress* (Penguin, 2018).
2. Xu, C., Kohler, T. A., Lenton, T. M., Svenning, J.-C., and Scheffer, M. Future of the human climate niche. *Proceedings of the National Academy of Sciences* 117, 11350–11355 (2020). https://doi.org/10.1073/pnas.1910114117.
3. Carpenter, S. R., Folke, C., Scheffer, M., and Westley, F. R. Dancing on the volcano: social exploration in times of discontent. *Ecology and Society* 24 (2019). https://doi.org/10.5751/es-10839-240123.
4. QuoteResearch. Quote origin: History does not repeat itself, but it rhymes, https://quoteinvestigator.com/2014/01/12/history-rhymes/ (2014).
5. Putnam, R. D. and Garrett, S. R. *The upswing: how America came together a century ago and how we can do it again* (Simon & Schuster, 2020).
6. Scheffer, M. *Ecology of shallow lakes*, 1st ed. (Chapman & Hall, 1998).
7. Scheffer, M., Carpenter, S. R., Foley, J. A., Folke, C., and Walker, B. Catastrophic shifts in ecosystems. *Nature* 413, 591–596 (2001), Scheffer, M. *Critical transitions in nature and society* (Princeton University Press, 2009).

1   The Trouble

1. Rockström, J. *et al.* A safe operating space for humanity. *Nature* 461, 472–475 (2009).
2. Polasky, S. *et al.* Corridors of clarity: four principles to overcome uncertainty paralysis in the Anthropocene. *BioScience* 70, 1139–1144 (2020). https://doi.org/10.1093/biosci/biaa115.
3. QuoteResearch, Quote origin.
4. Vitousek, P. M., Mooney, H. A., Lubchenco, J., and Melillo, J. M. Human domination of Earth's ecosystems. *Science* 277, 494–499 (1997).
5. Barnosky, A. D. *et al.* Approaching a state shift in Earth's biosphere. *Nature* 486, 52–58 (2012).
6. Kirchner, J. W. and Weil, A. Delayed biological recovery from extinctions throughout the fossil record. *Nature* 404, 177–180 (2000).

7. Folke, C. *et al.* Our future in the Anthropocene biosphere. *Ambio* 50, 834–869 (2021). https://doi.org/10.1007/s13280-021-01544-8.

8. Ibid.

9. Stern, N. H. *The economics of climate change: the Stern review* (Cambridge University Press, 2007).

10. Lenton, T. M. *et al.* Quantifying the human cost of global warming. *Nature Sustainability* 6, 1–11 (2023).

11. Xu *et al.* Future of the human climate niche.

12. Scheffer, M. *et al.* Anticipating the global redistribution of people and property. *One Earth* 7, 1151–1154 (2024).

13. Burke, M., Hsiang, S. M., and Miguel, E. Global non-linear effect of temperature on economic production. *Nature* 527, 235–239 (2015).

14. Lenton *et al.* Quantifying the human cost of global warming.

15. Xu *et al.* Future of the human climate niche.

16. Christensen, M.-B., Hallum, C., Maitland, A., Parrinello, Q., and Putaturo, C. Survival of the richest: how we must tax the super-rich now to fight inequality. Briefing paper, Oxfam International (2023). https://doi.org/10.21201/2023.621477.

17. Oreskes, N. and Conway, E. M. *Merchants of doubt: how a handful of scientists obscured the truth on issues from tobacco smoke to global warming* (Bloomsbury, 2010).

18. Harring, N., Jönsson, E., Matti, S., Mundaca, G., and Jagers, S. C. Cross-national analysis of attitudes towards fossil fuel subsidy removal. *Nature Climate Change* 13, 244–249 (2023).

19. Stigler, G. J. The theory of economic regulation, in *The political economy: readings in the politics and economics of American public policy*, ed. T. Ferguson and J. Rogers (Taylor & Francis, 2021), 67–81.

20. Christensen, M. The social facts of democracy: science meets politics with Mosca, Pareto, Michels, and Schumpeter. *Journal of Classical Sociology* 13, 460–486 (2013).

21. Robeyns, I. *Limitarianism: the case against extreme wealth* (Random House, 2024).

22. Suzman, J. *Work: a deep history, from the Stone Age to the age of robots* (Penguin, 2021).

23. Kohler, T. A. and Smith, M. E. *Ten thousand years of inequality: the archaeology of wealth differences* (University of Arizona Press, 2018).

24. Scheffer, M., van Bavel, B., van de Leemput, I. A., and van Nes, E. H. Inequality in nature and society. *Proceedings of the National Academy of Sciences* 114, 13154–13157 (2017). https://doi.org/10.1073/pnas.1706412114.

25. Khalfan, A. *et al.* Climate equality: a planet for the 99%. https://policy-practice.oxfam.org/resources/climate-equality-a-planet-for-the-99-621551/ (2023).

26. Neate, R. "Extra level of power": billionaires who have bought up the media, www.theguardian.com/news/2022/may/03/billionaires-extra-power-media-ownership-elon-musk (2022).

27. Applebaum, A. *Autocracy, Inc: the dictators who want to run the world* (Random House, 2024).

28. Krcmaric, D., Nelson, S. C., and Roberts, A. Billionaire politicians: a global perspective. *Perspectives on Politics* 22, 357–371 (2024).

29. Ibid.

30. Scheffer *et al.* Inequality in nature and society.https://url.avanan.click/v2/r02/__https://doi.org/10.1073/pnas.1706412114___.

31. Ibid, Van Nes, E. H. *et al.* A tiny fraction of all species forms most of nature: rarity as a sticky state. *Proceedings of the National Academy of Sciences of the United States of America* 121 (2024). https://doi.org/10.1073/pnas.2221791120.

32. Scheffer *et al.* Inequality in nature and society. https://url.avanan.click/v2/r02/__ https://doi.org/10.1093/biosci/biaa115__.

33. Ter Steege, H. *et al.* Hyperdominance in the Amazonian tree flora. *Science* 342 (2013). https://doi.org/10.1126/science.1243092.

34. Van Nes, E. H. *et al.* A tiny fraction of all species forms most of nature.

35. Scheffer *et al.* Inequality in nature and society.

36. Lierse, H. Globalization and the societal consensus of wealth tax cuts. *Journal of European Public Policy* 29, 748–766 (2022).

37. van Bavel, B. and Scheffer, M. Historical effects of shocks on inequality: the great leveler revisited. *Humanities and Social Sciences Communications* 8, 1–9 (2021).

38. Christensen *et al.* Survival of the richest.

39. Scheffer *et al.* Inequality in nature and society.

40. Welcome to the Anthropocene, *The Economist*, editorial. www.economist.com/leaders/2011/05/26/welcome-to-the-anthropocene (2011).

41. Barrett, S. *et al.* Social dimensions of fertility behavior and consumption patterns in the Anthropocene. *Proceedings of the National Academy of Sciences of the United States of America* 117, 6300–6307 (2020). https://doi.org/10.1073/pnas.1909857117.

42. ClimateWatch. Historical GHG emissions, www.climatewatchdata.org/ghg-emissions (2024).

43. FootprintNetwork. Ecological footprint, https://data.footprintnetwork.org/#/ (2024).

44. Raworth, K. *Doughnut economics: seven ways to think like a 21st century economist* (Chelsea Green Publishing, 2018).

45. Hickel, J. What does degrowth mean? A few points of clarification. *Globalizations* 18, 1105–1111 (2021), Hickel J. *Less is more: how degrowth will save the world* (Random House, 2020).

46. Fioramonti, L. *et al.* Wellbeing economy: an effective paradigm to mainstream post-growth policies? *Ecological Economics* 192, 107261 (2022).

47. McGreevy, S. R. *et al.* Sustainable agrifood systems for a post-growth world. *Nature Sustainability* 5, 1011–1017 (2022).

48. Strunz, S. and Schindler, H. Identifying barriers toward a post-growth economy: a political economy view. *Ecological Economics* 153, 68–77 (2018).

49. Judge, M., Bouman, T., Steg, L., and Bolderdijk, J. W. Accelerating social tipping points in sustainable behaviors: insights from a dynamic model of moralized social change. *One Earth* 7, 759–770 (2024), Otto, I. M. *et al.* Social tipping dynamics for stabilizing Earth's climate by 2050. *Proceedings of the National Academy of Sciences* 117, 2354–2365 (2020), Winkelmann, R. *et al.* Social tipping processes towards climate action: a conceptual framework. *Ecological Economics* 192, 107242 (2022), Lenton, T. M. Tipping positive change. *Philosophical Transactions of the Royal Society B* 375, 20190123 (2020), Lenton, T. M. *et al.* Operationalising positive tipping points towards global sustainability. *Global Sustainability* 5, e1 (2022), Tàbara, J. D. *et al.* Positive tipping points in a rapidly warming world. *Current Opinion in Environmental Sustainability* 31, 120–129 (2018).

2   The Tipping

1. Van Nes, E. H. *et al.* What do you mean, "tipping point"? *Trends in Ecology and Evolution* 31, 902–904 (2016).

2. Grodzins, M. *The metropolitan area as a racial problem* (University of Pittsburgh, Digital Research Library, 1958).

3. Hastings, A. *et al.* Transient phenomena in ecology. *Science* 361, eaat6412 (2018). https://doi.org/10.1126/science.aat6412.

4. Van Nes *et al.* What do you mean, "tipping point"?

5. Kopp, R. E. *et al.* "Tipping points" confuse and can distract from urgent climate action. *Nature Climate Change* 15, 29–36 (2025), Milkoreit, M. Social tipping points everywhere? Patterns and risks of overuse. *Wiley Interdisciplinary Reviews: Climate Change* 14, e813 (2023).

6. Strogatz, S. H. *Nonlinear dynamics and chaos: with applications to physics, biology, chemistry and engineering*, 1st ed. (Addison-Wesley, 1994), Kuznetsov, Y. A. *Elements of applied bifurcation theory* (Springer-Verlag, 1995).

7. Scheffer, M. Searching explanations of nature in the mirror world of math. *Conservation Ecology* 3, 11 (1999).

8. Scheffer, *Critical transitions in nature and society.*

9. Scheffer, M., van Nes, E. H., Bird, D., Bocinsky, R. K. & Kohler, T. A. Loss of resilience preceded transformations of pre-Hispanic Pueblo societies. *Proceedings of the National Academy of Sciences* 118, e2024397118 (2021). https://doi.org/10.1073/pnas.2024397118.

10. Scheffer, M. *et al.* A dynamical systems view of psychiatric disorders – practical implications: a review. *JAMA Psychiatry* 81, 624–630 (2024), Scheffer, M. *et al.* A dynamical systems view of psychiatric disorders – theory: a review. *JAMA Psychiatry* 81, 618–623 (2024). https://doi.org/10.1001/jamapsychiatry.2024.0215.

11. Scheffer, M. *et al.* Early-warning signals for critical transitions. *Nature* 461, 53–59 (2009). https://doi.org/10.1038/nature08227, Scheffer, M. *et al.* Anticipating critical transitions. *Science* 338, 344–348 (2012).

12. Scheffer *et al.* Early-warning signals for critical transitions.

13. Scheffer, M. and Carpenter, S. R. Catastrophic regime shifts in ecosystems: linking theory to observation. *Trends in Ecology and Evolution* 18, 648–656 (2003). https://doi.org/10.1016/j.tree.2003.09.002.

14. Dakos, V. *et al.* Slowing down as an early warning signal for abrupt climate change. *Proceedings of the National Academy of Sciences of the United States of America* 105, 14308–14312 (2008).

15. Judge *et al.* Accelerating social tipping points in sustainable behaviors, Otto *et al.* Social tipping dynamics for stabilizing Earth's climate by 2050, Winkelmann *et al.* Social tipping processes towards climate action, Lenton, Tipping positive change, Lenton *et al.* Operationalising positive tipping points towards global sustainability, Tàbara *et al.* Positive tipping points in a rapidly warming world.

16. Milkoreit, Social tipping points everywhere?

17. Monastersky, R. The greatest vanishing act in prehistoric America. *Nature* 527, 26–29 (2015). https://doi.org/10.1038/527026a.

18. Scheffer *et al.* Loss of resilience preceded transformations of pre-Hispanic Pueblo societies.

19. Ibid.

3   How Civilizations Transformed

1. Collingwood, R. G. *The idea of history* (Oxford University Press, 1993).

2. Turchin, P. *et al.* Quantitative historical analysis uncovers a single dimension of complexity that structures global variation in human social organization. *Proceedings of the National Academy of Sciences* 115, E144–E151 (2018).

3. Schwab, I. R. The evolution of eyes: major steps. The Keeler lecture 2017: centenary of Keeler Ltd. *Eye* 32, 302–313 (2018).

4. Broome, R. *Aboriginal Australians: black responses to white dominance 1788–1994* (Allen & Unwin Sydney, 1996).

5. Centeno, M., Callahan, P., Larcey, P., and Patterson, T., eds. *How worlds collapse: what history, systems, and complexity can teach us about our modern world and fragile future* (Taylor & Francis, 2023).

6. Jongman, W. M., Jacobs, J. P., and Goldewijk, G. M. K. Health and wealth in the Roman Empire. *Economics and Human Biology* 34, 138–150 (2019).

7. Scott, J. C. *Against the grain: a deep history of the earliest states.* (Yale University Press, 2017).

8. Pinker, *Enlightenment now.*

9. Cline, E. H. *1177 BC: the year civilization collapsed* (Princeton University Press, 2014), Cline, E. H. 1177 BC: the collapse of Bronze Age civilization. *Biblical Archaeology Review* 48, 40–47 (2022).

10. Cline, *1177 BC: the year civilization collapsed.*

11. Manning, S. W., Kocik, C., Lorentzen, B., and Sparks, J. P. Severe multi-year drought coincident with Hittite collapse around 1198–1196 BC. *Nature* 614, 719–724 (2023).

12. Kemp, L. and Cline, E. H., Systemic risk and resilience: the Bronze Age collapse and recovery, in *Perspectives on public policy in societal-environmental crises: what the future needs from history*, ed. A. Izdebski, J. Haldon, and P. Filipkowski (Springer International, 2022), 207–223.

13. Tainter, J. *The collapse of complex societies* (Cambridge University Press, 1988).

14. Van Schaik, C. and Michel, K. *The good book of human nature: an evolutionary reading of the Bible* (Basic Books, 2016), Powers, S. T., Van Schaik, C. P., and Lehmann, L. How institutions shaped the last major evolutionary transition to large-scale human societies. *Philosophical Transactions of the Royal Society B: Biological Sciences* 371, 20150098 (2016).

15. Morley, N. Decadence as a theory of history. *New Literary History* 35, 573–585 (2004).

16. Scheffer, M. *et al.* The vulnerability of aging states: a survival analysis across premodern societies. *Proceedings of the National Academy of Sciences of the United States of America* 120 (2023). https://doi.org/10.1073/pnas.2218834120.

17. Tainter, *The collapse of complex societies.*

18. Jongman *et al.* Health and wealth in the Roman Empire.

19. Ibid.

20. Scheffer, *Ecology of shallow lakes.*

21. Turchin, P. and Nefedov, S. A. *Secular cycles* (Princeton University Press, 2009).

22. Kemp, L. Diminishing returns on extraction: how inequality and extractive hierarchy create fragility, in Centeno *et al.* eds., *How worlds collapse*, 37–60.

23. Janssen, M. A., Kohler, T. A., and Scheffer, M. Sunk-cost effects and vulnerability to collapse in ancient societies. *Current Anthropology* 44, 722–728 (2003). https://doi.org/10.1086/379261.

24. Kohler and Smith, *Ten thousand years of inequality.*

25. Acemoglu, D. and Robinson, J. A. *Why nations fail: the origins of power, prosperity and poverty* (Profile Books, 2013).

26. Putnam and Garrett, *The upswing.*

27. Ibid.

28. Van Meerhaeghe, M. Bismarck and the social question. *Journal of Economic Studies* 33, 284–301 (2006).

29. Tuininga, M. J. Abraham Kuyper and the social order: principles for Christian liberalism. *Journal of Markets and Morality* 23, 337–361 (2020).

30. Ibid.

31. Piketty, T. *Capital in the twenty-first century* (Belknap Press of Harvard University Press, 2014), Scheidel, W. *The great leveler: violence and the history of inequality from the Stone Age to the twenty-first century* (Princeton University Press, 2017).

32. Wollstonecraft, M. *A historical and moral view of the origin and progress of the French Revolution* (Good Press, 2023), Doyle, W. *The Oxford history of the French Revolution* (Oxford University Press, 2018).

33. Darnton, R. An early information society: news and the media in eighteenth-century Paris. *American Historical Review* 105, 1–35 (2000).

34. Geddes, B., Wright, J., and Frantz, E. Autocratic breakdown and regime transitions: a new data set. *Perspectives on Politics* 12, 313–331 (2014).

35. Wright, G. Slavery and Anglo-American capitalism revisited. *Economic History Review* 73, 353–383 (2020).

36. Kaufmann, C. D. and Pape, R. A. Explaining costly international moral action: Britain's sixty-year campaign against the Atlantic slave trade. *International Organization* 53, 631–668 (1999).

37. Lauret, L. No emancipation without compensation: slave owners' petitions and the end of slavery in the Netherlands, c. 1833–1873. *BMGN: Low Countries Historical Review* 139, 94–117 (2024).

38. Mackie, G. Ending footbinding and infibulation: a convention account. *American Sociological Review* 61, 999–1017 (1996), Brown, M. J. and Satterthwaite-Phillips, D. Economic correlates of footbinding: implications for the importance of Chinese daughters' labor. *PloS one* 13, e0201337 (2018).

39. Mackie, Ending footbinding and infibulation, Brown and Satterthwaite-Phillips, Economic correlates of footbinding.

40. Ibid.

41. Hume, L. *The National Union of Women's Suffrage societies 1897–1914* (Routledge, 2016).

42. Oppenheimer, D. B. Kennedy, King, Shuttlesworth and Walker: the Events leading to the introduction of the Civil Rights Act of 1964. *University of San Francisco Law Review* 29, 645–679 (1994).

43. Nyborg, K. *et al.* Social norms as solutions. *Science* 354, 42–43 (2016).

44. Oreskes and Conway, *Merchants of doubt*.

45. Britton, J. Death, disease, and tobacco. *The Lancet* 389, 1861–1862 (2017).

46. Galor, O. *Unified growth theory* (Princeton University Press, 2011).

47. Barrett, S. *et al.* Social dimensions of fertility behavior and consumption patterns in the Anthropocene. *Proceedings of the National Academy of Sciences* 117, 6300–6307 (2020).

48. Thoreau, H. D. *Walden* (Yale University Press, 2006).

49. Livingston, A. Fidelity to truth: Gandhi and the genealogy of civil disobedience. *Political Theory* 46, 511–536 (2018).

50. Mann, C. C. *The wizard and the prophet: two remarkable scientists and their dueling visions to shape tomorrow's world* (Knopf, 2018).

51. Isenhour, C. Unearthing human progress? Ecomodernism and contrasting definitions of technological progress in the Anthropocene. *Economic Anthropology* 3, 315–328 (2016).

52. Lenton, T. M. *et al.* Survival of the systems. *Trends in Ecology and Evolution* 36, 333–344 (2021). https://doi.org/10.1016/j.tree.2020.12.003, Wrangham, R. W. and Carmody, R. N. Human adaptation to the control of fire. *Evolutionary Anthropology* 19, 187–199 (2010).

53. Scott, *Against the grain*.

54. Mummert, A., Esche, E., Robinson, J., and Armelagos, G. J. Stature and robusticity during the agricultural transition: evidence from the bioarchaeological record. *Economics and Human Biology* 9, 284–301 (2011).

55. Harari, Y. N. *Sapiens: a brief history of humankind* (Random House, 2014).

56. Hickel, *Less is more*.

57. Gollin, D., Hansen, C. W., and Wingender, A. M. Two blades of grass: the impact of the Green Revolution. *Journal of Political Economy* 129, 2344–2384 (2021), Hurt, R. D. *The Green Revolution in the Global South: science, politics, and unintended consequences* (University Alabama Press, 2020).

58. The man who saved a billion lives, *University of Minnesota News and Events*. https://twin-cities.umn.edu/news-events/man-who-saved-billion-lives (2016).

59. Gollin, Hansen, and Wingender, Two blades of grass.

60. Whitton, C., Bogueva, D., Marinova, D., and Phillips, C. J. Are we approaching peak meat consumption? Analysis of meat consumption from 2000 to 2019 in 35 countries and its relationship to gross domestic product. *Animals* 11, 3466 (2021).

61. Fan, S. and Rue, C. The role of smallholder farms in a changing world, in *The role of smallholder farms in food and nutrition security*, ed. S. Gomez y Paloma, L. Riesgo, and K. Louhichi (Springer, 2020), 13–28.

62. van Selm, B. *et al.* Recoupling livestock and feed production in the Netherlands to reduce environmental impacts. *Science of the Total Environment* 899, 165540 (2023).

63. Ritchie, H. and Roser, M. How many people does synthetic fertilizer feed? https://ourworldindata.org/how-many-people-does-synthetic-fertilizer-feed (2024).

64. Putnam and Garrett, *The upswing*.

65. Cline, 1177 BC: the collapse of Bronze Age civilization.

66. Sunstein, C. R. *How change happens* (MIT Press, 2019).

67. Staver, C. A. and Levin, S. A. Integrating theoretical climate and fire effects on savanna and forest systems. *American Naturalist* 180, 211–224 (2012). https://doi.org/10.1086/666648.

68. Lenton, T. M. and Williams, H. T. P. On the origin of planetary-scale tipping points. *Trends in Ecology and Evolution* 28, 380–382 (2013). https://doi.org/10.1016/j.tree.2013.06.001.

69. Gollin, Hansen, and Wingender, Two blades of grass.

70. Scott, *Against the grain*.

71. Tainter, *The collapse of complex societies*.

72. Cline, 1177 BC: the collapse of Bronze Age civilization.

73. Nicoll, K. and Zerboni, A. Is the past key to the present? Observations of cultural continuity and resilience reconstructed from geoarchaeological records. *Quaternary International* 545, 119–127 (2020).

74. Jongman, *et al.* Health and wealth in the Roman Empire.

75. van Bavel and Scheffer, Historical effects of shocks on inequality.

76. Geddes, Wright, and Frantz, Autocratic breakdown and regime transitions.

77. Brownlee, J., Masoud, T., and Reynolds, A. From dynamic events to deep causes: outcomes and explanations of the Arab Spring. *Middle East Law and Governance* 7, 3–15 (2015), Soffiantini, G. Food insecurity and political instability during the Arab Spring. *Global Food Security* 26, 100400 (2020).

78. Bacon, F. *The new organon* (Cambridge University Press, 2000).

4 How Social Tipping Works

1. Murray, J. A climate theory of everything. www.businessgreen.com/blog-post/4151704/climate-theory-everything (2023).
2. Stechemesser, A., Levermann, A., and Wenz, L. Temperature impacts on hate speech online: evidence from 4 billion geolocated tweets from the USA. *The Lancet Planetary Health* **6**, e714–e725 (2022).
3. Eberle, U. J., Rohner, D., and Thoenig, M. Heat and hate: climate security and farmer–herder conflicts in Africa. *Review of Economics and Statistics*, 1–47 (2025).
4. Brownlee, Masoud, and Reynolds, From dynamic events to deep causes, Soffiantini, Food insecurity and political instability during the Arab Spring.
5. Chamberlin, T. C. The method of multiple working hypotheses. *Journal of Geology* **5**, 837–848 (1897).
6. Scheffer, *Critical transitions in nature and society*, Scheffer, M. and Beets, J. Ecological models and the pitfalls of causality. *Hydrobiologia* **276**, 115–124 (1994), Oreskes, N., Shraderfrechette, K., and Belitz, K. Verification, validation, and confirmation of numerical models in the earth sciences. *Science* **263**, 641–646 (1994).
7. Centola, D., Becker, J., Brackbill, D., and Baronchelli, A. Experimental evidence for tipping points in social convention. *Science* **360**, 1116–1119 (2018).
8. Scheffer, *Critical transitions in nature and society*.
9. Ibid.
10. Scheffer *et al.* Early-warning signals for critical transitions.
11. Van Nes, E. H. and Scheffer, M. Slow recovery from perturbations as a generic indicator of a nearby catastrophic shift. *American Naturalist* **169**, 738–747 (2007).
12. Scheffer *et al.* A dynamical systems view of psychiatric disorders – practical implications, Scheffer *et al.* A dynamical systems view of psychiatric disorders – theory. https://url.avanan.click/v2/r02/__https://doi.org/10.1001/jamapsychiatry.2024.0215, van de Leemput, I. A. *et al.* Critical slowing down as early warning for the onset and termination of depression. *Proceedings of the National Academy of Sciences* **111**, 87–92 (2014). https://doi.org/10.1073/pnas.1312114110.
13. Dakos *et al.* Slowing down as an early warning signal for abrupt climate change.
14. Scheffer *et al.* Loss of resilience preceded transformations of pre-Hispanic Pueblo societies.
15. Tzedakis, P., Crucifix, M., Mitsui, T., and Wolff, E. W. A simple rule to determine which insolation cycles lead to interglacials. *Nature* **542**, 427–432 (2017).
16. Hall-Wallace, M. K. Can earthquakes be predicted? *Journal of Geoscience Education* **46**, 439–449 (1998).
17. Scheffer, M. and Westley, F. R. The evolutionary basis of rigidity: locks in cells, minds, and society. *Ecology and Society* **12**, 36 (2007).
18. Scheffer, M., Borsboom, D., Nieuwenhuis, S., and Westley, F. Belief traps: tackling the inertia of harmful beliefs. *Proceedings of the National Academy of Sciences of the United States of America* **119** (2022). https://doi.org/10.1073/pnas.2203149119.
19. Pinker, *Enlightenment now*.
20. Feinberg, M. and Willer, R. Apocalypse soon? Dire messages reduce belief in global warming by contradicting just-world beliefs. *Psychological Science* **22**, 34–38 (2011).
21. Sparkman, G., Geiger, N., and Weber, E. U. Americans experience a false social reality by underestimating popular climate policy support by nearly half. *Nature Communications* **13**, 4779 (2022).

22. Sunstein, *How change happens*.

23. Festinger, L. *A theory of cognitive dissonance*, vol. 2 (Stanford University Press, 1962).

24. Homer-Dixon, T. *et al.* A complex systems approach to the study of ideology: cognitive-affective structures and the dynamics of belief systems. *Journal of Social and Political Psychology* 1, 337–363 (2013).

25. Douglas, K. M. *et al.* Understanding conspiracy theories. *Political Psychology* 40, 3–35 (2019).

26. Scheffer *et al.* Belief traps.

27. Yellow Vest Movement. Demands of France's yellow vests. www.opendemocracy .net/en/can-europe-make-it/demands-of-frances-yellow-vests-as-uploaded-by-france-bleu-november-29/ (2018).

28. Grossman, E. and Mayer, N. A new form of anti-government resentment? Making sense of mass support for the Yellow Vest movement in France. *Journal of Elections, Public Opinion and Parties* 33, 746–768 (2023).

29. González, R. and Morán, C. L. F. The 2019–2020 Chilean protests: a first look at their causes and participants. *International Journal of Sociology* 50, 227–235 (2020).

30. Smith, S. A. *The Russian Revolution: a very short introduction* (Oxford University Press, 2002).

31. Caplan, J. *Nazi Germany: a very short introduction* (Oxford University Press, 2019).

32. Doyle, *The Oxford history of the French revolution*.

33. Davies, J. C. Toward a theory of revolution. *American Sociological Review* 27, 5–19 (1962).

34. Orbell, J. M. and Shay, R. C. Toward a theory of revolution: the legacy of James C. Davies in historical perspective. *Politics and the Life Sciences* 30, 85–90 (2011).

35. Gurr, T. R. *Why men rebel* (Routledge, 2015).

36. Grinin, L. and Korotayev, A., Revolutions, counterrevolutions, and democracy, in *Handbook of revolutions in the 21st century: the new waves of revolutions, and the causes and effects of disruptive political change*, ed. J. Goldstone, L. Grinin, and A. Korotayev (Springer, 2022), 105–136.

37. Wright, Slavery and Anglo-American capitalism revisited.

38. Newman, R. S. *Abolitionism: a very short introduction* (Oxford University Press, 2018), Lysack, M., The abolition of slavery movement as a moral movement: ethical resources, spiritual roots, and strategies for social change, in *Connecting spirituality and social justice* (Routledge, 2016), 150–171.

39. Sunstein, *How change happens*.

40. Oreskes and Conway, *Merchants of doubt*.

41. Supran, G., Rahmstorf, S., and Oreskes, N. Assessing ExxonMobil's global warming projections. *Science* 379, eabk0063 (2023).

42. Otto *et al.* Social tipping dynamics for stabilizing Earth's climate by 2050, Lenton, Tipping positive change, Lenton *et al.* Operationalising positive tipping points towards global sustainability.

43. Timperley, J. Why fossil fuel subsidies are so hard to kill. *Nature* 598, 403–405 (2021).

44. Vallone, S. and Lambin, E. F. Public policies and vested interests preserve the animal farming status quo at the expense of animal product analogs. *One Earth* 6, 1213–1226 (2023).

45. Lever, J. J. *et al.* Foreseeing the future of mutualistic communities beyond collapse. *Ecology Letters* 23, 2–15 (2020). https://doi.org/10.1111/ele.13401, Weinans, E.

et al. Finding the direction of lowest resilience in multivariate complex systems. *Journal of the Royal Society Interface* 16 (2019). https://doi.org/10.1098/rsif.2019.0629.

46. Gai, P. and Kapadia, S. Contagion in financial networks. *Proceedings of the Royal Society A: Mathematical, Physical and Engineering Sciences* 466, 2401–2423 (2010).

47. Battiston, S. *et al.* Complexity theory and financial regulation: economic policy needs interdisciplinary network analysis and behavioral modeling. *Science* 351, 818–819 (2016). https://doi.org/10.1126/science.aad0299.

48. May, R. M., Levin, S. A., and Sugihara, G. Complex systems: ecology for bankers. *Nature* 451, 893–895 (2008).

49. Scheffer *et al.* Anticipating critical transitions.

50. Figge, L., Oebels, K., and Offermans, A. The effects of globalization on ecological footprints: an empirical analysis. *Environment, Development and Sustainability* 19, 863–876 (2017).

51. Walker, B. *et al.* Response diversity as a sustainability strategy. *Nature Sustainability* 6, 621–629 (2023). https://doi.org/10.1038/s41893-022-01048-7.

52. Ibid.

53. Gheihman, N. Veganism as a lifestyle movement. *Sociology Compass* 15, e12877 (2021).

54. van de Leemput, I. A. *et al.* Transformation starts at the periphery of networks where pushback is less. *Scientific Reports* 14, 1–8 (2024).

55. Stein, R. A. Super-spreaders in infectious diseases. *International Journal of Infectious Diseases* 15, e510–e513 (2011).

56. van de Leemput *et al.* Transformation starts at the periphery of networks where pushback is less.

57. Judge *et al.* Accelerating social tipping points in sustainable behaviors.

58. Glückler, J. How controversial innovation succeeds in the periphery? A network perspective of BASF Argentina. *Journal of Economic Geography* 14, 903–927 (2014).

59. Uzzi, B. and Spiro, J. Collaboration and creativity: the small world problem. *American Journal of Sociology* 111, 447–504 (2005).

60. Gleick, J. *Genius: the life and science of Richard Feynman* (Vintage, 2011).

61. Wu, L., Wang, D., and Evans, J. A. Large teams develop and small teams disrupt science and technology. *Nature* 566, 378–382 (2019).

62. Judge *et al.* Accelerating social tipping points in sustainable behaviors.

63. Bak, P. *How nature works: the science of self-organized criticality* (Copernicus Books, 1996).

64. Stumpf, M. P. and Porter, M. A. Critical truths about power laws. *Science* 335, 665–666 (2012).

65. Pueyo, S. Self-organised criticality and the response of wildland fires to climate change. *Climatic Change* 82, 131–161 (2007). https://doi.org/10.1007/s10584-006-9134-2.

66. Yoshioka, N. A sandpile experiment and its implications for self-organized criticality and characteristic earthquake. *Earth Planets and Space* 55, 283–289 (2003).

67. Kron, T. and Grund, T. Society as a self-organized critical system. *Cybernetics & Human Knowing* 16, 65–82 (2009).

68. Turchin and Nefedov, *Secular cycles.*

69. Turchin, P. Dynamics of political instability in the United States, 1780–2010. *Journal of Peace Research* 49, 577–591 (2012).

70. Strauss, W. and Howe, N. *The fourth turning: what the cycles of history tell us about America's next rendezvous with destiny* (Crown, 1997).

71. Fukuyama, F. Big histories for the big future. www.nytimes.com/2023/07/18/books/review/the-fourth-turning-is-here-neil-howe-end-times-peter-turchin.html (2023).

72. Tainter, *The collapse of complex societies*.

73. Kemp, Diminishing returns on extraction.

74. Scheffer *et al.* The vulnerability of aging states.

75. Holling, C. S. The resilience of terrestrial ecosystems; local surprise and global change, in *Sustainable development of the biosphere*, ed. W. C. Clark and R. E. Munn (Cambridge University Press, 1986), 292–317.

76. Carpenter, S. R. and Peterson, G. D. C. S. "Buzz" Holling, 6 December 1930–16 August 2019. *Nature Sustainability* 2, 997–998 (2019).

77. Gunderson, L. and Holling, C. S. *Panarchy: understanding transformations in human and natural systems* (Island Press, 2001).

78. Pickrell, J. How the earliest mammals thrived alongside dinosaurs. *Nature* 574, 468–473 (2019).

79. Putnam and Garrett, *The upswing*.

80. Crucifix, M. Oscillators and relaxation phenomena in Pleistocene climate theory. *Philosophical Transactions. Series A, Mathematical, Physical, and Engineering Sciences* 370, 1140–1165 (2012). https://doi.org/10.1098/rsta.2011.0315.

81. Scheffer, M., Brovkin, V., and Cox, P. M. Positive feedback between global warming and atmospheric CO_2 concentration inferred from past climate change. *Geophysical Research Letters* 33, L10702 (2006).

82. Tzedakis *et al.* A simple rule.

83. Steffen, W. *et al.* Trajectories of the Earth system in the Anthropocene. *Proceedings of the National Academy of Sciences of the United States of America* 115, 8252–8259 (2018). https://doi.org/10.1073/pnas.1810141115.

84. Boon, E., van den Berg, P., Molleman, L., and Weissing, F. J. Foundations of cultural evolution. *Philosophical Transactions of the Royal Society B: Biological Sciences* 376, 20200041 (2021), Greenfield, P. M. Social change, cultural evolution, and human development. *Current Opinion in Psychology* 8, 84–92 (2016).

85. Darwin, C. *The origin of species* (Murray, 1859).

86. Dawkins, R. *The selfish gene* (Oxford University Press, 2016).

87. Lenton *et al.* Survival of the systems.

88. Pinker, *Enlightenment now*.

89. van Bavel, B. Back to the future: How economic history can gain more relevance by abandoning modernization thinking. *Economic History Review* 78, 401–423 (2025).

5   Reading our Times

1. Pinker, *Enlightenment now*.

2. Xu *et al.* Future of the human climate niche.

3. Britton, Death, disease, and tobacco.

4. Khalaf, A. M. and Alubied, A. A. The impact of social media on the mental health of adolescents and young adults: a systematic review. *Cureus* 15, e42990 (2023).

5. Scheffer, M., van de Leemput, I., Weinans, E., and Bollen, J. The rise and fall of rationality in language. *Proceedings of the National Academy of Sciences* 118, e2107848118 (2021).

6. Gerbaudo, P. and Treré, E. In search of the "we" of social media activism: introduction to the special issue on social media and protest identities. *Information, Communication and Society* 18, 865–871 (2015).

7. Haenfler, R., Johnson, B., and Jones, E. Lifestyle movements: exploring the intersection of lifestyle and social movements. *Social Movement Studies* 11, 1–20 (2012).

8. Breuer, A., Landman, T., and Farquhar, D. Social media and protest mobilization: evidence from the Tunisian revolution. *Democratization* 22, 764–792 (2015).

9. Weimann, G. *New terrorism and new media* (Commons Lab of the Woodrow Wilson International Center for Scholars, 2014).

10. Haenfler *et al.* Lifestyle movements.

11. McLoughlin, K. L. *et al.* Misinformation exploits outrage to spread online. *Science* 386, 991–996 (2024).

12. Southwell, B. G., Thorson, E. A., and Sheble, L. *Misinformation and mass audiences* (University of Texas Press, 2018).

13. Douglas *et al.* Understanding conspiracy theories.

14. Vosoughi, S., Roy, D., and Aral, S. The spread of true and false news online. *Science* 359, 1146–1151 (2018).

15. Douglas *et al.* Understanding conspiracy theories, Van Prooijen, J.-W. and Douglas, K. M. Conspiracy theories as part of history: the role of societal crisis situations. Memory Studies 10, 323–333 (2017).

16. Van Prooijen, J.-W., Krouwel, A. P., and Pollet, T. V. Political extremism predicts belief in conspiracy theories. *Social Psychological and Personality Science* 6, 570–578 (2015).

17. Bucher, E., Fieseler, C., and Lutz, C. What's mine is yours (for a nominal fee): exploring the spectrum of utilitarian to altruistic motives for Internet-mediated sharing. *Computers in Human Behavior* 62, 316–326 (2016).

18. Haenfler *et al.* Lifestyle movements, Amenta, E. and Polletta, F. The cultural impacts of social movements. *Annual Review of Sociology* 45, 279–299 (2019).

19. Haenfler *et al.* Lifestyle movements.

20. McPherson, M., Smith-Lovin, L., and Cook, J. M. Birds of a feather: homophily in social networks. *Annual Review of Sociology* 27, 415–444 (2001).

21. Herman, E. S. and Chomsky, N. *Manufacturing consent: the political economy of the mass media* (Random House, 2010).

22. Carpenter *et al.* Dancing on the volcano.

23. Pearson, H. The science of protests: how to shape public opinion and swing votes. *Nature* 630, 804–806 (2024).

24. Davies, Toward a theory of revolution.

25. Bollen, J., Gonçalves, B., van de Leemput, I., and Ruan, G. The happiness paradox: your friends are happier than you. *EPJ Data Science* 6, 4 (2017).

26. Shultziner, D. and Goldberg, S. The stages of mass mobilization: separate phenomena and distinct causal mechanisms. *Journal for the Theory of Social Behaviour* 49, 2–23 (2019).

27. Sunstein, *How change happens*, Sunstein, C. R. *Going to extremes: how like minds unite and divide* (Oxford University Press, 2009).

28. Bakshy, E., Messing, S., and Adamic, L. A. Exposure to ideologically diverse news and opinion on Facebook. *Science* 348, 1130–1132 (2015).

29. Smith, N. and Graham, T. Mapping the anti-vaccination movement on Facebook. *Information, Communication and Society* 22, 1310–1327 (2019), Hussain, A., Ali, S., Ahmed, M., and Hussain, S. The anti-vaccination movement: a regression in modern medicine. *Cureus* 10 e2919 (2018).

30. Weimann, *New terrorism and new media*.

31. Engesser, S., Ernst, N., Esser, F., and Büchel, F. Populism and social media: how politicians spread a fragmented ideology. *Information, Communication and Society* 20, 1109–1126 (2017).

32. Suiter, J., Farrell, D. M., and O'Malley, E. When do deliberative citizens change their opinions? Evidence from the Irish Citizens' Assembly. *International Political Science Review* 37, 198–212 (2016), Karpowitz, C. F., Raphael, C., and Hammond, A. S. IV. Deliberative democracy and inequality: two cheers for enclave deliberation among the disempowered. *Politics and Society* 37, 576–615 (2009), Dryzek, J. S. and Niemeyer, S. Deliberative democracy and climate governance. *Nature Human Behaviour* 3, 411–413 (2019).

33. Guess, A., Nagler, J., and Tucker, J. Less than you think: prevalence and predictors of fake news dissemination on Facebook. *Science Advances* 5, eaau4586 (2019). https://doi.org/10.1126/sciadv.aau4586.

34. Hassan, N., Yousuf, M., Mahfuzul Haque, M. A., Suarez Rivas, J., and Khadimul Islam, M. Examining the roles of automation, crowds and professionals towards sustainable fact-checking, in *Companion proceedings of the 2019 World Wide Web Conference*, ed. S. Amer-Yahia *et al.* (ACM, 2019), 1001–1006, Pennycook, G., Cheyne, J. A., Koehler, D. J., and Fugelsang, J. A. On the belief that beliefs should change according to evidence: implications for conspiratorial, moral, paranormal, political, religious, and science beliefs. *Judgment and Decision Making* 15, 476–498 (2020), Walter, N., Cohen, J., Holbert, R. L., and Morag, Y. Fact-checking: a meta-analysis of what works and for whom. *Political Communication* 37, 350–375 (2020).

35. Lorenz-Spreen, P., Oswald, L., Lewandowsky, S., and Hertwig, R. A systematic review of worldwide causal and correlational evidence on digital media and democracy. *Nature Human Behaviour* 7, 74–101 (2023).

36. Adams, T. David Cope: "You pushed the button and out came hundreds and thousands of sonatas." www.theguardian.com/technology/2010/jul/11/david-cope-computer-composer (2010).

37. Tarnoff, B. Weizenbaum's nightmares: how the inventor of the first chatbot turned against AI. www.theguardian.com/technology/2023/jul/25/joseph-weizenbaum-inventor-eliza-chatbot-turned-against-artificial-intelligence-ai (2023), Natale, S. If software is narrative: Joseph Weizenbaum, artificial intelligence and the biographies of ELIZA. *New Media and Society* 21, 712–728 (2019).

38. Hebb, D. O. *The organization of behavior: a neuropsychological theory* (Psychology Press, 2005).

39. Langille, J. J. and Brown, R. E. The synaptic theory of memory: a historical survey and reconciliation of recent opposition. *Frontiers in Systems Neuroscience* 12, 52 (2018).

40. Russell, S. J. and Norvig, P. *Artificial intelligence: a modern approach* (Pearson, 2016).

41. Harvey, F. Ban private jets to address climate crisis, says Thomas Piketty. www.theguardian.com/environment/2023/nov/22/ban-private-jets-to-address-climate-crisis-says-thomas-piketty> (2023).

42. European Parliament. Stopping greenwashing: how the EU regulates green claims. www.europarl.europa.eu/topics/en/article/20240111STO16722/stopping-greenwashing-how-the-eu-regulates-green-claims (2024).

43. Adams, David Cope: "You pushed the button and out came hundreds and thousands of sonatas."

44. Fischer, F. Knowledge politics and post-truth in climate denial: on the social construction of alternative facts. *Critical Policy Studies* 13, 133–152 (2019), Kofman, A. Bruno Latour, the post-truth philosopher, mounts a defense of science. www.nytimes.com/2018/10/25/magazine/bruno-latour-post-truth-philosopher-science.html (2018), Lewandowsky, S., Ecker, U. K., and Cook, J. Beyond misinformation: understanding and coping with the "post-truth" era. *Journal of Applied Research in Memory and Cognition* 6, 353–369 (2017), Flinders, M. Why feelings trump facts: anti-politics, citizenship and emotion. *Emotions and Society* 2, 21–40 (2019).

45. Hertz, N. *The lonely century: a call to reconnect* (Hachette UK, 2020), Thompson, S. A. Three weeks inside a pro-Trump QANON chat room. www.nytimes.com/interactive/2021/01/26/opinion/trump-qanon-washington-capitol-hill.html (2021).

46. Scheffer *et al.* The rise and fall of rationality in language, Bollen, J. *et al.* Historical language records reveal a surge of cognitive distortions in recent decades. *Proceedings of the National Academy of Sciences of the United States of America* 118 (2021). https://doi.org/10.1073/pnas.2102061118.

47. Scheffer *et al.* The rise and fall of rationality in language.

48. Kahneman, D. *Thinking, fast and slow* (Farrar, Straus & Giroux, 2011).

49. Jenkins, R. Disenchantment, enchantment and re-enchantment: Max Weber at the millennium. *Max Weber Studies* 1, 11–32 (2000).

50. Kofman, A. Bruno Latour, the post-truth philosopher, mounts a defense of science.

51. Latour, B. Why has critique run out of steam? From matters of fact to matters of concern. *Critical Inquiry* 30, 225–248 (2004).

52. Scheffer *et al.* The rise and fall of rationality in language.

53. Ibid.

54. Davenport, S. *et al.* Facts versus opinions: How the style and language of news presentation is changing in the digital age. Research report (2019). www.rand.org/pubs/research_briefs/RB10059.html.

55. Putnam and Garrett, *The upswing.*

56. Ibid.

57. Bollen *et al.* Historical language records reveal a surge of cognitive distortions in recent decades.

58. Ibid.

59. Bratsberg, B. and Rogeberg, O. Flynn effect and its reversal are both environmentally caused. *Proceedings of the National Academy of Sciences* 115, 6674–6678 (2018).

60. Pietschnig, J. and Voracek, M. One century of global IQ gains: a formal meta-analysis of the Flynn effect (1909–2013). *Perspectives on Psychological Science* 10, 282–306 (2015).

61. Dutton, E., van der Linden, D., and Lynn, R. The negative Flynn effect: a systematic literature review. *Intelligence* 59, 163–169 (2016), Dworak, E. M., Revelle, W., and Condon, D. M. Looking for Flynn effects in a recent online US adult sample: examining shifts within the SAPA Project. *Intelligence* 98, 101734 (2023).

62. OECD. *Do adults have the skills they need to thrive in a changing world? Survey of adult skills 2023* (OECD, 2024).

63. Bratsberg and Rogeberg, Flynn effect and its reversal are both environmentally caused.

64. Dworak *et al.* Looking for Flynn effects in a recent online US adult sample, Flynn, J. R., Secular changes in intelligence: the "Flynn effect", in *The*

Cambridge handbook of intelligence, ed. R. J. Sternberg and S. B. Kaufman (Cambridge University Press, 2020).

65. Johnson, S. L., Wibbels, E., and Wilkinson, R. Economic inequality is related to cross-national prevalence of psychotic symptoms. *Social Psychiatry and Psychiatric Epidemiology* 50, 1799–1807 (2015).

66. Milanovic, B. *Global inequality: a new approach for the age of globalization* (Harvard University Press, 2016), Piketty, T. and Saez, E. Inequality in the long run. *Science* 344, 838–843 (2014), Saez, E. and Zucman, G. Wealth inequality in the United States since 1913: evidence from capitalized income tax data. *Quarterly Journal of Economics* 131, 519–578 (2016).

67. Duménil, G. and Lévy, D. *The crisis of neoliberalism* (Harvard University Press, 2013), Steger, M. B. and Roy, R. K. *Neoliberalism: a very short introduction* (Oxford University Press, 2010).

68. Kennedy, G. Adam Smith and the invisible hand: from metaphor to myth. *Econ Journal Watch* 6, 239–263 (2009).

69. Scheffer, M., Westley, F., and Brock, W. Slow response of societies to new problems: causes and costs. *Ecosystems* 6, 493–502 (2003). https://doi.org/10.1007/s10021-002-0146-0.

70. Pickrell, How the earliest mammals thrived alongside dinosaurs.

71. Hayek, F. A. and Caldwell, B. *The road to serfdom: text and documents: the definitive edition* (Routledge, 2014).

72. Caldwell, B. *The road to serfdom* after 75 years. *Journal of Economic Literature* 58, 720–748 (2020).

73. Ibid.

74. Duménil and Lévy, *The crisis of neoliberalism*, Steger and Roy, *Neoliberalism*.

75. Stiglitz, J. E. *The road to freedom: economics and the good society* (Random House, 2024).

76. Pinker, *Enlightenment now*.

77. Becker, J. C., Hartwich, L., and Haslam, S. A. Neoliberalism can reduce well-being by promoting a sense of social disconnection, competition, and loneliness. *British Journal of Social Psychology* 60, 947–965 (2021).

78. Verhaeghe, P. Neoliberalism has brought out the worst in us. www.theguardian.com/commentisfree/2014/sep/29/neoliberalism-economic-system-ethics-personality-psychopathicsthic (2014).

79. Hyde, S. D. Democracy's backsliding in the international environment. *Science* 369, 1192–1196 (2020).

80. Conradt, L. and Roper, T. J. Democracy in animals: the evolution of shared group decisions. *Proceedings of the Royal Society B: Biological Sciences* 274, 2317–2326 (2007).

81. Galton, F. Vox populi (The wisdom of crowds). *Nature* 75, 450–451 (1907).

82. Lorenz, J., Rauhut, H., Schweitzer, F., and Helbing, D. How social influence can undermine the wisdom of crowd effect. *Proceedings of the National Academy of Sciences of the United States of America* 108, 9020–9025 (2011).

83. Sen, A. *Democracy as freedom* (Anchor, 1999), Steele, J. Food for thought – The Guardian profile: Amartya Sen. www.theguardian.com/books/2001/mar/31/society.politics (2001).

84. Applebaum, A. *Autocracy, Inc.*

85. Schoenegger, P., Tuminauskaite, I., Park, P. S., Bastos, R. V. S., and Tetlock, P. E. Wisdom of the silicon crowd: LLM ensemble prediction capabilities rival human crowd accuracy. *Science Advances* 10, eadp1528 (2024).

86. Mudde, C. Populism in Europe: an illiberal democratic response to undemocratic liberalism (the *Government and Opposition*/Leonard Schapiro Lecture 2019). *Government and Opposition* 56, 577–597 (2021), Berman, S. The causes of populism in the West. *Annual Review of Political Science* 24, 71–88 (2021).

87. Mudde, Populism in Europe, Mudde, C. The populist Zeitgeist. *Government and Opposition* 39, 541–563 (2004).

88. Gurr, *Why men rebel*.

89. Taylor, P. From Germany to Israel, it's "the will of the people" v the rule of law. Which will win?. www.theguardian.com/commentisfree/2024/jan/30/germany-israel-rule-of-law-democracy-populists?CMP=Share_iOSApp_Other (2024).

90. Phillips, T. The Cultural Revolution: all you need to know about China's political convulsion. www.theguardian.com/world/2016/may/11/the-cultural-revolution-50-years-on-all-you-need-to-know-about-chinas-political-convulsion (2016).

91. Peterie, M. and Neil, D. Xenophobia towards asylum seekers: a survey of social theories. *Journal of Sociology* 56, 23–35 (2020). https://doi.org/10.1177/1440783319882526, Bursztyn, L., Egorov, G., and Fiorin, S. From extreme to mainstream: the erosion of social norms. *American Economic Review* 110, 3522–3548 (2020).

92. Fine, G. A. Forgotten classic: the Robbers Cave Experiment. *Sociological Forum* 19, 663–666 (2004), Onyango, V. C. Reflections on the Robbers Cave Experiment: finding lessons on political conflict, racism, xenophobia, and business environments. *American Journal of Human Psychology* 1, 34–38 (2023).

93. De Dreu, C. K. and Kret, M. E. Oxytocin conditions intergroup relations through upregulated in-group empathy, cooperation, conformity, and defense. *Biological Psychiatry* 79, 165–173 (2016), Olff, M. *et al.* The role of oxytocin in social bonding, stress regulation and mental health: an update on the moderating effects of context and interindividual differences. *Psychoneuroendocrinology* 38, 1883–1894 (2013).

94. Edelman. Special report: trust and climate change. www.edelman.com/trust/2023/trust-barometer/special-report-trust-climate (2023).

95. Potential_Energy_Coalition. Later is too late: a comprehensive analysis of the messaging that accelerates climate action in the G20 and beyond. https://potentialenergycoalition.org/global-report/ (2023).

96. Darley, J. and Latane, B. Bystander intervention in emergencies: diffusion of responsibility. *Journal of Personality and Social Psychology* 8, 377–383 (1968).

97. Havlik, J. L. *et al.* The bystander effect in rats. *Science Advances* 6, eabb4205 (2020).

98. Zemanek, E. Between fragility and resilience: ambivalent images of nature in popular documentaries with David Attenborough. *Anthropocene Review* 9, 139–160 (2022).

99. Feinberg and Willer, Apocalypse soon?

100. Furnham, A. Belief in a just world: research progress over the past decade. *Personality and Individual Differences* 34, 795–817 (2003).

101. Potential_Energy_Coalition, Later is too late.

102. Habib, M. D., Alghamdi, A., Sharma, V., Mehrotra, A., and Badghish, S. Diet or lifestyle: consumer purchase behavior of vegan retailing. A qualitative assessment. *Journal of Retailing and Consumer Services* 76, 103584 (2024).

103. Gheihman, Veganism as a lifestyle movement, Haenfler *et al.* Lifestyle movements.

104. Loughnan, S., Haslam, N., and Bastian, B. The role of meat consumption in the denial of moral status and mind to meat animals. *Appetite* 55, 156–159 (2010).

105. Scheffer *et al.* Slow response of societies to new problems.

106. Haenfler *et al.* Lifestyle movements.

107. Carpenter *et al.* Dancing on the volcano.

108. Whitton *et al.* Are we approaching peak meat consumption?

109. Currid-Halkett, E. *The sum of small things: a theory of the aspirational class* (Princeton University Press, 2017).

110. Allen, F. L. *Since yesterday: The 1930s in America, September 3, 1929–September 3, 1939* (Open Road Media, 2015).

6 Three Plausible Futures

1. Ortiz-Ospina, E., Rosa, M., and Arriagada, P. Trust. https://ourworldindata.org/trust (2016).

2. Martela, F., Greve, B., Rothstein, B., and Saari, J. The Nordic exceptionalism: what explains why the Nordic countries are constantly among the happiest in the world, in *World happiness report* (Sustainable Development Solutions Network, 2020), 128–146. https://worldhappiness.report/ed/2020/the-nordic-exceptionalism-what-explains-why-the-nordic-countries-are-constantly-among-the-happiest-in-the-world/.

3. Stiglitz, *The road to freedom*.

4. Xu *et al.* Future of the human climate niche.

5. Milanovic, B. *Capitalism, alone: the future of the system that rules the world* (Harvard University Press, 2019).

6. Schleussner, C.-F. *et al.* Overconfidence in climate overshoot. *Nature* 634, 366–373 (2024).

7. Xu *et al.* Future of the human climate niche.

8. Scheffer *et al.* Anticipating the global redistribution of people and property.

9. Polasky, S., Scheffer, M., and Anderies, J. M. Meltdown of trust in weakly governed economies. *Proceedings of the National Academy of Sciences* 122, e2320528122 (2025). https://doi.org/10.1073/pnas.2320528122.

10. Fukuyama, F. Trust: the social virtues and the creation of prosperity. *World and I* 10, 264–268 (1995), Coleman, J. S. Social capital in the creation of human capital. *American Journal of Sociology* 94, S95–S120 (1988).

11. Rothstein, B. and Stolle, D. The state and social capital: an institutional theory of generalized trust. *Comparative Politics* 40, 441–459 (2008).

12. Schultz, G. Life and learning after one hundred years: trust is the coin of the realm: reflections on trust and effective relationships across a new hinge of history. www.hoover.org/sites/default/files/research/docs/shultz_finalfile_web-ready.pdf (2020).

13. Kong, D. T. and Yao, J. Advancing the scientific understanding of trust and culture in negotiations. *Negotiation and Conflict Management Research* 12, 117–130 (2019).

14. Lenton, T. M., Boulton, C. A., and Scheffer, M. Resilience of countries to COVID-19 correlated with trust. *Scientific Reports* 12 (2022). https://doi.org/10.1038/s41598-021-03358-w.

15. Ortiz-Ospina *et al.* Trust.

16. Oreskes and Conway, *Merchants of doubt*.

17. van Bavel, B. Power concentration and state capture: insights from history on consequences of market dominance for inequality and environmental calamities, in *UN human development report 2019* (UNDP, 2019), 60–63.

18. Becker, S. O., Boeckh, K., Hainz, C., and Woessmann, L. The empire is dead, long live the empire! Long-run persistence of trust and corruption in the bureaucracy. *Economic Journal* 126, 40–74 (2016).

19. Dawson, C. How persistent is generalised trust? *Sociology* 53, 590–599 (2019).

20. De Dreu and Kret, Oxytocin conditions intergroup relations through upregulated in-group empathy, cooperation, conformity, and defense, Olff *et al.* The role of oxytocin in social bonding, stress regulation and mental health.

21. Scheffer *et al.* Belief traps.

22. Pfefferbaum, B. and North, C. S. Mental health and the Covid-19 pandemic. *New England Journal of Medicine* 383, 510–512 (2020).

23. Perry, N. B., Donzella, B., Troy, M. F., and Barnes, A. J. Mother and child hair cortisol during the COVID-19 pandemic: associations among physiological stress, pandemic-related behaviors, and child emotional-behavioral health. *Psychoneuroendocrinology* 137, 105656 (2022).

24. Charlson, F. *et al.* New WHO prevalence estimates of mental disorders in conflict settings: a systematic review and meta-analysis. *The Lancet* 394, 240–248 (2019).

25. Smeeth, D. *et al.* War exposure, post-traumatic stress symptoms and hair cortisol concentrations in Syrian refugee children. *Molecular Psychiatry* 28, 647–656 (2023).

26. Dziurkowska, E. and Wesolowski, M. Cortisol as a biomarker of mental disorder severity. *Journal of Clinical Medicine* 10, 5204 (2021).

27. Scheffer *et al.* Belief traps.

28. Douglas *et al.* Understanding conspiracy theories, Van Prooijen and Douglas, Conspiracy theories as part of history.

29. Mani, A., Mullainathan, S., Shafir, E., and Zhao, J. Poverty impedes cognitive function. *Science* 341, 976–980 (2013), Troller-Renfree, S. V. *et al.* The impact of a poverty reduction intervention on infant brain activity. *Proceedings of the National Academy of Sciences* 119, e2115649119 (2022).

30. Mani *et al.* Poverty impedes cognitive function.

31. Neckerman, K. M. and Torche, F. Inequality: causes and consequences. *Annual Review of Sociology* 33, 335–357 (2007).

32. Wilson, N. and McDaid, S. The mental health effects of a universal basic income: a synthesis of the evidence from previous pilots. *Social Science and Medicine* 287, 114374 (2021).

33. Hertz, *The lonely century*, US Public Health Service. *Our epidemic of loneliness and isolation: The US Surgeon General's Advisory on the healing effects of social connection and community.* www.hhs.gov/sites/default/files/surgeon-general-social-connection-advisory.pdf (2023).

34. De Dreu and Kret, Oxytocin conditions intergroup relations through upregulated in-group empathy, cooperation, conformity, and defense, Olff *et al.* The role of oxytocin in social bonding, stress regulation and mental health.

35. De Dreu and Kret, Oxytocin conditions intergroup relations through upregulated in-group empathy, cooperation, conformity, and defense, Olff *et al.* The role of oxytocin in social bonding, stress regulation and mental health.

36. Peterie and Neil, Xenophobia towards asylum seekers. https://url.avanan.click/v2/r02/__https://doi.org/10.1177/1440783319882526___.

37. Osborne, D., Costello, T. H., Duckitt, J., and Sibley, C. G. The psychological causes and societal consequences of authoritarianism. *Nature Reviews Psychology* 2, 220–232 (2023).

38. Hickman, C. *et al.* Climate anxiety in children and young people and their beliefs about government responses to climate change: a global survey. *Lancet Planetary Health* 5, e863–e873 (2021).

39. Kemp, L. *et al.* Climate endgame: exploring catastrophic climate change scenarios. *Proceedings of the National Academy of Sciences of the United States of America* 119, e2108146119 (2022). https://doi.org/10.1073/pnas.2108146119, Bradshaw,

C. J. *et al.* Underestimating the challenges of avoiding a ghastly future. *Frontiers in Conservation Science* 1, 615419 (2021).

40. Brysse, K., Oreskes, N., O'Reilly, J., and Oppenheimer, M. Climate change prediction: erring on the side of least drama? *Global Environmental Change* 23, 327–337 (2013).

41. Armstrong McKay, D. I. *et al.* Exceeding 1.5 C global warming could trigger multiple climate tipping points. *Science* 377, eabn7950 (2022).

42. Steffen *et al.* Trajectories of the Earth system in the Anthropocene.

43. Abrams, J. *et al.* Divergent impacts of ocean tipping and global warming on habitability. (2025). Under review. https://doi.org/10.21203/rs.3.rs-4402479/v1, Jackson, L. *et al.* Global and European climate impacts of a slowdown of the AMOC in a high resolution GCM. *Climate Dynamics* 45, 3299–3316 (2015).

44. Xu *et al.* Future of the human climate niche, Lenton *et al.* Quantifying the human cost of global warming.

45. Homer-Dixon, T. *et al.* Synchronous failure: the emerging causal architecture of global crisis. *Ecology and Society* 20 (2015). https://doi.org/10.5751/es-07681-200306, King, N. and Jones, A. An analysis of the potential for the formation of "nodes of persisting complexity". *Sustainability* 13, 8161 (2021).

46. Drake, B. L. The influence of climatic change on the Late Bronze Age collapse and the Greek dark ages. *Journal of Archaeological Science* 39, 1862–1870 (2012). https://doi.org/10.1016/j.jas.2012.01.029.

47. Cline, 1177 BC: the collapse of Bronze Age civilization.

48. Makoond, N., Setiawan, A., Buitrago, M., and Adam, J. M. Arresting failure propagation in buildings through collapse isolation. *Nature* 629, 592–596 (2024).

49. Johnstone, S. and Mazo, J. Global warming and the Arab Spring. *Survival* 53, 11–17 (2011).

50. Kemp *et al.* Climate endgame.

51. Meng, X., Qian, N., and Yared, P. The institutional causes of China's Great Famine, 1959–1961. *Review of Economic Studies* 82, 1568–1611 (2015).

52. McDoom, O. S. Contested counting: toward a rigorous estimate of the death toll in the Rwandan genocide. *Journal of Genocide Research* 22, 83–93 (2020).

53. Yongyi, S. Chronology of mass killings during the Chinese Cultural Revolution (1966–1976), in *Online encyclopedia of mass violence* (Sciences Po, 2011), 315–327. www.massviolence.org/Article?id_article=551.

54. Roser, M. Nuclear weapons: why reducing the risk of nuclear war should be a key concern of our generation. https://ourworldindata.org/nuclear-weapons-risk (2023).

55. Ibid.

56. Ibid.

57. King and Jones, An analysis of the potential for the formation of "nodes of persisting complexity".

58. Scheffer, M. *et al.* A heart model of Earth stewardship: shaking up science for positive futures. *Earth Stewardship* 1, e12019 (2024).

59. Cork, S. *et al.* Exploring alternative futures in the Anthropocene. *Annual Review of Environment and Resources* 48, 25–54 (2023).

60. Tzung, S. Carbon negativity in Bhutan: an inverse free rider problem. https://hir.harvard.edu/carbon-negativity-in-bhutan-an-inverse-free-rider-problem/ (2022).

61. Perissi, I. and Jones, A. Investigating European Union decarbonization strategies: evaluating the pathway to carbon neutrality by 2050. *Sustainability* 14, 4728 (2022).

62. Krishnan, M. *et al.* The net-zero transition: what it would cost, what it could bring. https://coilink.org/20.500.12592/od6rdj (2022).

63. Cuff, M. Key carbon plan is unworkable. *New Scientist* 262, 8–9 (2024). https://doi.org/10.1016/S0262-4079(24)00711-5.

64. Dudley, N. and Alexander, S. Agriculture and biodiversity: a review. *Biodiversity* 18, 45–49 (2017).

65. Khan, N. *et al.* Current progress and future prospects of agriculture technology: gateway to sustainable agriculture. *Sustainability* 13, 4883 (2021).

66. Leclère, D. *et al.* Bending the curve of terrestrial biodiversity needs an integrated strategy. *Nature* 585, 551–556 (2020).

67. Ritchie, H. and Roser, M. If the world adopted a plant-based diet, we would reduce global agricultural land use from 4 to 1 billion hectares. https://ourworldindata.org/land-use-diets (2024).

68. Willett, W. *et al.* Food in the Anthropocene: the EAT–Lancet Commission on healthy diets from sustainable food systems. *The Lancet* 393, 447–492 (2019).

69. Haines, A. and Frumkin, H. *Planetary health: safeguarding human health and the environment in the Anthropocene* (Cambridge University Press, 2021).

70. Suzman, *Work*, Scott, *Against the grain*.

71. Suzman, *Work*.

72. Ibid.

73. Hatzius, J. The potentially large effects of artificial intelligence on economic growth (Briggs/Kodnani). Goldman Sachs (2023). https://publishing.gs.com/content/research/en/reports/2023/03/27/d64e052b-0f6e-45d7-967b-d7be35fabd16.html.

74. Suzman, *Work*.

75. Skidelsky, R. *Keynes: a very short introduction* (Oxford University Press, 2010).

76. Rifkin, J. *The end of work* (Putnam, 1995).

77. Galbraith, J. K. *The affluent society* (Houghton Mifflin Harcourt, 1998).

78. Bettelheim, M. P. Flânerie or flimflammery? The urban myth of the flâneur and turtle-walking. *Bibliotheca Herpetologica* 16, 1–13 (2022), Solnit, R. *Wanderlust: a history of walking* (Penguin, 2001).

79. Lamont, M. Toward a comparative sociology of valuation and evaluation. *Annual Review of Sociology* 38, 201–221 (2012).

80. Currid-Halkett, *The sum of small things*, Bellezza, S. Distance and alternative signals of status: a unifying framework. *Journal of Consumer Research* 50, 322–342 (2023).

81. Katz, D. Eleven Madison Park: the triumph of vegan fine dining. www.gastromondiale.com/eleven-madison-park/ (2024).

82. Reasons to be cheerful about generation Z., *The Economist* (2024). https://www.economist.com/leaders/2024/04/18/reasons-to-be-cheerful-about-generation-z.

83. Bellezza, Distance and alternative signals of status.

84. Milanovic, *Capitalism, alone.*

85. Brosnan, S. F. and de Waal, F. B. M. Monkeys reject unequal pay. *Nature* 425, 297–299 (2003). https://doi.org/10.1038/nature01963.

86. Nuzzo, R. Profile of Frans BM de Waal. *Proceedings of the National Academy of Sciences* 102, 11137–11139 (2005).

87. de Waal, F. Capuchin monkeys reject unequal pay. https://youtu.be/lKhAdoTynyo?si=WRorBLq3Qg76fZjX.

88. de Waal, F. B. Putting the altruism back into altruism: the evolution of empathy. *Annual Review of Psychology* 59, 279–300 (2008).

89. Bregman, R. *Humankind: a hopeful history* (Bloomsbury, 2020).

90. Wu, Y. E. and Hong, W. Neural basis of prosocial behavior. *Trends in Neurosciences* 45, 749–762 (2022).

91. Gneezy, U. and Rustichini, A. A fine is a price. *Journal of Legal Studies* 29, 1–17 (2000).

92. Vohs, K. D. Money priming can change people's thoughts, feelings, motivations, and behaviors: an update on 10 years of experiments. *Journal of Experimental Psychology: General* 144, e86 (2015), Vohs, K. D., Mead, N. L., and Goode, M. R. The psychological consequences of money. *Science* 314, 1154–1156 (2006).

93. Turchin *et al.* Quantitative historical analysis uncovers a single dimension of complexity that structures global variation in human social organization.

94. Medvedev, D., Davenport, D., Talhelm, T., and Li, Y. The motivating effect of monetary over psychological incentives is stronger in WEIRD cultures. *Nature Human Behaviour* 8, 456–470 (2024).

95. Scheffer *et al.* The rise and fall of rationality in language.

96. Becker *et al.* Neoliberalism can reduce well-being by promoting a sense of social disconnection, competition, and loneliness, Verhaeghe, Neoliberalism has brought out the worst in us.

97. Hickel, What does degrowth mean?, Hickel, *Less is more*, Fioramonti *et al.* Wellbeing economy, McGreevy *et al.* Sustainable agrifood systems for a post-growth world.

98. Strunz and Schindler, Identifying barriers toward a post-growth economy.

99. Hickel, *Less is more*, Milanovic, *Capitalism, alone*.

100. Chancel, L. and Piketty, T. Global income inequality, 1820–2020: the persistence and mutation of extreme inequality. *Journal of the European Economic Association* 19, 3025–3062 (2021).

101. Schleussner *et al.* Overconfidence in climate overshoot.

102. Barrett, S. *et al.* Climate engineering reconsidered. *Nature Climate Change* 4, 527–529 (2014). https://doi.org/10.1038/nclimate2278, Sovacool, B. K., Baum, C., and Low, S. The next climate war? Statecraft, security, and weaponization in the geopolitics of a low-carbon future. *Energy Strategy Reviews* 45, 101031 (2023).

103. Smith, W. The cost of stratospheric aerosol injection through 2100. *Environmental Research Letters* 15, 114004 (2020).

104. Krishnamohan, K. and Bala, G. Sensitivity of tropical monsoon precipitation to the latitude of stratospheric aerosol injections. *Climate Dynamics* 59, 151–168 (2022).

105. Barrett *et al.* Climate engineering reconsidered, Sovacool *et al.* The next climate war?

106. National Academies of Sciences, Engineering, and Medicine. *Reflecting sunlight: recommendations for solar geoengineering research and research governance* (National Academies Press, 2021).

107. Pecl, G. T. *et al.* Biodiversity redistribution under climate change: impacts on ecosystems and human well-being. *Science* 355, eaai9214 (2017).

108. Lenton *et al.* Quantifying the human cost of global warming.

109. Adger, W. N. *et al.* Urbanization, migration, and adaptation to climate change. *One Earth* 3, 396–399 (2020).

110. UN. *Global Compact for Safe, Orderly and Regular Migration.* www.iom.int/global-compact-migration (2018).

111. Adger *et al.* Urbanization, migration, and adaptation to climate change.

112. Fan and Rue, The role of smallholder farms in a changing world.

113. Baldassarri, D. and Abascal, M. Diversity and prosocial behavior. *Science* 369, 1183–1187 (2020).

114. Stanley, S. K. and Williamson, J. Attitudes towards climate change aid and climate refugees in New Zealand: an exploration of policy support and ideological barriers. *Environmental Politics* 30, 1259–1280 (2021), Spilker, G., Nguyen, Q., Koubi, V., and Böhmelt, T. Attitudes of urban residents towards environmental migration in Kenya and Vietnam. *Nature Climate Change* 10, 622–627 (2020).

115. Balvin, N. and Christie, D. J. *Children and peace: from research to action* (Springer Nature, 2020), Monroe, M. C., Plate, R. R., Oxarart, A., Bowers, A., and Chaves, W. A. Identifying effective climate change education strategies: a systematic review of the research. *Environmental Education Research* 25, 791–812 (2019).

116. Vince, G. *Nomad century: how climate migration will reshape our world* (Flatiron Books, 2022).

7 The Invisible Strangling Hand

1. Plato. *Critias*. www.platonicfoundation.org/translation/critias/.

2. Holmgren, M. and Scheffer, M. To tree or not to tree: cultural views from ancient Romans to modern ecologists. *Ecosystems* 20, 62–68 (2017). https://doi.org/10.1007/s10021-016-0052-5.

3. Tyrrell, I. America's national parks: the transnational creation of national space in the Progressive Era. *Journal of American Studies* 46, 1–21 (2012).

4. Supran *et al.* Assessing ExxonMobil's global warming projections.

5. Rockström, J. *et al.* Safe and just Earth system boundaries. *Nature* 619, 102–111 (2023). https://doi.org/10.1038/s41586-023-06083-8.

6. Livingston, Fidelity to truth.

7. Nye, J. S. Soft power. *Foreign Policy* 80, 153–171 (1990).

8. Buckley, W. Society as a complex adaptive system, in *Systems research for behavioral science*, ed. W. Buckley (Routledge, 2017), 490–513, Lansing, J. S. Complex adaptive systems. *Annual Review of Anthropology* 32, 183–204 (2003), Levin, S. Complex adaptive systems: exploring the known, the unknown and the unknowable. *Bulletin of the American Mathematical Society* 40, 3–19 (2003).

9. Mitchell, K. J. *Free agents: how evolution gave us free will* (Princeton University Press, 2023).

10. Bockting, C. L. *et al.* Effectiveness of preventive cognitive therapy while tapering antidepressants versus maintenance antidepressant treatment versus their combination in prevention of depressive relapse or recurrence (DRD study): a three-group, multicentre, randomised controlled trial. *The Lancet Psychiatry* 5, 401–410 (2018).

11. Peskin, S. M. Is it really a sin if it's hardwired in? The neurological basis for "bad" behaviour. *Nature* 635, 543–544 (2024).

12. Aquino, K. and Reed, A. II. The self-importance of moral identity. *Journal of Personality and Social Psychology* 83, 1423 (2002).

13. Barkan, R., Ayal, S., and Ariely, D. Ethical dissonance, justifications, and moral behavior. *Current Opinion in Psychology* 6, 157–161 (2015).

14. Ibid.

15. Shimizu, M., Kubota, Y., Toichi, M., and Baba, H. Folie à deux and shared psychotic disorder. *Current Psychiatry Reports* 9, 200–205 (2007).

16. Giurge, L. M., Van Dijke, M., Zheng, M. X., and De Cremer, D. Does power corrupt the mind? The influence of power on moral reasoning and self-interested behavior. *Leadership Quarterly* 32, 101288 (2021).

17. Peskin, Is it really a sin if it's hardwired in?

18. Giurge *et al.* Does power corrupt the mind?

19. McPhedran, R. *et al.* Psychological inoculation protects against the social media infodemic. *Scientific Reports* 13, 5780 (2023).

20. Polasky *et al.* Corridors of clarity. https://url.avanan.click/v2/r02/__https://doi.org/10.1093/biosci/biaa115___.

21. Turns, A. The photo that made the plastics crisis personal. www.bbc.com/future/article/20230531-the-photo-that-changed-the-worlds-response-to-the-plastics-crisis (2023).

22. Koelmans, A. A. *et al.* Risks of plastic debris: unravelling fact, opinion, perception, and belief. *Environmental Science and Technology* 51, 11513–11519 (2017). https://doi.org/10.1021/acs.est.7b02219.

23. Grennfelt, P. *et al.* Acid rain and air pollution: 50 years of progress in environmental science and policy. *Ambio* 49, 849–864 (2020).

24. Roser, M. Data review: how many people die from air pollution? https://ourworldindata.org /data-review-air-pollution-deaths (2024).

25. Fuller, R. *et al.* Pollution and health: a progress update. *The Lancet Planetary Health* 6, e535–e547 (2022).

26. Willsher, K. France halts €100-a-month electric car leasing scheme after huge demand. www.theguardian.com/world/2024/feb/13/france-halts-100-a-month-electric-car-leasing-scheme-after-surge-in-demand (2024).

27. Harvey, Ban private jets to address climate crisis, says Thomas Piketty.

28. Khalfan *et al.* Climate equality.

29. Solnit, R. *Hope in the dark: the untold history of people power* (Canongate Books, 2010).

30. de Freitas Netto, S. V., Sobral, M. F. F., Ribeiro, A. R. B., and Soares, G. R. d. L. Concepts and forms of greenwashing: a systematic review. *Environmental Sciences Europe* 32, 1–12 (2020).

31. Ibid.

32. Mazar, N. and Zhong, C.-B. Do green products make us better people? *Psychological Science* 21, 494–498 (2010).

33. Supran *et al.* Assessing ExxonMobil's global warming projections.

34. Frankfurt, H. G. *On bullshit* (Princeton University Press, 2005).

35. Black, M. *The prevalence of humbug and other essays* (Cornell University Press, 1985).

36. van der Lee, R., Ellemers, N., Zarzeczna, N., and Scheepers, D. Threatened by the immoral, challenged by the incompetent: cardiovascular responses to intragroup morality vs. competence evaluations. *Group Processes and Intergroup Relations* 27, 62–75 (2024).

37. Ibid, van Nunspeet, F. and Ellemers, N. Regulating other people's moral behaviors: turning vicious cycles into virtuous cycles. *Group Processes and Intergroup Relations* 27, 196–213 (2024).

38. Eastwood, J. The role of ideas in Weber's theory of interests. *Critical Review* 17, 89–100 (2005).

39. Ritchie, H. and Roser, M. Cars, planes, trains: where do CO_2 emissions from transport come from? https://ourworldindata.org/co2-emissions-from-transport (2024).

40. Koelmans *et al.* Risks of plastic debris.

41. Carroll, L. *Sylvie and Bruno concluded* (Macmillan, 1894).

42. Peters, J. D. Resemblance made absolutely exact: Borges and Royce on maps and media. *Variaciones Borges* 25, 1–23 (2008).

43. Chapin, F. S. III *et al.* Earth stewardship: shaping a sustainable future through interacting policy and norm shifts. *Ambio* 51, 1907–1920 (2022).

44. Ibid.

45. Scheffer *et al.* Anticipating critical transitions, Lever *et al.* Foreseeing the future of mutualistic communities beyond collapse, Weinans *et al.* Finding the direction of lowest resilience in multivariate complex systems.

46. van de Leemput *et al.* Transformation starts at the periphery of networks where pushback is less.

8   What Can Be Done

1. Applebaum, *Autocracy, Inc.*

2. Chen, Y.-H., Paolino, P., and Mason, T. D. Who protests and why: hierarchical government trust and protest participation in China. *Journal of East Asian Studies* 21, 499–513 (2021).

3. Hepburn, C. *et al.* Towards carbon neutrality and China's 14th Five-Year Plan: clean energy transition, sustainable urban development, and investment priorities. *Environmental Science and Ecotechnology* 8, 100130 (2021).

4. Hickel, What does degrowth mean?, Hickel, *Less is more*, Fioramonti *et al.* Wellbeing economy.

5. Strunz and Schindler, Identifying barriers toward a post-growth economy.

6. Thaler, R. H. and Sunstein, C. R. *Nudge: the final edition* (Yale University Press, 2021).

7. Sunstein, *How change happens.*

8. Sparkman *et al.* Americans experience a false social reality by underestimating popular climate policy support by nearly half.

9. Mudde, Populism in Europe, Mudde, The populist Zeitgeist, Peterie and Neil, Xenophobia towards asylum seekers, Bursztyn *et al.* From extreme to mainstream.

10. Gandour, J., Riddell, R., and Ahmed, N. Multilateralism in an Era of Global Oligarchy. How Extreme Inequality Undermines International Cooperation, Oxfam media briefing. www.oxfam.org/en/research/multilaterialism-era-global-oligarchy (2024).

11. Watts, J. Interview Bruno Latour: "This is a global catastrophe that has come from within". www.theguardian.com/world/2020/jun/06/bruno-latour-coronavirus-gaia-hypothesis-climate-crisis (2020).

12. Wong, C. Do climate lawsuits lead to action? Researchers assess their impact. *Nature* 628, 698–699 (2024).

13. Shanor, A. and Light, S. E. Greenwashing and the first amendment. *Columbia Law Review* 122, 2033–2118 (2022).

14. European Parliament, Stopping greenwashing.

15. Stone, C. D., *Should trees have standing? Toward legal rights for natural objects, in environmental rights,* ed. S. Vanderheiden (Routledge, 2017), 283–334, Epstein, Y., Ellison, A. M., Echeverría, H., and Abbott, J. K. Science and the legal rights of nature. *Science* 380, eadf4155 (2023).

16. Aksoy, C. G., Carpenter, C. S., De Haas, R., and Tran, K. D. Do laws shape attitudes? Evidence from same-sex relationship recognition policies in Europe. *European Economic Review* 124, 103399 (2020).

17. Jefferson, T. From Thomas Jefferson to James Madison, 30 January 1787, letter. https://founders.archives.gov/documents/Jefferson/01-11-02-0095 (1787).

18. Goldberg, S. and Bächtiger, A. Catching the "deliberative wave"? How (disaffected) citizens assess deliberative citizen forums. *British Journal of Political Science* 53, 239–247 (2023).

19. Karpowitz *et al.* Deliberative democracy and inequality, Grönlund, K., Herne, K., and Setälä, M. Does enclave deliberation polarize opinions? *Political Behavior* 37, 995–1020 (2015).

20. Decourcy, E. Just a grain of salt? Symbolic construction during the Indian nationalist movement. *Melbourne Historical Journal* 38, 57–73 (2010).

21. Mishra, M. Swedish climate activist Greta Thunberg is the new Gandhi. https://timesofindia.indiatimes.com/blogs/mind-the-gap/swedish-climate-activist-greta-thunberg-is-the-new-gandhi/ (2019).

22. Ryalls, E. D. and Mazzarella, S. R. "Famous, beloved, reviled, respected, feared, celebrated": media construction of Greta Thunberg. *Communication, Culture and Critique* 14, 438–453 (2021).

23. Gheihman, Veganism as a lifestyle movement, Haenfler *et al.* Lifestyle movements.

24. Blood, R. Should NGOs be viewed as "political corporations"? *Journal of Communication Management* 9, 120–133 (2005).

25. Baur, D. and Schmitz, H. P. Corporations and NGOs: when accountability leads to co-optation. *Journal of Business Ethics* 106, 9–21 (2012).

26. Lerner, M. J. *The belief in a just world* (Springer, 1980).

27. Klein, E. *Why we're polarized* (Simon & Schuster, 2020).

28. Perry, S. L. American religion in the era of increasing polarization. *Annual Review of Sociology* 48, 87–107 (2022). https://doi.org/10.1146/annurev-soc-031021-114239.

29. Chapin *et al.* Earth stewardship, Fry, L. W. and Egel, E. Global leadership for sustainability. *Sustainability* 13, 6360 (2021).

30. Hearn, A. X., Huber, F., Koehrsen, J., and Buzzi, A.-L. The perceived potential of religion in mitigating climate change and how this is being realized in Germany and Switzerland. *Journal of Environmental Studies and Sciences* 14, 342–357 (2024). https://doi.org/10.1007/s13412-023-00884-z.

31. Folke, C. *et al.* Transnational corporations and the challenge of biosphere stewardship. *Nature Ecology and Evolution* 3, 1396–1403 (2019). https://doi.org/10.1038/s41559-019-0978-z.

32. Griffin, P. and Heede, C. R. *The Carbon Majors Database.* https://carbonmajors.org/briefing/The-Carbon-Majors-Database-26913 (2024).

33. Folke *et al.* Transnational corporations and the challenge of biosphere stewardship.

34. Ibid.

35. QuoteResearch. History does not repeat itself, but it rhymes.

36. Folke *et al.* Transnational corporations and the challenge of biosphere stewardship.

37. Polman, P. and Bhattacharya, C. Engaging employees to create a sustainable business. *Stanford Social Innovation Review* 14, 34–39 (2016).

38. Jónasson, J. T. Educational change, inertia and potential futures: why is it difficult to change the content of education? *European Journal of Futures Research* 4, 1–14 (2016).

39. Skidelsky, *Keynes.*

40. Scheffer *et al.* A heart model of Earth stewardship.

41. Robinson, K. S. *The ministry for the future* (Hachette UK, 2020).

42. Scheffer *et al.* A heart model of Earth stewardship.

43. Herbert, D. L., Barnett, A. G., and Graves, N. Funding: Australia's grant system wastes time. *Nature* 495, 314 (2013). https://doi.org/10.1038/495314d.

44. Fang, F. C., Bowen, A, and Casadevall, A. NIH peer review percentile scores are poorly predictive of grant productivity. *eLife* 5, e13323 (2016). https://doi.org/10.7554/eLife.13323.

45. Bollen, J., Carpenter, S. R., Lubchenco, J., and Scheffer, M. Rethinking resource allocation in science. *Ecology and Society* 24 (2019). https://doi.org/10.5751/es-11005-240329, Bollen, J., Crandall, D., Junk, D., Ding, Y., and Börner, K. From funding agencies to scientific agency: collective allocation of science funding as an alternative to peer review. *EMBO reports* 15, 131–133 (2014). https://doi.org/10.1002/embr.201338068.

46. Scheffer *et al*. A heart model of Earth stewardship, Lamont, M. *How professors think: inside the curious world of academic judgment* (Harvard University Press, 2009).

47. Scheffer and Beets, Ecological models and the pitfalls of causality, Carpenter, S. R. Replication and treatment strength in whole-lake experiments. *Ecology* 70, 453–463 (1989).

48. Oreskes, N., Shraderfrechette, K., and Belitz, K. Verification, validation, and confirmation of numerical models in the earth sciences. *Science* 263, 641–646 (1994).

49. Scheffer *et al*. A heart model of Earth stewardship.

50. Holden, J. How we value arts and culture, in *Sustaining cultural development*, ed. B. Mickov and J. Doyle (Routledge, 2016), 17–28.

51. Milanovic, *Capitalism, alone*.

52. Österblom, H., Jouffray, J.-B., Folke, C., and Rockström, J. Emergence of a global science–business initiative for ocean stewardship. *Proceedings of the National Academy of Sciences* 114, 9038–9043 (2017).

53. Falguera, E., Jones, S., and Ohman, M. *Funding of political parties and election campaigns: a handbook on political finance* (Idea, 2014).

54. Vallone and Lambin, Public policies and vested interests preserve the animal farming status quo at the expense of animal product analogs.

55. Harring *et al*. Cross-national analysis of attitudes towards fossil fuel subsidy removal.

56. Segerson, K. *et al*. A cautious approach to subsidies for environmental sustainability. *Science* 386, 28–30 (2024).

57. Riemer, K. and Peter, S. Algorithmic audiencing: why we need to rethink free speech on social media. *Journal of Information Technology* 36, 409–426 (2021).

58. Bouman, T., Bolderdijk, J. W., and Smith, E. K. Local fossil fuel ad ban as a catalyst for global change. *Nature Climate Change* 15, 348–350 (2025).

59. Woodcock, R. A. The obsolescence of advertising in the information age. *Yale Law Journal* 127, 2270–2341 (2017).

60. Karppinen, K. and Moe, H. What we talk about when we talk about "media independence". *Javnost – The Public* 23, 105–119 (2016).

61. Robinson, *The ministry for the future*.

62. Disco, C. and van der Vleuten, E. The politics of wet system building: balancing interests in Dutch water management from the Middle Ages to the present. *Knowledge, Technology and Policy* 14, 21–40 (2002).

63. Torry, M. *The Palgrave international handbook of basic income* (Springer, 2019).

64. Bregman, R. *Utopia for realists: how we can build the ideal world* (Hachette UK, 2017).

65. Mani *et al*. Poverty impedes cognitive function, Troller-Renfree *et al*. The impact of a poverty reduction intervention on infant brain activity.

66. Van Prooijen and Douglas, Conspiracy theories as part of history.

67. Osborne *et al.* The psychological causes and societal consequences of authoritarianism.

68. De Dreu and Kret, Oxytocin conditions intergroup relations through upregulated ingroup empathy, cooperation, conformity, and defense, Olff *et al.* The role of oxytocin in social bonding, stress regulation and mental health.

69. Robinson, *The ministry for the future*, Chen, D. B., van der Beek, J., and Cloud, J. Climate mitigation policy as a system solution: addressing the risk cost of carbon. *Journal of Sustainable Finance and Investment* 7, 233–274 (2017).

70. van Bavel and Scheffer, Historical effects of shocks on inequality.

71. Christensen *et al.* Survival of the richest.

72. Robeyns, *Limitarianism*.

73. Patriotic Millionaires *et al.* Proud to pay more. https://proudtopaymore.org (2024).

74. Jacques, O. Explaining willingness to pay taxes: the role of income, education, ideology. *Journal of European Social Policy* 33, 267–284 (2023).

75. van Bavel and Scheffer, Historical effects of shocks on inequality.

76. Reich, R. *Just giving: why philanthropy is failing democracy and how it can do better* (Princeton University Press, 2020).

77. Dear, K., Dutton, K., and Fox, E. Do "watching eyes" influence antisocial behavior? A systematic review and meta-analysis. *Evolution and Human Behavior* 40, 269–280 (2019).

78. Judge *et al.* Accelerating social tipping points in sustainable behaviors, Otto *et al.* Social tipping dynamics for stabilizing Earth's climate by 2050, Winkelmann *et al.* Social tipping processes towards climate action, Lenton, Tipping positive change, Lenton *et al.* Operationalising positive tipping points towards global sustainability, Tàbara *et al.* Positive tipping points in a rapidly warming world, Chapin *et al.* Earth stewardship, Chapin, F. S. III *Grassroots stewardship: sustainability within our reach* (Oxford University Press, 2020).

79. Otto *et al.* Social tipping dynamics for stabilizing Earth's climate by 2050.

80. Potential_Energy_Coalition. Later is too late.

Epilogue

1. Raes, F. *et al.* Overgeneralization as a predictor of the course of depression over time: the role of negative overgeneralization to the self, negative overgeneralization across situations, and overgeneral autobiographical memory. *Cognitive Therapy and Research* 47, 598–613 (2023). https://doi.org/10.1007/s10608-023-10385-6.

2. Maier, S. F. and Seligman, M. E. Learned helplessness at fifty: insights from neuroscience. *Psychological Review* 123, 349–367 (2016).

3. Hickman *et al.* Climate anxiety in children and young people and their beliefs about government responses to climate change.

4. Watts, Interview Bruno Latour.

5. Dannenberg, A. and Barrett, S. Cooperating to avoid catastrophe. *Nature Human Behaviour* 2, 435–437 (2018), Barrett, S. and Dannenberg, A. Tipping versus cooperating to supply a public good. *Journal of the European Economic Association* 15, 910–941 (2017).

6. Dannenberg and Barrett, Cooperating to avoid catastrophe.

7. Geddes, L. Scientists whose work enabled mRNA Covid vaccine win medicine Nobel Prize. www.theguardian.com/science/2023/oct/02/scientists-whose-work-enabled-mrna-covid-vaccine-win-nobel-prize-for-medicine-katalin-kariko-drew-weissman (2023).

8. Feist, G. J. A meta-analysis of personality in scientific and artistic creativity. *Personality and Social Psychology Review* 2, 290–309 (1998).

9. Geddes, Scientists whose work enabled mRNA Covid vaccine win medicine Nobel Prize.

INDEX

Printed by Integrated Books International,
United States of America